Rhinegold Study Guides

A Student's Guide to AS Religious Studies

for the **AQA** Specification

by

Dennis Brown and Stephen Morris

with Jonathan Knight

Edited by

Lucien Jenkins

with Hugh Sadleir and Emma Whale

R·

Rhinegold Publishing Ltd
241 Shaftesbury Avenue
London WC2H 8TF
Telephone: 01832 270333
Fax: 01832 275560
www.rhinegold.co.uk

Rhinegold Religious Studies Study Guides
(series editor: Lucien Jenkins)

A Student's Guide to AS Religious Studies for the AQA Specification
A Student's Guide to AS Religious Studies for the Edexcel Specification
A Student's Guide to AS Religious Studies for the OCR Specification

A Student's Guide to A2 Religious Studies for the AQA Specification
A Student's Guide to A2 Religious Studies for the Edexcel Specification
A Student's Guide to A2 Religious Studies for the OCR Specification

Other Rhinegold Study Guides
Students' Guides to GCSE Music for the AQA, Edexcel, OCR and WJEC Specifications
Listening Tests for Students: AQA, Edexcel and OCR GCSE Music Specifications
Students' Guides to AS and A2 Music for the AQA, Edexcel and OCR Specifications
Listening Tests for Students: AQA, Edexcel and OCR AS and A2 Music Specifications
A Student's Guide to Music Technology for the Edexcel AS and A2 Specification
Listening Tests for Students: Edexcel Music Technology AS and A2 Music Specification

Students' Guides to AS and A2 Drama and Theatre Studies for the AQA and Edexcel Specifications
Students' Guides to AS and A2 Performance Studies for the OCR Specification

Rhinegold Publishing also publishes Classical Music, Classroom Music, Early Music Today, Music Teacher, Opera Now, Piano, The Singer, British and International Music Yearbook, British Performing Arts Yearbook, Music Education Yearbook, Rhinegold Dictionary of Music in Sound.

First published 2003 in Great Britain by
Rhinegold Publishing Ltd
241 Shaftesbury Avenue
London WC2H 8TF
Telephone: 01832 270333
Fax: 01832 275560
www.rhinegold.co.uk

© Rhinegold Publishing Ltd 2003, reprinted 2003, 2004, 2005

All rights reserved. No part of this publication may be reproduced,
stored in a retrieval system, or transmitted in any form or by any means,
electronic, mechanical, photocopying, recording or otherwise,
without the prior permission of Rhinegold Publishing Ltd.

Rhinegold Publishing Ltd has used its best efforts in preparing this guide.
It does not assume, and hereby disclaims, any liability to any party
for loss or damage caused by errors or omissions in the Guide
whether such errors or omissions result from negligence, accident or other cause.

You should always check the current requirements of the examination, since these may change.
Copies of the AQA specification may be obtained from the Assessment and Qualifications Alliance at
Publications Department, Stag Hill House, Guildford, Surrey GU2 5XJ
or Aldon House, 39 Heald Grove, Rusholme, Manchester M14 4PB
See also the AQA website at www.aqa.org.uk

A Student's Guide to AS Religious Studies for the AQA specification
British Library Cataloguing in Publication Data.
A catalogue record for this book is available from the British Library.

ISBN 1-904226-08-6

Printed in Great Britain by WPG Group Ltd

Contents

Introduction 5
Religion and human experience 18
    Religious experience, 18
    Religious authority, 33
Old Testament 50
    God and the covenant, 50
    Development of prophecy, 55
    Prophecy in the 8th century BCE, 61
New Testament 65
    Biblical criticism, 65
    Jesus and the early Church, 68
    Jesus and the Evangelists, 70
Religion and ethics 80
    Utilitarianism, 80
    Kantian ethics, 83
    Christian ethics, 86
    Medical issues, 88
    Environmental issues, 95
World faiths 98
    Buddhism, 98
    Christianity, 101
    Hinduism, 105
    Islam, 110
    Judaism, 113
    Sikhism, 116
Religion and science 121
    The origins of the universe, 121
    Arguments for the existence of God, 126
    Miracles, 132

The authors

Dennis Brown is an experienced teacher of Religious Studies and Philosophy, and is currently head of the Religion and Philosophy department at Manchester Grammar School. He has been an examiner for AQA and has worked for this board in developing several courses, including the new AS and A2 Specifications in Religious Studies. He is also the author of a book on Saint Jerome (*Vir Trilinguis*, Peeters, Leuven) and several articles for books on early Church history. He would like to dedicate this book to the three most important people in his life: Catherine, Brian and Patrick.

Stephen Morris is head of sixth form at Brentwood School, Essex. He read Theology at Hull University, going on to the posts of head of Religious Education at Beverley Grammar School in East Yorkshire, and head of Religious Education at Bedford School. He has examined for AQA and OCR, and edited the HMC schools' web portal for Religious Studies. He is a member of the council of the Independent Schools' Religious Studies Association.

Acknowledgements

In the writing of a guide such as this many people have contributed. The authors and publishers are grateful to the following people for their specific advice, support and expert contributions: Hallam Bannister, Wendy Dossett, Susan Gillingham, Richard Maloney, Abigail Walmsley, Keith Ward and Andrew Wright. But the authors are also conscious of having drawn on a lifetime's reading. More recently the growth in use of the Internet has made an unparalleled amount of exciting information and challenging opinion widely available. Although every attempt has been made to acknowledge both the primary and secondary sources drawn on, it is impossible to do justice to the full range of material that has affected the creation of this book. The authors would therefore like to apologise if anyone's work has not been properly acknowledged. They would be happy to hear from authors or publishers so that any such errors or omissions may be rectified in future editions.

Warning. Photocopying any part of this book without permission is illegal.

Introduction

Religious Studies attracts people from many backgrounds and interest groups – members of different religions, philosophers, atheists, agnostics, ethicists and textual students. What binds all of these people together is a passion for thinking seriously about the fundamental questions of life and about how people have responded to these questions.

How does AS differ from GCSE?

If you have already done GCSE Religious Studies, you may find that you draw on some of the skills and knowledge you learned there, but you will now be studying the subject from a different point of view and at a higher level. You will also be studying new material and learning new skills.

Your AS grade in Religious Studies will depend on how well you do in three written examinations lasting 1 hour each. Whether you are taking AS as a free-standing qualification or as the first half of an A level, you will take three modules out of the six on offer. You MUST take:

Module 1: An Introduction to Religion and Human Experience

and then you choose any TWO other modules from:

Module 2: An Introduction to the Old Testament

Module 3: An Introduction to the New Testament

Module 4: An Introduction to Religion and Ethics

Module 5: An Introduction to Aspects of a Major World Faith

Module 6: An Introduction to Religion and Science.

If you are taking AS as the first half of an A level, you will go on to take another three modules, this time from the ones on offer at A2 level. See *A Student's Guide to A2 Religious Studies for the AQA Specification* by Dennis Brown and Stephen Morris (Rhinegold Publishing Ltd 2003).

Modules

Module 1

Module 1 is designed to give you a broad understanding of what religion is about and is intended to be an introductory module for the whole course. This is because it introduces you to two fundamental ideas in religious faith and practice:

✦ Religious experience

✦ Religious authority.

Although only one aspect of authority is examined – the authority and inspiration of sacred writings – you will need to know something about other sources of religious authority, such as holy people, tradition and dogma.

Modules 2–6

Within Modules 2–6 there are essentially three different kinds of course. These are:

✦ Textual study (Modules 2 and 3)

✦ Study of a particular religion (Module 5)

✦ Philosophical study (Modules 4 and 6).

Modules 2 and 3

For Modules 2 and 3, you will learn to use a Bible. You are allowed to use any version, but any quotes from the Bible in examination questions will be taken from the Revised Standard Version (RSV).

Introduction 5

You will not gain any marks for writing out lengthy quotations from the Bible because you are allowed to take your copy into the examination room. Do remember, though, that you must not make any notes or other annotations on your copy of the Bible.

In both of these modules you will be looking at certain important themes such as 'God and Covenant' (Module 2) or 'Reflections on Jesus by the Evangelists' (Module 3). You will be studying the specified texts in relation to these themes, so, in a sense, it is the *themes* that are the more important focus of your study, not the details of the text.

Module 5 If you take Module 5, you will have the opportunity to study the following aspects of one of the major world faiths (Buddhism, Christianity, Hinduism, Islam, Judaism and Sikhism):

- Historical foundations and overall development (how it began, how it developed)
- Central concepts (what it preaches)
- Practices and their significance (how believers practise their religion).

The examination paper for this module will be arranged in sections, one for each of the religions. Make sure that you answer questions from only one section.

Modules 4 and 6 If you take Module 4 and/or Module 6, you will be looking in a philosophical way at some of the important questions that affect religious believers. Module 4 concerns the relation between religion and ethics. Here you will look at three different ways of approaching ethics (a Utilitarian, Kantian and religious perspective), and then apply each of these to some important medical and environmental issues. If you study Module 6, you will be looking at aspects of the interaction between religion and science in three areas: creation, miracles, and design arguments for the existence of God. In both of these modules, you will examine religion in a somewhat different way than if you are taking any of the other modules. For instance, in Modules 4 and 6, you will be analysing religious teaching, doctrine and concepts in a more general, overarching way than you might be in Module 2 or 3.

You might be concerned about how much detail you will be expected to know for Modules 4 and 6 on specific ethical or scientific issues. For example how much science do you need to know in order to answer a question on the Big Bang theory? Or how much do you need to know about the medical techniques involved in abortion? Let us try to answer this with reference to Module 4.

The focus of questions in Module 4 will be on the ethical theories. You will not need to know detailed scientific or medical terminology or debates. This is particularly relevant to the section on medical issues you have to study. Below is an indication of the kind of detail you would be expected to bring to any question you would have to answer.

Abortion. It will be useful for you to know some detail on the contemporary legal position in Britain on abortion. Obviously some facts on foetus development may be relevant to the ethical issues, but there is no need to go into detail on methods of abortion other than where these details are used in ethical arguments for and against the issues.

Euthanasia. You will be expected to know the meaning of terms such as 'voluntary euthanasia', 'involuntary euthanasia', 'active euthanasia' and 'passive euthanasia'. Some very basic knowledge of contemporary UK and Netherlands (where euthanasia is now legal) law would be useful.

Value and use of embryo and foetus. You will only be expected to know a few examples of when embryos may be used for medical research (for example, surplus embryos resulting from IVF can be used in research to improve subsequent IVF techniques). You will also be expected to know at least one example of the circumstances when embryos may be discarded, because only the healthy ones are kept (for example, recent cases of Pre-Implantation Genetic Diagnosis which were widely discussed in the media). Some basic biological knowledge about the nature of embryos may also be useful.

Allocation of resources. You should have some knowledge of the central dilemmas facing doctors in this area, and in particular of the problem of limited funds and rising demands. It would be helpful for you to have some awareness of individual cases. You will not be expected to know precise NHS methods for calculating what money goes where. Rather you should investigate how the basic issue might be approached by Bentham, Mill, Kant or from a religious perspective.

Transplantation. You will need to know the different types of transplantation and the ethical problems surrounding them.

How to study

Sources

Sources enable you to find the information you need to develop your understanding of topics and to write your essays. Good sources include:

- Notes taken from lectures
- Notes given out by teachers
- Reference books
- Text books
- Specialist books on the topic
- Journals and magazines
- Websites.

You should be able to obtain the basic information you need from these sources, and you should also get examples of the way in which this information has been understood and evaluated by others.

Don't neglect current affairs: read newspapers, looking for articles related to the issues you are studying. You will find there are

Because anyone has the freedom to set up a website and post material on it, you need to be careful about the reliability of what you find on the Internet. You should double-check any information you find against another source. Be selective and you will learn which sites are reliable. Remember to bookmark good sites so that you can find them again easily, and always acknowledge websites as sources in any written work you do.

Newspapers

frequent articles about ethical issues which could help if you are studying Module 4. There are sometimes articles about the beliefs and current political activities of different religious groups which could prove interesting if you are studying Module 5. For instance if you are studying Christianity in Module 5, look out for articles or editorials on issues like the relationship between Church and State, the views of the Archbishop of Canterbury, statements from Church leaders about topical issues and the like. For Module 6, Religion and Science, there are often articles about scientific discoveries that may be relevant to the topics you are studying. Read any such articles, cut them out and keep them in a file for future reference.

Places Try to visit relevant places of religious interest, or museums. If you are studying Hinduism in Module 5, try to visit a mandir (temple) and talk to some of the Hindu community. Most members of religious communities are happy for people to show an interest in their religion and will welcome the opportunity to talk to you about their beliefs. This kind of encounter can bring out quite different emphases from reading a book about religious beliefs. It can also highlight some of the regional differences about religious belief – being a Hindu in a British city or town is different from being a Hindu in rural India, for instance. Many museums have sections that are relevant to your studies. If you can't find anything of interest, such as religious artefacts, simply ask a member of staff. They will be pleased to help you, perhaps by explaining the significance of an artefact, or by pointing you to some other source of information.

Organisations Equally, you could contact some relevant organisations. To help with Module 4, Religion and Ethics, for example, you could contact organisations concerned with euthanasia or pollution. Ask them for any literature they may have on the issues involved and examples of the kind of work they do (for example lobbying governments, publishing literature, work in developing countries, case studies and so on).

Further study You will also find some additional reference points in the margins of this guide. The 'Further study' sections do not contain information that will directly gain you marks in your exams, but the recommended activities will help to enhance your general knowledge of the topic. They invite you to look at an issue in a different and interesting way: you might be advised to listen to a piece of music or to watch a film, for example.

Organising your work

During your course your teachers will give you notes, handouts, exercises, tasks and homework. You need to learn how to deal with the large amount of material coming your way or you won't be able to learn, understand and evaluate it. Three useful ways of helping to cope with all this material are to:

◆ Make good notes

◆ Create a good filing system

◆ Manage your time effectively.

Making notes

There are essentially three kinds of notes you will have to make:

Notes from books. Your teacher will ask you to do this so that you can learn to select the most important points from an article or chapter and then condense them for yourself. Usually (though not always) the most important point comes at the beginning of each paragraph. The rest of the paragraph normally then elaborates or explains the main point. Try to learn to look carefully at the beginnings of paragraphs so that you can see the progression of the points the author is making.

Class notes. Your teacher will expect you to note down important points for yourself. At first you may try to write down every single word they say. But unless your teacher speaks very slowly indeed, you will simply not be able to do this. What you will need to learn is how to listen, assimilate what you hear and sift the most important phrases to write down. If your teacher is talking about John Stuart Mill's version of Utilitarianism, they may talk for 15 minutes about what Mill says and how his theory differs from that of Jeremy Bentham. You may write down only the key words:

consequentialist – hedonist (happiness) – pleasure – qualitative not quantitative – higher and lower pleasures – competent judges

What you have done is listened carefully, understood what the teacher is saying, and written down – in a very concise form – the essential features of Mill's theory to help you remember the lesson. The purpose of class notes is for you to consolidate what you have learned in class, so that these notes provide you with the structure of everything you need to know for the examination.

Revision notes. When it comes to revision for your module examinations, you will need to distil all your notes into a more manageable body of information. The usual way to do this is by rewriting your notes. Use your class notes as the basis of the distilled version, but add in useful information from the other notes you have made during the course. Distilling notes means cutting them down to the bare essentials – for example reducing one module to two sides of A4 paper, or a 'mind map' diagram. At a later stage of revision, you could distil these further on to, say, two postcards or one diagram.

A mind map is a more sophisticated form of spider diagram, using space, colour and imagery to help you remember key themes. For information on 'how to mind map' go to www.peterussell.com/Mindmaps/HowTo.html.

Filing

It is absolutely essential that you have a manageable filing system if you are to succeed at AS. Keep a different-coloured file at home for each module you are taking and label each one clearly. Then have a *separate* file that you take to school or college each day. This is the file in which you put the day's notes and handouts. When you return home in the evening, transfer the notes from this daily file to the appropriate module file.

When you get to the revision stage, get another file and use it to store just your distilled revision notes in. This will make any last-minute revision easier.

Managing your time

Unlike at GCSE, at AS you will find yourself having free (ie non-taught) periods during the day. You may also find that teachers do not set you specific homework to do every night, and they may give you a week or longer to complete a task. You will therefore have

Warning. Photocopying any part of this book without permission is illegal.

to learn how to manage your time effectively. Make sure you plan ahead with your work rather than leaving it all to the last possible moment. List the tasks or assignments you are given (have a special book or diary to do this in), noting when they are to be handed in. Use your available time to do the must-do tasks first, then the can-do things, then the could-do tasks if you have time left over.

Revision

Revision is essential for examination success and it does not have to be terminally boring! Organising your work effectively is as essential in revision as it is in studying. Here are a number of suggestions:

The Revision Process	
About two months before the exam, complete Stages 1–5:	
Stage 1: Filing system	Put together a separate file which contains your revision notes and sample questions
Stage 2: Outline	Make sure you have an outline guide of what you need to know: ask your teacher for one
Stage 3: Sorting and filling	Use the outline to identify irrelevant material and any important gaps. Fill any gaps by getting information from teachers, friends or books
Stage 4: Checklist	Using the outline and your own notes, make a list of topics you need to cover. Prioritise the list, putting least-known topics at the top. In revision, work down the list
Stage 5: Examination	Look at the sort of questions you will be answering in the examination. This book has some examples at the end of each chapter
About a month before the module, you should begin revising about two hours a day. This is Stage 6:	
Stage 6: Note, learn, do	Your different modules may require different revision techniques. Whatever the technique, make it **active**. Make lists, mind maps, timelines or condense notes
In the final weeks before the module, finalise notes and move to Stage 7:	
Stage 7: Past questions	Your teacher will give you some past examination questions, and there are also some in this book. Work through these yourself, trying to complete them in the time allowed
Stage 8: Problem solving	When you reach this stage, you may encounter some difficulties. Ask friends and teachers to help you solve them
Stage 9: The night before	You should by now be working from notes condensed to key words or ideas: remind yourself of these and try to get a good night's sleep

It is very difficult to prescribe an optimal study time for revision. Many people can work effectively for about 40 minutes at a time, with breaks of 15 minutes in between. Three sessions of this would be sufficient. On the other hand, Tony Buzan, a leader in the field of study skills, recommends study periods of 25 minutes with a five-minute break in between and with a longer break after 2½ hours. These are good guidelines to consider, but you should find a schedule that works for you, checking first with your teacher that it is sufficient.

The ideal place for revision is somewhere away from distractions like your stereo, television or computer, where you can leave your files and books out while working. Find an upright chair so that you stay awake, and work at a table or desk. Different people learn in different ways and you will need to find the way that is best for you, but here are some suggestions:

+ Use colour to highlight certain facts or types of idea in your notes – colour stimulates memory

+ Use flashcards, index cards with brief revision notes on – you can revise them while travelling to school or college

+ Translate your notes into spider diagrams, tables, lists or flowlines of linked ideas

+ Use mnemonics, rhymes or short poems to help you remember ideas or facts.

Examinations

One of the major differences between GCSE level and AS level is the style of the examination questions. At GCSE, you probably had to answer three different types of question: short answer, slightly

Warning. Photocopying any part of this book without permission is illegal.

longer explanatory answer and structured essay. At AS the style of questions will be different, but in general will be more akin to the structured-essay type.

What are you being examined on?

In each module or section of the course, you will be doing work that will give you the opportunity to show **knowledge, understanding** and the ability to make informed **judgements** about:

- The key concepts in each module (ie, the concept of authority in Module 1) and how these are shown in texts or practices
- The contribution of important people, traditions or movements to each module (ie, Gotama for Buddhism, Module 5)
- Religious language and terminology (ie, covenant for Module 2)
- Major issues and questions arising from the study (ie, whether religion and science are contradictory)
- The relationship between each module and other specified aspects of human experience (ie, how important mysticism is for Christians).

You can do this by demonstrating that you are able to:

- Recall, select and deploy the knowledge you have learned
- Identify, investigate and analyse questions and issues arising from your course
- Use appropriate language and terminology in context
- Interpret and evaluate religious concepts, issues, ideas, and the relevance of arguments and the views of scholars
- Communicate using reasoned arguments substantiated by evidence
- Make connections between the module studied and other specified aspects of human experience.

Assessment Objectives

To make sure that you do all of these things in each of the modules you take, the examiners have set out two Assessment Objectives (AOs) for AS. These are:

- **AO1.** You show that you can select and demonstrate clearly relevant knowledge and understanding through the use of evidence, examples, and correct language and terminology appropriate to the course of study
- **AO2.** You show that you can sustain a critical line of argument and justify a point of view.

Trigger words

Your exam questions are likely to contain a number of trigger words that give you clues about what the examiner wants you to write in your answer. Here they are, with explanations of what they are asking for and a guide to which AO they are tied:

Warning. Photocopying any part of this book without permission is illegal.

Introduction 11

AO1	
State	This looks for a straightforward account of the topic: write a few sentences about the main points
Identify	This is used to elicit a list of main points (characteristics, causes etc): explain/expand each point in a few sentences
Outline; Summarise	These require a brief or concise account of the main points
Describe; Give/write an account	The focus here is on factual information: more detail than outline is needed
Define	Explain the meaning and give some examples or illustrations
Explain	The focus is on understanding, not knowledge: give reasons for and examples of the main points
Examine	This requires knowledge and understanding: unpack the meaning of concepts by explaining them and giving reasons or illustrations
What? Why? How?	These triggers can require knowledge, understanding or both

AO2	
Assess; Evaluate; To what extent? How far?	Set out the arguments for and against a statement or viewpoint, consider alternatives, weigh up strengths and weaknesses or evidence or arguments, and draw a conclusion

How to get a high grade

To get a high grade, you need to show a full, accurate knowledge of the topics studied. Your understanding and analysis of the issues needs to be excellent. You will need to be able to compare, contrast and evaluate the views of scholars as well as offering your own ideas and insights. Use evidence to support your arguments, explain what the opposing views are and show why you disagree with those views. Keep your eye out for the connections between the areas you have studied, and their contribution to the nature of religion and aspects of human experience.

Clear use of language is also an important skill. To gain a high grade, you need to write well and communicate ideas expressively. You should also use technical language fluently and in a variety of contexts, though you should make sure that it is appropriate and effective – don't just cram in technical terms.

Exam structure

Two different types of question are set in the AS examinations and the format of the examination is the same in each module. Let us set out the important points below:

✦ Each examination lasts 1 hour

✦ Question 1 is compulsory

✦ Question 1 consists of a short stimulus text, followed by two sub-questions

✦ Each of these sub-questions is worth 10 marks (therefore maximum 20 marks) and both test AO1.

There will be two other questions on the paper, of which you must answer one:

✦ Questions 2 and 3 are divided into two parts: (a) and (b)

✦ These parts will be worth 15 (AO1) and 25 (AO1=10; AO2=15) marks respectively (therefore maximum 40 marks).

Try to keep the amount of time you spend on the two questions relative to the marks available: ie, you should try and spend 20 minutes on part (a) and 40 minutes on part (b).

The total number of marks for each module examination is 60, and each AS module examination is worth one third of the overall AS qualification.

Warning. Photocopying any part of this book without permission is illegal.

Examination technique

Many candidates do less well than they should in examinations because they do not follow some very basic advice. Below are some tried and tested ideas:

Read the instructions. There are some important instructions on the front page of the examination paper. Make sure you read them carefully. This will help you to remember that you MUST answer question 1, but that you only answer ONE other question, not BOTH.

Read the questions. Do not panic when the examination starts; take a minute to read ALL the questions before you start writing. For instance you may find that you can answer question 3 better than question 2.

Underline the key words in the question. This will help you to structure your answer, because it will show you what the examiners want and how they expect you to answer.

Timing. Many people do badly in examinations because they do not have time to finish all the questions. Make sure you are aware of the available time for each question and sub-question. For example, in question 1, you will have approximately 37 minutes to answer all four sections, ie about 8 minutes per 10 marks, with 5 minutes' thinking time.

Keep it simple. Because you will not have much time for your answers, do not bother with a florid introduction or elaborate prose. Make the point, explain it and give an example (see PEER *below*).

Be specific. Do not generalise by using phrases like 'all Buddhists believe…'. Instead be aware of the diversity of opinion within religions or philosophical systems: 'Most Theravada Buddhists believe…'.

Answer the question. Make sure that you answer THIS year's question, not the one you did as part of your revision. Keep looking back at the question to make sure you are doing what it asks you to do. Using words from the question in your answer will help keep you on the right topic.

Balance. Try to give a balanced answer, particularly when dealing with the second part of each question. If you fail to show different points of view you will limit the number of marks you can gain.

Finally here are two useful ideas that will help you in the examination. The recipe for writing a good answer at AS level is:

The P-plan and PEER

> **Prior Planning and Punchy Purposeful Paragraphs Prevent Pathetically Poor Performance.**

- ✦ **Planning.** Know exactly what you need to say before you start writing. Think of four or five ideas or key points, put them into logical order and use them to structure your answer.

- ✦ **Punchy.** You do not have time to waffle. Make your points precisely and clearly, then explain them and give an example.

- ✦ **Purposeful.** Split your answer up into paragraphs, and make the beginning of each paragraph obvious and clearly relevant to the question asked. At every stage try to link what you are saying to the question.

✦ **Poor performance.** A paragraph will be poor if it is unclear, lacks examples to support the point you are making or is irrelevant to the question.

And how do you write those punchy, purposeful paragraphs? PEER at them!

P Make your **point** concisely at the beginning of the paragraph – your opening sentence should be short and to the point.

E Give a clear **explanation** of your point – what it means, how it works, and why it is important in explaining your answer.

E Provide an **example** or **evidence** to show that you know what you are talking about.

R Show how what you have written is **relevant** to the question. Refer back to the question to show how your point answers it.

If you follow these hints, you should be able to show the examiner that you are a top-class candidate.

Sample answers

Let's look at a real answer to a Module 1 question 1. It was written under examination conditions and is quoted exactly as it was written. We have made some comments about the answer in the margin.

The question Read this passage and answer questions (a) and (b) which follow.

'The religious experience of important figures played a critical part in the origin and development of many different traditions. However, whilst the religious experience of those important figures from the past is still relevant, the religious experience of ordinary believers is not important in religion today.'

With reference to the tradition(s) you have studied:

(a) Describe the religious experience of **one** important figure.
(10 marks)

(b) Explain why the religious experience of such important people may have no authority for non-believers. (10 marks)

The answer

(a) Saul, later St. Paul, had a conversion experience on the road to Damascus, in Acts 9. He was confronted by Jesus who asked: 'Why do you persecute me?'. 'Who are you Lord?' came Paul's response, to which Jesus revealed his identity.

Prior to this, Saul had been a member of an aggressive Jewish tribe and persicuted [sic] Christians, in an attempt to create a Jewish race that was pure enough for the Messiah to arrive. He believed that using violence, he could force his beliefs upon others, a marked contrast to his views after conversion.

- After his experience, Paul had an immediate conversion (not gradual like those of C. S. Lewis and Leo Tolstoy), however it left him blind. Paul remained blind until Jesus sent Simon to restore his vision. Upon recovering his sight, Paul embarked on his new mission, to spread the word of Jesus. He now believed that love and faith were the principal aspects of the religion rather than practice as he had previously believed.

(b) Without having had a religious experience yourself, it is hard to relate to those of others. There are also many problems encountered with religious experiences, such as why was this
- particular person chosen? Paul is a particularly good example of this having previously persicuted [sic] Christians.

Alistair MacIntyre questioned the role of God in religious experience, for if he is infinite, he can not be one designated shape and therefore can not be a part of a religious experience. Religious experiences can be vague and therefore misinterpreted or can be radical and therefore contradict the institution it is trying to serve i.e. the church, undermining the credibility of both.

It is also hard to determine whether the experience is from a divine source or being induced by such things as hallucinations or the passing of electrical currents through the brain, or something more sinister such as the devil.

Schizophrenia can often lead to experiences which are seemingly religious, however they are merely mental instability.

Address the question correctly. This question asks for a description, not an analysis, of the religious experience of an important person. This candidate has focused on conversion, and has included some material that is relevant (confrontation with Jesus, immediate effect of the experience, preaching as the result of the conversion). Quite a lot of what is written is not relevant, however. For example, most of the second paragraph would not gain any marks because it does not help to answer the question.

Be succinct. The candidate makes several good points here, though they are written in a rather wordy style. They show a good understanding of the issues surrounding the authority (or lack of it) of religious experiences.

End your answer appropriately. Even if your question deals with a description rather than analysis calling for a balanced conclusion, try not to leave your answer in mid-air because of time constraints, as this candidate appears to have done.

Here is a second Module 1 answer. This answer is very good and got a high grade.

The question

(a) With reference to one religious tradition you have studied, identify and explain the different ways in which scripture may be interpreted. (15 marks)

(b) 'In religion today, the authority of religious leaders is more important than the authority of scripture'. Explain and assess this view. (25 marks)

Warning. Photocopying any part of this book without permission is illegal.

The answer

> Do not waste time with a wordy introduction, but immediately begin to demonstrate your knowledge.

> Use religious terminology, where relevant, with confidence.

> This is an impressive paragraph: clear and well-written with effective use of candidate's own judgment.

> Combine a clear identification of the relevant issues with a sophisticated explanation of them.

> Get to grips with the question in a relevant and concise introduction.

(a) In Christianity, there are three main schools of scriptural interpretation: fundamentalist, conservative and liberal.

Fundamentalists maintain a very close link between scripture and divine truth. They stress the literal sense of the text as the 'Word of God', looking particularly at passages like 2 Timothy 3:16. They believe that scripture is the product of direct divine revelation, so that prophets or apostles, although appointed by God, were merely messengers and had no personal effect on the eternal truths contained in the Bible. Scripture is therefore understood by fundamentalists as a fixed point against which the cultural changes of our contemporary society are to be measured and judged. If, for example, the findings of evolutionary biology are seen to contradict a literal reading of Genesis 1 and 2, then the Bible, which contains eternal truth, must be right and the evolutionary theories incorrect. However when fundamentalists are faced with dispute over the central issues of the Christian faith and by apparently contradictory passages in the Bible, they tend to be narrow in their definition of 'Orthodoxy' and selective in their literal reading.

Conservative Christians differ from fundamentalists mainly by giving greater place to reason in their understanding of the Bible. They would reject a literal reading of Genesis 1 and 2, and prefer to see the creation story as symbolic picture language. But conservatives try to integrate the findings of modern science with their interpretation of the Bible, while still holding to its authority. For them, all truth is God's truth, whether received through 'Special Revelation' in scripture, or through 'General Revelation' in the natural world.

The liberal approach is based on a shift in people's world-view, from a simple acceptance of the biblical word and an unquestioning belief in the authority of the Church to a more critical, scientific approach to religious belief. Liberals believe that the documents in the Bible were written by religious men who reflected profoundly on their experience of God and his relationship with the universe. But these men were very much the product of their times and their work was affected by their circumstances. Consequently, liberals feel free to dispense with some passages in the Bible, such as teaching on slavery and homosexuality, which they see as a result of a world-view different from our own. Liberals still call the Bible the 'Word of God', but they use this term in a much looser sense: biblical books show evidence of inspiration and perceptive insight, but in much the same way as do the works of Shakespeare or Dickens.

(b) This statement expresses the view that the authority of the Bible is not as important as the pronouncements of religious leaders such as the Pope, the Archbishop of Canterbury, or even a parish priest.

In the Roman Catholic Church, the Pope is called the 'Vicar of Christ'. The Second Vatican Council (1962–65) declared that the Pope, as the successor of Peter, is the perpetual and visible source of the unity of the Church. This means that the Pope is the principle source of authority for Roman Catholics and that, when he speaks, all Roman Catholics must listen to and obey what he says. This is particularly the case when the Pope speaks 'Ex Cathedra' ('from the chair') to the whole Church, because on these occasions the words and teaching of the Pope are equivalent to the words and teaching of God, and are thus understood as having greater authority than the words of the Bible. In fact the First Vatican Council (1869-70) declared that anything pronounced 'Ex Cathedra' was believed to be infallible. However, the Pope does not usually speak 'Ex Cathedra', having done so on only two occasions since Vatican I.

The words of the Archbishop of Canterbury have a similar importance for Anglicans. In recent years, the Archbishop has made statements concerning many contemporary ethical issues, including care for the environment, homosexuality and the ordination of women priests. Many such issues are not discussed directly in the Bible, and hence statements on them by the Archbishop can be seen as particularly important and authoritative.

> It is vital to demonstrate that you recognise the diversity within your chosen religion. This is a very important skill at this level.

In assessing this statement, it is important to bear in mind the distinction between 'internal' and 'external' authority. External authority is that which is attached to a person because of their position or office. So the Pope and the Archbishop of Canterbury both have external authority in this way. Internal authority on the other hand rests in a convincing argument or in the weighty moral or spiritual example provided by someone's life. An example of such a person is Mahatma Gandhi or perhaps a classical Christian saint, like St Francis of Assisi.

The Bible is the ultimate example of internal authority. Many Christians believe that the Bible is the divinely inspired 'Word of God', that the books of the Bible come from God himself. This means that, because the Bible comes ultimately (either directly or indirectly) from God, it must have greater authority than the words or teaching of any religious leader.

Another major argument against the statement in the question is that, even if we concede that Christian religious leaders have authority, they get this authority ultimately from the Bible. For instance, when the Pope speaks about poverty, he derives his teaching from various passages in the Bible. Similarly, when the Archbishop of Canterbury speaks about caring for the environment, he uses biblical teaching, such as God's gift of 'dominion' over everything in creation in Genesis 1: 27, to support his statements. Even when a religious leader speaks about an issue on which there is no specific discussion in the Bible, such as genetic engineering, he will still attempt to base his argument on general biblical principles. In every circumstance, therefore, religious leaders depend upon the authority of the Bible.

Finally it should be said that all religious people accept that absolute authority resides neither in the Bible nor religious leaders, but in God himself. All Christians, be they fundamentalists or liberals, Roman Catholics or Protestants, accept that God is the single, only creator of everything. Moreover it was God who revealed himself in the books of the Bible and it is God who inspires religious leaders. As a result, both those who believe that the authority of the Bible is more important than that of religious leaders, and those who believe the opposite, agree that God is ultimately the source of all authority within the Church.

> The candidate assesses this question clearly and comprehensively, backing up their points with effective use of evidence, and reaching a sophisticated conclusion.

Warning. Photocopying any part of this book without permission is illegal.

Religion and human experience

Religious experience

The nature of religion

Different people interpret and use words like 'religion' in different ways, and these interpretations themselves are constantly evolving. This makes the word religion quite hard to pin down. Some notable modern scholars have tried to define it in the following ways:

Bronislaw Malinowski (1884–1942) pioneered the **Anthropological Definition**, seeing religion as part of what human communities use to unite and share their experience of life's mysteries and their understanding of life's meaning. It is also one of the key ways in which human communities codify acceptable patterns of human behaviour.

Emile Durkheim (1858–1917) established the **Sociological Definition**, which emphasises the social dimension of religion, seeing it as a way in which societies provide an agreed way of interpreting the world and offer the individual a sense of meaning and significance. Durkheim argued that society itself possesses Godlike powers: it exists before we are born, continues after our death, and it constructs our language and concepts.

Mircea Eliade (1907–1986) developed the **Historical Definition**, which focuses on the events which result from beliefs (for example, the Middle-Eastern conflict which results from beliefs about the Holy Land and about the sacredness of various sites).

The **Theological Definition** concentrates on the meaning and significance of the beliefs themselves, the truth or falsehood of those beliefs and the question of how they affect believers' lives. Theology is often associated with the adherents of a religion, who themselves use scholarship to advance understanding of the central concepts and expectations of their faith.

Ninian Smart (1927–2001) was a leading figure in the development of the **Phenomenological Definition** which seeks to classify the different characteristics which belong to all religious traditions, rather like a linguist may identify a language in terms of verbs, nouns, adjectives etc. Smart described religion as having seven key features:

- **Ritual.** Behaviour that seeks to express an inner reality, such as closing your eyes for prayer, meditation, yoga or any other action performed symbolically
- **Myths.** Narrative stories that illustrate a spiritual truth; they may or may not be factually and historically true
- **Doctrine.** A systematic code of beliefs and teachings
- **Ethics.** Persuading followers to live by a common set of values
- **Social effects.** The way in which the religion directs the customs of the society in which it is based
- **Experiential.** How it feels to be part of the religion, to be a believer

---

We shall frequently refer to the following texts in this chapter:

The Varieties of Religious Experience by William James (Longman 1902).

The Religious Experience of Mankind by Ninian Smart (Collins 1969).

> **Further study**
>
> Read the quotations below, make sure you understand each one, and then decide which definition of religion each expresses:
>
> a) Karl Marx: 'Religion is the sigh of the oppressed creature, the heart of a heartless world, and the soul of soulless conditions. It is the opium of the people.'
>
> b) Anthony Wallace: 'A set of rituals, rationalised by myth, which mobilises supernatural powers for the purpose of achieving or preventing transformations of state in man or nature.'
>
> c) Paul Tillich: 'Religion is the state of being grasped by an ultimate concern'.
>
> d) William James: 'The belief that there is an unseen order, and that our supreme good lies in harmoniously adjusting ourselves thereto.'
>
> e) J. Z. Smith: 'While there is a staggering amount of data, phenomena, of human experiences and expressions that might be characterised in one culture or another, by one criterion or another, as religion – there is no data for religion. Religion is solely the creation of the scholar's study. It is created for the scholar's analytic purposes by his imaginative acts of comparison and generalisation. Religion has no existence apart from the academy.'

- **Material.** Religions produce buildings, artwork and other cultural artifacts.

The nature of religious experience

William James (1842–1910) defined religion as 'the feelings, acts and experiences of individual men in their solitude, so far as they apprehend themselves to stand in relation to whatever they may consider as divine'. He taught that there were four basic features of religious experience:

- Ineffable: it is impossible to find words adequately to describe the experience
- Noetic: the experiences are felt to be absolutely real
- Transient: the experience is temporary but the impact of the experience is long-lasting
- Passive: the person who has the experience feels controlled by a force outside themselves.

W. T. Stace (1886–1967) also tried to define religious experience, and used eight dimensions:

W. T. Stace *Mysticism and Philosophy* (Macmillan 1960).

- Unified vision: a sense that all things are together in harmony
- Timelessness and spacelessness: a feeling of being detached from the world
- Sense of reality: life feels more real, not less, as a result of the experience
- Blessedness: joy, happiness, peace
- Appreciation of the holy: the sacred aspect of life
- Paradox: normal rules of logic do not apply
- Ineffability: being unable to describe what has happened adequately in words
- Loss of sense of self: one's own wants and priorities become less important as those of the god become more important.

St Francis of Assisi (c.1181–1226) referred to the moon as his sister and the sun as his brother, because his religious experiences had made him feel in harmony with all creation.

Do James' and Stace's definitions contradict or complement one another?

Rejecting the view of religion as a sociological phenomenon, **Rudolph Otto** (1869–1937) maintained that God must be transcendent, above and beyond human understanding, and that religion is rooted in **numinous** experience, bypassing reason. This view has been criticised by scholars who feel that it makes God impersonal and distant. Christian theologians point to the Incarnation as evidence of God's closeness to humanity.

The Idea of the Holy by Rudolph Otto (Oxford University Press 1968) uses the word 'numinous' to refer to the feeling of being in the presence of an awesome power.

What 'brings on' religious experiences? Alister Hardy of the Oxford Religious Experience Research Unit surveyed 3,000 people who claimed to have had religious experiences. He compiled the following list of triggers (listed in order of frequency):

1. Depression or despair
2. Prayer or meditation
3. The beauty of nature
4. Participation in religious worship

5. Literature, drama or film
6. Illness
7. Music
8. Crises in personal relationships
9. The death of others
10. Sacred places
11. Visual arts
12. Creative work
13. The prospect of death
14. Silence or solitude
15. Anaesthetic drugs
16. Physical activity
17. Relaxation
18. Childbirth
19. Happiness
20. Psychedelic drugs
21. Sexual relations.

For more details on these findings, see *The Relevance of Bliss* by N. Coxhead (St Martin's Press 1985).

Conversions

'To be converted is the process, gradual or sudden, by which a self, hitherto divided and consciously wrong, inferior and unhappy, becomes unified and consciously right, superior and happy, in consequence of its former hold upon religious realities.'
William James

Lewis R. Rambo *Understanding Religious Conversion* (Yale University Press 1993).

One key religious experience is conversion, turning one's life toward religious goals. Conversion can be from one religion to another, or more commonly either from no religion to a faith, or from nominal religious affiliation to a fuller religious commitment. Not all religions actively seek converts. Christianity, Islam and Buddhism all have marked missionary histories. On the other hand, Judaism abandoned missionary work to focus on consolidation within the faith itself, while the missionary efforts of Hinduism in the west is a new phenomenon.

Lewis Rambo and **Charles Farhadian** offer a more systematic explanation of conversion, identifying seven causal factors:

1. **Context.** We may need to take into account such diverse things as the politics of the country, the local religious organisations, the social acceptability of religion, the convert's family and friends

2. **Crisis.** An experience such as a bereavement, a divorce or a near-death experience which makes the person begin asking questions about the big issues of life

3. **Quest.** What were the person's own inner motives in being converted? What did they have to gain (political influence, promotion, etc), if anything? Were their motives centred upon a quest for truth and reality, or on the less noble 'going along with the crowd'?

4. **Encounter.** What happened in the encounter that brought about the conversion? Was pressure put upon the convert? Was anyone else involved?

5. **Interaction.** How did the convert learn the roles, behaviour and attitudes expected of them now they are converted? What

demands are made upon their life? From whom did they learn what is now expected of them?

6. **Commitment.** Does the conversion lead on to a personal commitment and become real and permanent, or is it short-lived? To whom is commitment made, and how?

7. **Consequences.** What effect does the conversion have upon the life of the convert in a long-term sense? What are the life-changing results of the conversion?

Undoubtedly many conversions are genuine and long lasting. A person may be persuaded that a particular faith is true; they may be attracted by other adherents to that faith or they may have a religious experience that leads to conversion. On the other hand, some conversions can be short-lived emotional affairs, pushed through by evangelists working like door-to-door salesmen.

We should not assume that conversion is always the beginning. Lewis Rambo points out that sometimes faith comes after a person has begun to follow the practices of a religion, rather than the other way round:

> Many social scientists are saying that, in many cases, it is belief that follows practice, and not practice that follows belief. There's always a debate about the sequence, but I think one could argue that, in many groups, learning to behave in certain ways, and to affiliate in certain ways, often takes priority over some sort of belief system. The belief system is often something that people acquire much later, at least in its more sophisticated terms.

See more of Lewis Rambo's speech, delivered at the International Coalition for Religious Freedom conference in Germany (1998) at www.religiousfreedom.com/conference/germany/rambo.htm.

Ninian Smart acknowledged that religious experience can take many forms, and therefore described it as involving: 'Some kind of perception of the invisible world, or... a perception that some visible person or thing is a manifestation of the invisible world.' This perception of the invisible world can take the form of a vision.

Adherents of most religions report themselves as having experienced visions. People usually interpret them in terms of their own faith (Christians may see Mary; Hindus may see Vishnu). The visions have a positive message or purpose. The person may feel afraid, even overcome, but not psychologically destroyed by the experience. Some neuro-scientists have speculated that the people who have visions have a highly developed right-side of the brain which is particularly attuned to creative and religious things (in a similar way to someone with a highly developed left-side of the brain may be very good at maths). It is helpful to categorise visions into three types:

Visions

'[The] apparent difference in the experiences of different men and women does not point to any difference between the source of the experiences, which is always the pure divine Overself. Rather it points to the fact that each recipient colours and interprets the experience in the light of their own mentality, culture and personal history – that is, the form of the experience is contributed by the recipient himself.' Peter K. Cross, http://website.lineone.net/~peter_cross/mystic.htm

✦ **Corporeal vision.** An actual figure may really be present but it is perceived in a luminous way suggesting that it has been seen and appreciated more deeply than usual. Alternatively something is seen or heard for which there is no apparent day-to-day justification or other people present cannot see it. The figure may be a religious icon such as Mary or a dead person

✦ **Imaginative vision.** A person is imaginatively aware of a figure that they cannot see. The experience is beyond the control of the person and is accompanied by a feeling of holiness. It is usually short-lived and may give way to intellectual visions

Imaginative visions often occur during sleep: see Genesis 41 and Daniel 2.

> 'We see nothing, either interiorly or exteriorly… But without seeing anything the soul conceives the object and feels whence it is more clearly than if it saw it, save that nothing in particular is shown to it. It is like feeling someone near one in a dark place.' St Teresa of Avila.

Küng sees a contrast with institutional religion, which tends to emphasise the importance of external activity and ritual. See *Does God exist?* by Hans Küng (Collins 1980).

St Bonaventure was an Italian scholastic theologian. He taught the theologian St Thomas Aquinas: see pages 86–87, 121 and 126–127.

Revelations

Monotheism is the belief that only one god exists.

> 'I do not understand so that I may believe: I believe in order that I may understand.' St Augustine of Hippo.

The veracity of religious experience

See *The Doors of Perception/Heaven and Hell* by Aldous Huxley (Flamingo 1994) which both give an account of the author's experiments with drugs.

> **Warning.** Photocopying any part of this book without permission is illegal.

- ✦ **Intellectual vision.** The person becomes aware not of a figure but an abstraction or concept, such as the essence of the soul or the grace of God. It may be accompanied by a similar imaginative or sensual experience such as persistent light, inner peace or a call toward a religious life.

A particular kind of vision, which you may decide belongs under the third category, is that of the mystic. The modern liberal Catholic theologian Hans Küng describes **mysticism** as a closing of the senses to the outside world in order to lose oneself in God. As a specific category of experience mysticism involves the spiritual recognition of truths beyond normal understanding. A mystical experience may be a sudden, brief insight or it may be a prolonged experience of union with God. **St Bonaventure** (1221–1274) recorded that the mystical experience has three stages:

- ✦ **Purgative.** Purification by prayer and self-denial
- ✦ **Illuminative.** Experiences which are spiritually enlightening, and which are free from the limitations of time, space and self
- ✦ **Unitive.** Reaching oneness with God and achieving a sense of bliss or serenity.

Some religious experiences are recorded to form a core written tradition. What marks out monotheistic religions is the centrality of the resulting scriptures. The authorities in monotheistic religions have tended to teach that scripture holds all the truths about God that need to be known: the Guru Granth Sahib, the Torah, the Qur'an and the Bible. To know about God one only has to read scripture. Other things may also be held to be revelations of God, but a genuine revelation will amplify or enlarge what is already set out in scripture, not contradict it.

These scriptural revelations of God are held to be perfect. However as human understanding of that revelation may be imperfect, religious systems grow up to define an orthodox understanding of the revelation. The definition of **orthodoxy** is an attempt to bring reason to bear on revelation. Reason is here a necessary addition to revelation, not a replacement. Human reason is limited in its scope and usefulness, but it allows access to certain types of knowledge and understanding. But where revelation is not dependent upon intelligence levels, reason is. The defence of orthodoxy thus tends to create hierarchies, while revelation tends to break them down.

When we attempt to measure the veracity (truth) of religious experiences, several problems arise. These experiences are usually individual, and therefore the only evidence of the experience is the individual's own account. They are difficult to measure against another individual's response in the same circumstances. They tend to make sense within the individual's own religious tradition. They may resemble the effects of drugs, including alcohol: William James performed experiments with nitrous oxide and anaesthetics that produced results very similar to religious experiences.

How do religions determine whether a religious experience is 'true' or 'false'? The Bible is full of good advice on this point and the following list is drawn from it. True religion:

- ✦ Emphasises commitment rather than emotion or feelings

22 Religion and human experience

- ✦ Produces an improvement in the individual's behaviour
- ✦ Leads to action against social wrongs such as injustice
- ✦ Leads to humility not pride
- ✦ Is marked by a leadership that guides but does not control
- ✦ Believes regardless of miracles or signs
- ✦ Is consistent with the message of the scriptures.

The Religious Experience Argument claims that these experiences prove the existence of God. The argument suggests that if someone claims to have experienced God, then either they are lying or they have experienced something significant. If they define that something as God, then they are either mistaken, or they did experience God. But isn't such an assertion in fact on a par with claiming to have been abducted by aliens? Perhaps we should test out how normal such an experience is. Research done at Oxford's Religious Experience Research Unit (published 1987) indicated that up to 80% of people in the UK had been aware of a presence or power beyond themselves. This unexpectedly high number suggested that religious experiences were widespread. The research found that those who had undergone such an experience usually found it to be a profound experience which changed their perception of the world and of their own lives. These results tend to suggest that visionary or mystical experiences are actually normal.

The positive respondents to this survey included all of the UK's cultures, races and religions, and even atheists and agnostics.

One philosopher who believes religious experience provides an important argument for the existence of God is **Richard Swinburne**. He has categorised five types of religious experiences in which people seem to recognise God:

Richard Swinburne *The Existence of God* (Oxford University Press 1979).

- ✦ A normal but impressive experience such as a beautiful sunset
- ✦ An unusual and impressive experience such as witnessing someone in a wheelchair being inexplicably healed
- ✦ A describable visionary experience such as seeing an angel in a dream
- ✦ An indescribable mystical experience
- ✦ An awareness of God without any sensation, perhaps achieved retrospectively, such as when an individual looks back on a crisis and believes that God accompanied them through it.

Swinburne uses two principles to make an argument that religious experiences are not internal imaginings but genuine experiences of a superior being beyond us. They are:

Principle of Credulity. If someone believes that they have experienced something, then they probably have.

Principle of Testimony. Unless someone is a liar or disturbed, their description of a religious experience is probably true.

If we refused to believe normally honest and sane people, then we would never believe anything anybody said. If sceptics can't prove the person who has had a religious experience wrong, argues Swinburne, then it is most reasonable to believe them to be right.

A number of challenges to alleged religious experiences can be mounted. Let's group these under four headings:

Disputing the veracity of religious experience

Challenges to description. To describe any event as an experience of 'God' is to describe it as an experience of something beyond proof, and therefore the description that an experience was one 'of God' is a false one. It was simply an experience which the recipient did not understand.

Challenges to subject. Claims of religious experiences are evidence of mental ill health, and the individuals involved are therefore unreliable and unable properly to evaluate what has happened to them. Equally many religious experiences can be explained in terms of psychological factors, and are purely internal and not dependent upon any external factor such as God.

Challenges to object. Claims to have experienced God are as incredible as claims to have seen flying pigs and cows jumping over the moon.

Challenges to conflicting claims. Religions often use reports of religious experiences to support the idea that their particular faith is true. But all religions claim to be true, and all seem to report similar kinds of religious experiences. The point is obvious: different people did indeed have religious experiences, but they were wrong to conclude that this established the primacy of their own experience.

There is no doubt that all religious experiences raise complex philosophical and psychological issues. When considering them, ensure you have a clear understanding of the main models and challenges in the contemporary study of the phenomena. You will find it helpful to study specific traditions, authors, notions and phenomena.

Religious experience in Judaism

The Jewish scriptures are called the Tenakh, a word based on the acronym TNKH. These letters stand for Torah, Neviim (the Prophets) and Ketuvim (the Writings) respectively.

The types of religious experience found in the Tenakh can be categorised into three types – revelations, visions and mystical experiences. God is shown as intervening in the human story through key historical figures and events. The two examples below are foundational in nature for Judaism in the succeeding centuries, offering insights into the nature of God and his relationship with the chosen people.

Moses

Moses is confronted by the presence of God who calls him by name and allows him to approach the divine presence, albeit with shoes removed out of respect (Ex 3). Moses is overawed and afraid. God reveals to him (and through him to the Jewish people) his essential nature:

> **Further study**
>
> Looking at this account, can you see the four features of religious experience as proposed by William James? See page 19.

+ **Rooted in history and tradition.** He calls himself the God of Abraham, Isaac and Jacob, thus establishing the authority of the patriarchs and the traditions attached to them

+ **Forever in the present.** He calls himself 'I am' rather than 'I was' because he is always present – not confined to history like Abraham, Isaac and Jacob, but an ongoing dynamic force

+ **Nameless and unique.** Moses asks his name and is not given one because God needs no name as he is the only God, incomparable to anything else in human experience.

These three facets of God underpin Judaism from Moses onwards. Another important thing to notice is that the revelation is not simply given to Moses to satisfy his interest or for the sake of having a spiritual experience, but in order to send him to free the oppressed in Egypt. This imperative to act morally is a normal element of religious experience in the Bible (see page 23 and see *below*).

Ezekiel's momentous vision took place in the historical context of the 6th century BCE, the time of the invasion of the Jewish homeland by the Babylonian King Nebuchadnezzar and the exile of many leading Jews to Babylon (in modern Iraq) (Ezek 1–3). It was a political, economic and religious crisis. It may have seemed to people that the gods of the Babylonians were stronger than the God of Israel, or that God had abandoned his covenant with the chosen people. Ezekiel was probably a young priest, taken into exile in 597 BCE, who sought to understand the situation from God's viewpoint. His vision has the usual hallmarks of a biblical 'call' – an encounter with God, a commission, an objection by the prophet-to-be, reassurance and then a sign from God.

Ezekiel's vision of God leads on to a call to preach his word to the people. These are some of the significant aspects of the experience:

◆ It resembled the Jerusalem Temple where winged creatures surrounded the holy of holies (the content of the vision represented something he was already familiar with)

◆ It was completely beyond ordinary human experience (he had never known an experience like it)

◆ It was radiant with glory (it was more powerful than anything he had previously encountered)

◆ His response was to fall face down – to prostrate himself (he was overcome)

◆ He is told to take God's message into his life (symbolised by his eating the scrolls) and preach it to others

◆ He is to confront corruption and injustice (this is the reason *for* the vision and the result *of* the vision).

Ezekiel's vision is typically biblical: visions in the Bible always happen for a clear reason. They are not for the benefit of the individual, but are designed to communicate an urgent message to the world.

The Kabbalah is a complex, secret, mystical tradition followed by Jews of different communities. It was initially associated with Sephardic Jews. Hasidic Jews are also closely associated with the exploration of the Kabbalah, and their piety and scholarship became very important in communicating it to Ashkenazi Jews.

A vital text of the Kabbalah is the **Zohar** (c.1280) but many writings have been added since. A lot of the literature is passed on through an esoteric tradition that bypasses most Jews. The Kabbalah is used by different groups who hold widely different perceptions about how to receive the mystical writings. The Kabbalah creates complex diagrams and writings that seek to demonstrate the ten cre-

Ezekiel

For more on the covenant between God and the Israelites, see pages 50–55.

Compare Ezekiel 3 with Jeremiah 1: 4–10.

> **Further study**
>
> For a striking contrast, look at the way in which the Book of Job links the nature of God with human suffering. Job shows the difficulties we have trying to understand the way life works in the context of a God whose ways and means are beyond our minds' limit. You might find the following book useful: *Job The Silent* by Bruce Zuckerman (Oxford University Press 1998). Zuckerman suggests that a key purpose of the Book of Job is to 'underscore the more positive aspects of God's incomprehensible nature'.

Kabbalah

You may also see this spelt other ways, such as 'cabala' and 'qabala'.

You may also see Hasidic spelt 'Chasidic'.

Sephardic Jews are of Spanish or Portuguese origin and tend to live around the Mediterranean. Ashkenazi Jews are those with roots in northern and eastern Europe, including Russia.

ative forces that intervene between the transcendent unknowable God (Ein Sof) and the created world. Kabbalism holds that through the careful balancing of these forces humans are able to encourage God to send forces of either compassion or judgement. The mystical life is then spent trying to bring about the correct balance in one's own life in order that divine light should be channelled into the lower sphere of existence – our own – through human thoughts and deeds, and then on from humans to the rest of material reality.

Hasidism

During the 17th and 18th centuries Judaism went through a period of instability and upheaval. The activities of self-proclaimed prophets foretelling the coming of the Messiah and the persecution abounding in eastern Europe left many Jews feeling that traditional Judaism had failed them. In this context Israel ben Eliezer (also known as Ba'al Shem Tov, 'Master of the Good Name' or Besht) (c.1700–1760) began to attract a large following through his teaching, which blended popular religious practices with mystical Judaism.

Besht is a designation for Israel ben Eliezer that comes from the acronym of **Ba**'al **Sh**em **T**ov.

Although the **Torah** and traditional ritual still lay at the centre of his vision of Jewish life, the Besht demanded a holistic sense of worship. He taught that worship should be joyful, full of singing, dancing and human involvement, and this energy provided the standard religious experience for the faithful. Sadness and joylessness were seen as a barrier to a productive relationship with God; joy allowed love for creation in its entirety to flow forth and create positive energy. The act of worship was not enough on its own, so the Besht encouraged Jews to worship God in everything. The awareness of God mattered to the Besht and he believed that Jews should be aware of God in all their actions.

Further study

It is often suggested that Kabbalists were influenced by Christian and Islamic mysticism and vice versa: can you find similarities between the Besht's teaching and the concept of Dhikr in Sufism? See page 31. Look at www.jewfaq.org/kabbalah.htm for more details on Jewish mysticism and the Kabbalah.

The Besht's followers became known throughout eastern Europe as the **Hasidim** (the 'pious ones'). He did not write books and his teachings were passed down in oral form. The leaders of the Hasidic community who succeeded the Besht also took on a semi-mystical role. Such a leader is known as a **Tzaddik** ('righteous one'). These leaders are capable of becoming spiritual conduits for God's grace and base their religious authority in their closeness to God. Even at a lower level the special nature of the Hasidic religious leader continues. In individual Hasidic communities the leaders are called **Rebbes** and are believed to exist in a higher state of spirituality, **devekus**, the meaning of which transmits the mystical idea of 'clinging to God'.

Hasidism stresses the importance of mystical books and the religious experience of the faithful; experiences that could be as simple as trances induced by singing and dancing or the more complex experiences of visions, ecstasies and miracles. This emphasis on piety, ecstatic prayer and Kabbalah have been rejected as extreme by many Jews.

The Hasidim have a central role in the mystical life of Judaism though it is important to remember that the Torah is at the centre of their religious consciousness, not the Kabbalah. It is how the Torah is received in the life of the community that sets the Hasidim aside from mainstream Jewish thinking.

Religious experience in Christianity

The account of the Transfiguration in Mark's Gospel shows a small group of apostles undergoing a revelatory experience (Mk 9). Features of this revelation are:

Transfiguration of Jesus

- The transformation of Jesus' appearance reveals to those present his hidden divine identity
- Jesus appears with Moses (representing the Jewish Law) and Elijah (representing the Jewish Prophets). This in turn represents the fact that Jesus is held by Christianity to fulfil the messianic promises of the Jewish Scriptures (to Christians, the Old Testament)
- Elijah and Moses fade away, implying that Jesus is now the focus of God's revelation, not the Jewish Scriptures
- A voice is heard revealing Jesus as God's Son and urging the disciples to listen to him (rather than to Jewish law and prophecy).

Saul of Tarsus was at one time a major persecutor of Christians. Following a conversion he became the new religion's most important apostle and the author of one third of the New Testament. Here is his conversion set out in terms of the seven stages identified by Lewis Rambo and Charles Farhadian (see pages 20–21).

Conversion of Paul

St Paul, one of the most important leaders in the 1st-century Church, was a dedicated preacher, theologian and philosopher. He travelled throughout the Mediterranean world spreading the Christian faith and developing its teaching. He was executed in Rome c.62 CE, accused of inciting violence and disorder through his preaching.

Background. He was well-educated, training to be a rabbi and a member of the Pharisaic politico-religious party.

Crisis. Saul was present at the death of a Christian called Stephen, who died forgiving his killers (Acts 7 and 8).

Quest. He was a religious enthusiast, strict in his observance of religious law (Acts 26).

Encounter. On a journey to Damascus he has a vision of Jesus (Acts 9).

Interaction. He meets with Ananias (Acts 9).

Commitment. He is baptised a Christian and takes the name Paul.

Consequences. He becomes a missionary and teacher for Christianity.

Look also at Paul writing about his conversion in Galatians 1.

Visions

At different times individual Roman Catholics have claimed to have had a vision, for example of Mary the mother of Christ. The Catholic Church has accepted some of these visions as genuine and classes them as 'private revelations', to distinguish them from the public revelation completed during Apostolic times. Private revelations are viewed as being given to an individual or group for their own good or that of others: they are not an addition to the public revelation and Catholics are not obliged to believe in them.

One such apparition is recorded as taking place in Lourdes, a town in south-west France. At the age of 14 a French peasant girl called **Bernadette Soubirous** claimed that she had experienced numerous visions of the Virgin Mary and that the Virgin had imparted miraculous powers of healing to the waters of a spring near a grotto in Lourdes. The visions were declared authentic by the Roman Catholic Church, the Lourdes grotto became a shrine for pilgrims and each year millions visit it.

Bernadette Soubirous (1844–1879) joined the Sisters of Charity, a group of women dedicated to religious and charitable work, in 1866. She was canonised (declared a saint) in 1933.

Conversions

Christians believe that Jesus has commanded them to seek to win other people over to the religion (Mk 16: 15). The most influential people who do this are called **evangelists**, the vast majority of whom are little known and ordinary. Three well-known modern evangelists are Billy Graham, Luis Palau and Reinhard Bonnke. Each of these figures comes from the Evangelical Protestant branch of Christianity. Other branches of Christianity see conversion as a more gradual process, perhaps even taking a lifetime in some cases.

John Wesley

Revelation is an insight, a new understanding of reality, given by God to believers. John Wesley (1703–1791), the founder of the Methodist Church writes thus:

> In the evening I went very unwillingly to a society in Aldersgate-Street, where one was reading Luther's preface to the Epistle to the Romans. About a quarter before nine, while he was describing the change which God works in the heart through faith in Christ, I felt my heart strangely warmed. I felt I did trust in Christ, Christ alone for salvation: And an assurance was given me, that he had taken away my sins, even mine, and saved me from the law of sin and death.

Mystical experiences

Teresa of Avila was born in 1515 and grew into a flirtatious and rebellious teenager. When she was 16 her father decided to take control of the situation and sent her to a convent. Her life there did not begin well but in time she learned to love it: her relationship with God grew and the convent was actually less strict than her father. But despite meditating on Christ, she felt that she was getting nowhere. Then she became so dangerously ill that her grave was dug. She recovered but was initially paralysed and never regained her previous health.

After a period in which her religious observances halted, she resumed and on beginning to pray again, she began to have mystical experiences. For example she became convinced that God was lifting her bodily into the air: she would even call on her fellow nuns to help hold her down. She wrote in detail about these experiences, analysing them almost like an academic researcher. She saw the experiences not as God singling her out for something special but God's way of keeping her disciplined. Her writings became very influential initially in Spain and then throughout Catholic Europe. She died in 1582 and was canonised in 1622.

St Teresa defined her mystical progression in this order:

- The Prayer of Quiet (constant meditation)
- The Prayer of Union (more intense prayer than that gained through quietness)
- Ecstasy with God (loss of physical control, involuntary movements)
- Spiritual Marriage (feeling totally at one with God).

> **Further study**
> - Some commentators have adopted a Freudian approach and compared Teresa of Ávila's mystical experiences with sexual ones. To find out more about Freud's anti-religious stance, see *Freud and Jung on Religion* by Michael Palmer (Routledge 1997).
> - Find out about Spanish Carmelite John of the Cross (1542–1591), who was spiritual adviser to Teresa of Ávila's convent. Persecuted by enemies, he was imprisoned and wrote *The Dark Night of the Soul*.
> - Julian of Norwich was an anchoress in Medieval England. Find out more about her life and her visions, which she wrote about in *Revelations of Divine Love*. She is unusual in emphasising the motherhood of God.

For more on Buddhism, see pages 98–101.

Religious experience in Buddhism

You may also see this spelt 'Gautama'. We have used the Pali transliteration here.

Siddhartha Gotama is commonly known as the Buddha, a Sanskrit word meaning 'one who is awake' or 'the enlightened one'. How was this 'awakening' achieved?

There is some scholarly debate about the Buddha's precise dates. See page 99.

Gotama was born either in 563 or 448 BCE into a prosperous family in what we now call Nepal. As a young man he was well-schooled in philosophy and the study of religion, yet existed in a state of noble separation from the rest of society as his Father's intention was to keep Gotama from the difficulties and problems faced by other people in order to protect his future as a great warrior. Tradition has it that the beginnings of young Gotama's dissatisfaction with his privileged life began when he persuaded a chariot driver to take him for a ride outside the palace walls on four consecutive days. On these covert trips Gotama saw examples of old age, disease and death. Having not been exposed to the frailty of existence previously, Gotama began to question the purpose of existence. On the fourth excusion he saw a **sadhu**, a religious man who had given up all his wealth to seek the truth about life and its meaning.

A religious experience will often involve a shift in worldview; in Gotama's case this shift was seismic. At the age of 29 he waved goodbye to his wife and parents, his palace, his servants and his opulent life and set out on six years of wandering as an **ascetic**.

An ascetic is someone who deprives themselves of physical sustenance and sensual pleasure in order to focus fully on the religious. The idea of this lifestyle is that without material distraction an individual will only be aware of spirituality as the fundamental aspect of his or her existence.

It became apparent that this way of life was not leading him any closer to fulfilment, in fact the opposite was happening and he was losing focus on the spiritual as his health nearly collapsed several times. Consequently Gotama rejected the ascetic life and formulated the doctrine of the middle way. He argued that while materialism causes an undue focus on possessions and worldly goods, the ascetic life causes so much bodily pain that it too causes the individual to lose sight of the spiritual aspect of life.

Gotama sat meditating under a tree, recollecting the tranquillity of a day spent in a similar way when he was a child. He allowed himself to move into deeper levels of concentration, not trying to force depth into his meditation. As he sat there, possibly for weeks, he saw existence as it was, a perpetual struggle against earthly desire, and saw too the actions that brought about happiness. He emerged from his meditation with the realisation that he had discerned the truth and was liberated from the restrictions of the material world. Gotama had become the Buddha, the enlightened one.

Further study

To what extent can the stages of conversion identified by Rambo and Farhadian be detected in Siddhartha Gotama's experience? See pages 20–21.

Religious experience in Hinduism

The *Bhagavad Gita* is found within the epic Hindu poem the *Mahabharata*. Although scholars are unsure as to when it was actually written, it is thought to predate Buddhism and a date of 500 BCE or earlier is generally accepted for its creation (but see *right*). The *Gita* consists of a series of dialogues between **Arjuna**, who represents humanity, and **Krishna**, whom Hindus understand to be an incarnation of Vishnu, the preserver.

Dates in Hinduism are problematic. Hinduism traditionally recognises a very different history for sacred writing from that ascribed to it by western scholars, generally regarding it as much older.

In Chapter 11 Arjuna expresses his desire to see God in his fullness. Previously Arjuna had gained intellectual knowledge of Krishna's essence through discussion. Krishna warns Arjuna of the futility of trying to see his divine essence with human eyes but promises him divine sight to do so. When Arjuna sees Krishna in his celestial form he gazes on infinity, seeing the universe entirely encapsulated in the divine Krishna: 'Arjuna saw in that radiance the whole universe in its variety, standing in a vast unity in the body of the God of gods.' His reaction is to tremble with awe, bow his head and declare: 'Nowhere I see a beginning, middle or end of thee, O God of all, Form Infinite.'

Arjuna's vision

Warning. Photocopying any part of this book without permission is illegal.

Arjuna understands that God is everywhere, that there is no escaping his presence, that everyone is subject to his control and that we are hurtling through life towards God and our own physical destruction. Arjuna recognises that this experience is personal and ineffable – and confusing. He is both exultant and terrified. As if to stress his new understanding of God in his majesty, Arjuna issues an apology: 'If in careless presumption, or even in friendliness, I said "Krishna! Son of Yadu! My friend!", this I did unconscious of thy greatness.' Now that Arjuna sees the fullness of God, the concept is no longer the more simple, comfortable and personal God of his earlier relationship. The experience is fascinating and wonderful but the new knowledge of the full picture is terrifying, causing him to beg for mercy, aware of the tremendous power that Krishna truly possesses.

In the end Krishna returns to his human form, which is far easier for Arjuna to cope with. Arjuna speaks of the peace he feels return when Krishna puts on his 'gentle, human face'. Krishna makes it clear that many seek to see God in his fullness yet few do so. But ritual and austerity are not enough to see him in his fullness, explains Krishna: this makes Arjuna's vision yet more profound, ineffable and special.

Bhakti also means devotion, and is most often used in Hinduism to describe devotional practices.

In his vision of God Arjuna has gained knowledge and insight no one else can easily obtain; his experience is unique, terrifying yet utterly compelling. Happily, Krishna gives all humans hope when he returns to the main theme of the *Gita*, **bhakti**, the loving union between God and human beings which is also the love between people. It is bhakti that will allow people access to the truth experienced so vividly by Arjuna and expressed by Krishna in the final two sentences of Chapter 11:

> Only by love can men see me, and know me, and come unto me. He who works for me, who loves me, whose end supreme I am, free from attachment to all things, and with love for all creation, he in truth comes unto me.

Religious experience in Islam

Muhammad

See *Muhammad* by Karen Armstrong (Phoenix 2001).

Qur'an 96: 1–5.

Muhammad's vision in a cave on Mount Hira when he was aged 40 is seen by Muslims as the most profound and influential of religious experiences. Tradition has it that Muhammad found the Angel **Jibra'il** (Gabriel) standing before him while he was meditating. Muhammad may have been illiterate, for when Jibra'il demanded he 'Read in the name of thy Lord', Muhammad told him he could not. The angel then squeezed Muhammad to the point of suffocation three times. After this Muhammad found himself reciting the beautiful poetry of the Qur'an as if it were 'inscribed on his heart'. This first revelation was one of a series that extended over 20 years, each revealed text being held to be the direct word of God.

For Muhammad's preaching see pages 110–112.

Doubting his own sanity as a result of this first message, Muhammad sought reassurance from his wife Khadija, who gave him her support. Muhammad was next troubled when Waraqa ibn Nawfal, a **hanif** (pre-Islamic monotheist), found out about these revelations and the Prophet had to decide whether or not to acknowledge them and begin preaching. After much inner turmoil Muhammad began to spread the message that Jibra'il had brought to him from God.

The distinctive aspect in Muhammad's vision of the Angel Jibra'il is the reception of textual revelation. Clearly it is central to the development of not only his religious consciousness but also to the Islamic faith. Muhammad's revelations are the foundations of Islam, containing theology, ethics and eschatology. His revelations are held to be transcriptions of the actual word of God, in contrast to the inspiration of the Christian canon. The experience was profound on a personal level for Muhammad himself, and is considered to be the final complete, universal revelation of God and thus for Muslims is completely central to the religious experience of humankind as they seek to encounter religious truth.

As with all Muslims, the Sufis see the religious experience of Muhammad, and therefore the Qur'an, as absolutely central to their understanding of human existence and the nature of God. However they stand out markedly from other Islamic groups as they practise mysticism.

Sufism grew out of a reaction against increased materialism in Umayyad Islam, and was an attempt to get back to the piety, simplicity and prayer that characterised Muhammad's life and the lives of the Caliphs (see page 111).

The Sufis use ritual, and meditative and ascetic practices to move towards a closer relationship with God. These include music, rhythmic movement and chanting. The aim is to reach a higher level of awareness of the divine and to purify the human soul. The Qur'an describes the knowledge brought by the prophets as **dhikr** (remembrance). Sufism extends the meaning of this term by using it to describe the meditative focus on (or heightened, mystical awareness of) God, particularly of God as the beloved.

The Sufi movement produced a substantial body of writings over the first few centuries of its development. These consisted of teachings which stood in contrast to the intellectualism of mainstream Islam, and its ever-expanding and influential schools of sacred law (Shari'ah). Many of the Sufi writers, such as al-Ghazali (1058/9–1111) and ibn Arabi (1165–1240), wrote poetry, using metaphor and analogy to communicate the complex nature of experiential truth.

Sufism is a significant part of Islamic thinking: perhaps 2%–3% of Muslims align themselves with Sufi Islam and it is practised in many different Islamic societies. It is important to note that a Sufi is a Muslim first and Sufi second. This means that the external orthodox duties and obligations of Islam are paramount in maintaining a good Islamic life. However Sufis also focus on the inward path called **tariqah** which, if followed correctly, can lead to **haqiqah**, which is the inner discovery of truth. The path cannot be followed alone and the inexperienced Sufi is lead along the path by a **shaykh**, a teacher who passes on their experience and helps the pupil mature spiritually.

According to Sufi tradition Muhammad, said that 'Shari'ah is my words, tariqah is my deeds and haqiqah is my inner state'. This shows that a Muslim should fulfil the duties of Islam to family, community and law, even while following the path of inner purifi-

Sufism
The words 'Sufi' and 'Sufism' are generally agreed to come from the Arabic word 'tasawwuf' meaning wool and to refer to the Sufis' modest clothes.

The Umayyad dynasty ruled Islam from Damascus c.660–750 CE. Although it was overthrown there by a rebellion and replaced by the Abbasids, an Umayyad seized power in Muslim Spain and he and his descendants ruled there 756 CE–1031 CE.

The Qur'an describes the content of both the Torah and the Gospels as dhikr. For more on dhikr, see *Sufism, A Short Introduction* by William C. Chittick (Oneworld 2001), particularly pages 52–60.

'Sufism is the spiritual path ('tariqah') of Islam and has been identified with it for well over a thousand years… It has been call "Islamic Mysticism" by Western scholars because of its resemblance to Christian and other forms of mysticism elsewhere. Unlike Christian mysticism, however, Sufism is a continuous historical and even institutionalized phenomenon in the Muslim world that has millions of adherents down to the present day.' Victor Danner *The Islamic Tradition* (Amity House 1988).

cation in order to reach a greater and deeper personal knowledge of Allah.

Religious experience in Sikhism

Guru Nanak (1469–1539) was exposed to both Islam and Hinduism. His family were of good standing, though, unlike the family of the Buddha, they were not especially wealthy or important.

Nanak composed many poems and hymns which encapsulate his religious thinking. These give us insights into the lifestyle and central principles of the Sikh faith. When reading Nanak's writings we should remember that he was seen by his disciples in the Punjab as a teacher and a leader, and he describes his religious experiences in order to communicate the insights into the human condition and of the nature of God that he had developed through them.

> Nanak is the first Sikh Guru. The last is the Guru Granth Sahib (also called the Adi Granth), which is not a person but the holy Sikh scriptures containing the writings of all the Gurus. See pages 116–118.

Nanak rejected wealth and saw a sense of community as essential in reaching a higher level of religious life. He felt that personal experience of God was paramount in heightening his religious sense and used a variety of spiritual techniques to gain deeper insights. Meditation and singing played a great part in Nanak's private and public worship, and chanting and recitation still play a central part in Sikh life today. He describes his meditative experiences in the poems and songs contained in the Adi Granth:

> 'Satguru' means 'true guru' and is frequently used to refer to God. A Gurmukh is someone who has become filled with God rather than being self-centred.

> The basis of my teaching is the first breath.
> My thought belongs to the age of the Satguru.
> The word is my Guru, I am a disciple of the sound of meditation;
> The exposition of the inexplicable keeps me in detachment.
> Nanak, in each succeeding age the Guru is God.
> I meditate on the exposition of the one word,
> For the Gurmukh, self-interest is consumed in its fire.

> This passage is quoted in *Man's Religious Quest: A Reader,* ed. W. Foy (Open University Press 1978).

Nanak uses a combination of poetic description, metaphor and allegory to try to 'describe the indescribable'. It is then for Sikhs to unravel this mystery through their own personal devotion and religious development in the worship of the community.

> 'When the self is overcome, then doubt and fear are also overcome and the sorrow of death and rebirth removed.
>
> 'The teaching of the Guru makes the Unmanifest manifest, by His perfect wisdom we are saved.
>
> 'Nanak, repeat the formula: "He is me, I am He." The three levels of existence are summed up in that.'
> Rag Maru; A. G. P. 1092; page 285.

Public worship was particularly important to Guru Nanak as he felt that individuals should see themselves as part of a community. To that end, women worshipped with men, Sikhs shared a communal meal and the worship itself was in Punjabi so that everyone could understand it. Nanak felt that this allowed his followers to reach inside themselves and encounter God. His early community consisted of morning meditations followed by hymn singing in the evening.

Nanak's composition and singing of hymns is still important to Sikhs today. Their religious experiences are often centred around the repetitive chanting of **Waheguru** ('wonderful Lord'). This is not restricted to the confines of public worship but can be uttered while at work, at leisure or in private meditation. Chanting enables Sikhs to focus on God. They put aside all worldly distractions and reach towards the presence of God, thus deepening their religious understanding.

> You might find this term spelt 'Vahiguru'.

The Guru was aware of the difficulty of describing God and his descriptions of his experiences often end with him recognising the transcendence and unknowability of God: 'Though I think a hundred thousand thoughts of God, thought alone cannot reach him.' Nanak stressed that a diversity of public and private worship, meditation, poetry, singing, communal living and simplicity brings together the myriad religious experiences that enhance the believer's relationship with God.

Religious authority

Religious experience, as we have seen, can be an individual and (at least initially) intensely personal matter. But a religious institution is inevitably a collective and public affair. How can such an institution ensure that it retains intact the original vibrant message of its founders without becoming merely that message's lifeless container? All major religious traditions have had to debate what the sources of authority are that can determine the truth about that tradition's message.

Founders

Most of these religions trace their origins back to a key founder-figure. The founder of a religion can serve as:

- Figurehead
- Example
- Inspiration
- God's messenger or representative
- Especially enlightened
- The person through whom God acts or acted.

Myths can attach themselves easily to the founder as a way of underlining his importance and authority. Successive leaders of religions will often try to trace their own authority back to that of the founder. These features can be seen clearly in operation in three of the most important foundational figures in religion: Abraham, Jesus and Muhammad.

Jews claim to be the descendants of Abraham, both in their faith in the one God who made a covenant with him and in their lineage which the Tenakh traces back to his second son, Isaac. Abraham is seen as the ideal Jew who kept the Law perfectly, even though it was not revealed until Moses and the events on Sinai some 800 years later. Abraham's authority for Jews consists both in this bold leap into monotheistic faith and his complete commitment to it even when under severe strain.

Christianity is traced back to the teaching and life of Jesus, a 1st-century CE rabbi who lived and died a Jew. Jesus' teaching, with its emphasis on forgiveness, justice for all and peace among peoples, is at the heart of the Christian ethic, and the events of Jesus' life as recounted in the Gospels are believed to be the means by which God has acted in human history. Jesus' authority for Christians results from his perceived role as the saviour of humanity, not simply because he is seen to have lived a perfect life, but because he is considered to be God incarnate.

Abraham

See pages 51–52. Abraham is also claimed as a founder-figure by Christians (who see themselves as his descendants since the Church is the new Israel) and Muslims (Arabs trace their lineage in the Qur'an back to Abraham's first son, Ishmael).

Jesus

Whether Jesus ever intended to found a new religion is much debated, and the Jewish scholar Geza Vermes (see his *Jesus the Jew* SCM Press 1983) is not alone in thinking that Jesus would not easily identify with Christian teachings today.

Muhammad

See pages 110–111.

Muhammad is known as the 'Seal of the Prophets' because he is the final prophet.

Tradition holds that the founder of Islam was a devout young man who experienced angelic visitations which led him to seek God more fully. The Arabian peninsula, where Muhammad lived, was in the 6th century CE a place of refuge from persecution for Jews and some non-orthodox Christians, even though many areas including Mecca practised various forms of polytheistic worship. Muhammad was called in a vision by the Angel Jibra'il to become the prophet of Allah and lead people away from polytheism to a monotheistic faith. The moral dimension to his message was a call to unity and brotherhood between all peoples, a logical consequence of the belief that everyone originated from the same God. Muhammad's authority for Muslims comes from his role as the final prophet whose recitations, preserved in the Qur'an, are uniquely significant because they are the last and most authoritative word from Allah, and because they have not been corrupted by the community that received them.

Scriptures

From the Greek 'kanon', meaning 'rule'.

Scriptures are the sacred texts of religions. They are usually regarded as inspired and authoritative, and they typically form part of a collection of writings, known as a **canon**. Many religious texts were originally part of an oral tradition that came to be written down over time. For instance the Hindu **Vedas** (veda means knowledge) were regarded as truths which only those sufficiently spiritually developed could realise. The families of the priestly wise-men (or 'seer-poets') who comprehended the essential truths transmitted their content and meanings orally. In Islam, the revelations of the Qur'an were collated and written down (sometimes on banana skins and pieces of pottery) by Muhammad's wives and friends.

The Old Testament books of the Apocrypha are afforded different statuses by different Churches, while no mainstream Church recognises the New Testament Apocrypha.

The establishment of a canon is a long and often controversial process. It took centuries to gain any form of consensus on the content of the Christian canon (see page 42), and there is still a good deal of dispute about the issue. In fact, Catholics and Protestants acknowledge different numbers of books in the Old and New Testaments.

Judaism, Christianity, Sikhism and Islam all hold, in varying degrees, to the idea of the inerrancy of scripture. This means that scripture does not teach error in any way, which is the key to its authority – in the scriptures, the infallible and inerrant God is communicating with humanity.

Leaders

In many religious traditions teachings and rituals are mediated through an official leadership. History is littered with examples of religious leaders exploiting their spiritual authority for personal gain, which has resulted in strong anticlerical traditions (see page 35 for some examples). However there are also examples of inspirational religious leadership standing up for the dignity of humanity and for human rights. The role of Archbishop Desmond Tutu in the ending of apartheid in South Africa is an example.

In ancient Judaism, priesthood belonged to a sacred hereditary class which was charged with performing rituals in the Temple in Jerusalem. Within the Jewish Scriptures there is division of opinion about who may become a priest – Leviticus 8 teaches that this right belongs to the descendants of Aaron alone, whereas Deuteronomy 33: 8–10 widens the right to the entire tribe of Levi. Following the Roman destruction of the Second Temple in 70 CE and the consequent end of sacrifices, leadership passed to the rabbinate. A rabbi is a Jewish man (or, since 1972 in Reform Judaism, a woman) who has been instructed in the Torah and has been ordained (officially set apart) to be a religious teacher and leader. Orthodox Judaism emphasises the rabbi's duty of interpreting the Torah; in this respect he carries huge authority within the individual community. On the other hand, Reform rabbis are more concerned with pastoral care of the community than the intricacies of the Law.

The role of the Christian priesthood is not specified in the New Testament: it has developed from the elders referred to in its pages. The sacrificial and sacramental aspects of the Christian priesthood developed in response partly to Old Testament Jewish examples, and partly to the pagan priesthoods of the Roman Empire. There are three orders of priesthood in Orthodox, Roman Catholic and Anglican Christianity: bishops, priests and deacons. The bishops are successors to the Apostles and are a focus of unity for the local church. They perform the entire range of sacramental functions. The priest is subordinate to the bishop and his priestly powers are derived from him (or more recently in some Anglican churches, from him or her). A priest can perform all the sacramental functions except ordination (and confirmation, in the Anglican churches). The lowest rank is the deacon, who has only limited sacramental functions and who is usually a priest in training, although there are also permanent deacons.

In Roman Catholicism, all the bishops together have joint authority to lead the Church, and their collective teaching is seen as infallible. As Bishop of Rome, the Pope is seen as 'first among equals' in regard to the bishops, and their collective authority to teach the faith is focused particularly in him. The Pope can thus be said to be infallible when he teaches on important matters of faith or ethics, but in practice the church usually regards his teaching as 'authoritative and binding' rather than as infallible. The Pope teaches through encyclicals, which are letters addressed to the bishops and the faithful. Encyclicals set the direction of the Church and address modern dilemmas. An example of this is the famous 1968 encyclical, written by Pope Paul VI, *Humanae Vitae* ('Human Life') which condemns as unnatural and sinful any use of artificial contraception by Catholics. This is a good example of the authority of the Pope – there is no word about artificial contraception in the Bible so as Pope it was his role is to magnify its general teachings about the sacred nature of human life and the sexual act, and apply them to this modern dilemma.

Protestant Christians, Jews (since the destruction of the Temple in 70 CE) and Muslims have tended to dismiss any sacramental and sacrificial authority in religious leaders. Protestants regard all Christians equally as priests before God. As a result, Protestant ministers and clergymen, Jewish rabbis and Muslim imams often tend to adopt a teaching and pastoral role in the community.

> **Further study**
>
> Look at these four expressions of fierce anticlericalism. What do you think creates this kind of hostility to priests?
>
> 'There is in every village a torch – the teacher; and an extinguisher – the clergyman.' Victor Hugo.
>
> 'In every country and every age, the priest had been hostile to Liberty.' Thomas Jefferson.
>
> 'Theology is not what we know about God, but what we do not know about Nature. In order to increase our respect for the Bible, it became necessary for the priests to exalt and extol that book, and at the same time to decry and belittle the reasoning powers of man. The whole power of the pulpit has been used for hundreds of years to destroy the confidence of man in himself – to induce him to distrust his own powers of thought, to believe that he was wholly unable to decide any question for himself, and that all human virtue consists in faith and obedience.' Robert G. Ingersoll.
>
> 'In a sense, the religious person must have no real views of his own and it is presumptuous of him, in fact, to have any. In regard to sex-love affairs, to marriage and family relations, to business, to politics, and to virtually everything else that is important in his life, he must try to discover what his god and his clergy would like him to do; and he must primarily do their bidding.' Albert Ellis.

Protestant Christians would point in particular to 1 Peter 2: 5, 9.

Tradition

Tradition is the handing down over the years of beliefs and rituals, and the reflection upon the meaning of those beliefs and rituals. Tradition carries weight within religions because it is in part what religion is all about – the application of the wisdom of the past to the world of today. Holding to tradition ensures stability through continuity, though it may also stifle reform and renewal.

In early Christianity, in the face of a threat to Christian teaching from **Gnosticism**, tradition came to be valued highly. Second-century CE theologians such as St Irenaeus (c.130–200 CE) who was Bishop of Lyons, saw the need to have not only the scriptures as an authoritative record of the Church's teaching, but additionally to have an official interpretation of the scriptures which was in keeping with the way in which the message of the scriptures had been understood by mainstream Christianity since the apostles. The message of scripture was not to be interpreted in any way by anyone, it could only be rightly understood in the historical context of the faithful community in which the scriptures belonged.

An alternative approach is to view tradition as a separate and distinct form of authority. In matters on which the central sacred text(s) of the religion may be silent, tradition can serve as the authoritative guide. Such tradition may not be written down, but could be oral or simply the summary of an attitude that had prevailed throughout the religion's history. For example, during the **Reformation** in the 16th century, the Catholic Church felt that Protestant reformers were casting aside tradition in favour of a Bible-only approach. The Catholic Church affirmed the importance of tradition as an authority alongside that of the Bible in 1546 at the Council of Trent, when it was made clear that the Gospel of Christ was contained 'in written books and in unwritten traditions'.

In modern Christianity, the attitude of the Protestant theologian **Karl Barth** (1886–1968) is a good illustration of an attempt to work out the role of tradition in religion. He viewed the Word of God as speaking to people in every age through scripture, and saw tradition as the record of the ways in which the message of scripture had been received at different times by different peoples. For Barth, tradition should be shown 'love and respect', but not held to be in any way equal in authority to scripture.

Tradition is afforded a similar role in Judaism and is seen as the authoritative interpretation of the Torah, handed down in oral form through rabbinic teaching. It is considered so important that it is called 'the Second Torah'. Jewish oral Law ('Torah she be'al peh') is said to have been revealed on Mount Sinai to Moses in the same way as the written Law was. Jewish tradition includes history, folklore, law and custom, and is referred to in general as **masoret**.

For Islam, tradition is also crucial. The Qur'an is a steadfastly established code or revelation from Allah and the most important source of guidance for Muslims. The **sunnah** (Muhammad's life and example) and the **hadith** (Muhammad's sayings) provide a basis for interpreting the Qur'an and for Muslim law as a whole.

Gnosticism takes its name from the Greek word 'gnosis' (knowledge). The Gnostics claimed that the present material world was evil and that only the world of the spirit was good. For more on this see page 122.

The Anabaptists rejected the tradition of infant baptism because the Bible contains no examples of babies being baptised. Modern Baptists continue to reject baptism of infants because they are seen as being too young to make an informed personal commitment to Christianity.

Further study

How would you answer the challenges these two views of tradition mount?

'When we ask on what the claim [of religious teachings] to be believed is founded, we are met with three answers, which harmonise remarkably badly with one another. Firstly, these teachings deserve to be believed because they were already believed by our primal ancestors; secondly, we possess proofs which have been handed down to us from those same primaeval times; and thirdly, it is forbidden to raise the question of their authentication at all.' Sigmund Freud.

Warning. Photocopying any part of this book without permission is illegal.

Experience

How reliable a guide is personal experience to learning about reality? In one sense it must be the primary guide. A child learns about the world around him by experience. People travel the world in order to experience other traditions, places and cultures. But no one refuses to believe in Russia just because they have not been there. They trust the authority of books and the testimony of others.

Do you need to have experienced God to believe in God? What if your religious experience is hard to understand, or at odds with other forms of religious authority? For example the conversion of St Paul's religious experience was unexpected and, initially, unwelcome. It went against the sources of religious authority which Saul of Tarsus (Paul's original name) embraced as a trainee rabbi – the authority of scripture as he had understood it up to that time, and the authority of tradition and religious leaders. But the experience of his conversion overruled all these other factors.

The problem with the subjective nature of religious experience is the reverse of that with tradition. Holding to tradition ensures stability through continuity, but can stifle reform and renewal. Religious experience, on the other hand, is a source of reform and renewal, but can lead to delusion, deception and instability.

Philosophical scepticism will always surround religious experience. **Thomas Hobbes** (1588–1679) questioned what the difference was between a person who said that God spoke to them in a dream, and a person who simply dreamed that God spoke to them. But **William James**, while acknowledging that claims of religious experience were extremely subjective and unlikely to convince those who had not had such experiences, nevertheless felt that they had value for those who had them, and that they could enrich society by giving people renewed moral lives and a strong sense of hope.

> **Further study**
>
> How reliable is personal experience in religious matters? Weigh up the following two statements:
>
> 'Religious experience is absolute... it cannot be disputed. Those who have had it possess a great treasure, a source of life, meaning and beauty which gives a new splendour to the world. It is overwhelming and healing and is therefore of great validity.' Carl Gustav Jung.
>
> 'From a scientific point of view, we can make no distinction between the man who eats little and sees heaven and the man who drinks much and sees snakes.' Bertrand Russell.

Revelation

Some religions depend to a great extent upon the concept that God chooses to reveal himself to humankind. Religious believers think revelation is God speaking in human language for the instruction and benefit of humankind.

That God reveals himself does not mean that he is no longer shrouded in mystery. **Martin Luther** (1483–1546) taught that God can only be known partially, yet that partial revelation is reliable and adequate for salvation. In fact Luther was seeking to reconcile two seemingly irreconcilable ideas: that God can be known and that God is a mystery. Religions seem to need to make both these points – God revealing himself through the religion underlines the importance of believing in and following the main tenets of the religion. Yet if God can be fully known at any point, what is the point of continuing one's religious quest? The 19th-century theologian **John Henry Newman** (1801–1890) believed in the idea of reserve: that God never revealed himself completely and that there was always something in reserve, always more to know.

Newman was an Anglican who converted to Roman Catholicism in 1845. He was later made a Cardinal.

Believers often argue that God reveals himself in part through nature itself, that even by looking at the world around us and conscience within us, human beings can deduce the existence and nature of God. This kind of revelation through nature, expressed in several faiths, is called **natural revelation** and the Book of Psalms is an early expression of it: 'The heavens declare the glory of God, and the skies proclaim the work of his hands' (Ps 19: 1).

> For more on the covenant, see pages 50–55.

In Judaism God was first revealed through nature and then through the covenant he made with the Jewish people. The Jewish people themselves are a revelation of God to the world, according to the biblical tradition. God further revealed himself in the writings of the prophets, but essentially all that is ever to be revealed about him is contained in the Torah, and although later revelations may amplify and clarify its meaning, they never contradict it.

In Christianity God reveals himself first through nature, second through the 'Old (Jewish) covenant' and thirdly through Jesus Christ. Here is a prayer from the Roman Catholic Mass expressing this idea:

> Even when mankind disobeyed you and lost your friendship, you did not abandon him to the power of death, but time and again you offered a covenant to man and through the prophets taught him to hope for salvation. In the fullness of time you sent your only Son to be our Saviour.

Reason

What is the place of reason in religion? Believing in something your physical senses can't detect may be thought to be irrational: by this argument religion and reason are opposites.

Accordingly sceptics do indeed contrast the apparent clarity of reason with the credulity of religion. The moral philosopher **John Stuart Mill** (1806–1873) wrote in *Theism* (1870):

> For more on Mill, see pages 81–82.

> The rational attitude of a thinking mind toward the supernatural, whether in natural or revealed religion, is that of scepticism as distinguished from belief on one hand, and from atheism on the other hand... The notion of a providential government by the omnipotent Being for the good of his creatures must be entirely dismissed... The possibility of life after death rests on the same footing – of a boon which this powerful Being who wishes well to man, may have the power to grant... The whole domain of the supernatural is thus removed from the region of Belief into that of simple Hope.

Yet some religious traditions embrace reason. Unitarian Universalism (a liberal Protestant Church) has as part of its creed: 'We believe in the authority of reason and conscience. The ultimate arbiter in religion is not a church, or a document, or an official, but the personal choice and the decision of the individual.'

The Anglican churchman and theologian **Richard Hooker** (1554–1600) endorsed reason as a source of authority in religion on the basis that the universe is an unfolding of the mind of God, that all created beings in some way participate in the mind of God, and that God has planted a seed of his mind in every human being.

The modern-day Anglican priest, and former Professor of Mathematical Physics at Cambridge University, **John Polkinghorne** holds this view of reason:

> For more on John Polkinghorne see pages 130–131.

> There is some deep-seated relationship between the reason within (the rationality of our minds...) and the reason without (the rationale order and structure of the physical world around us). The two fit together like a glove.

> Warning. Photocopying any part of this book without permission is illegal.

38 Religion and human experience

Other religious traditions are more wary, holding that reason is a tool for understanding God's revelation (through the scriptures, for example) but can never replace or be equal in authority to that revelation. Of course the whole question of authority in these matters is problematic. The presentation of arguments may seem reasoned. Let's look at how an appeal to authority can work.

+ An individual is claimed to be an authority on a subject
+ They make a claim about that subject
+ Their followers accept that claim to be true.

How believable is that claim going to be, though?

+ The individual would have to be an expert on the subject
+ The claim itself would also have to be within their area of expertise
+ The area of expertise would have to be a legitimate discipline
+ The individual would need to be unbiased, or to have the agreement of other experts on the topic.

Followers will usually claim that their founders, scriptures or leaders do indeed fulfil these conditions. But an outsider might conclude that this claim in itself is also a matter of faith, not of fact.

Conflict within a faith

There are often conflicts between the different sources of religious authority. Sometimes reason conflicts with scripture, or leaders appear to contradict scripture.

The following illustrations of this problem are drawn from the Bible and Christianity, but the principles are important ones for people of whatever religion. Essentially the problem is that the various sources of religious authority do not always seem to say the same thing, and when conflicts between sources arise, some kind of judgement has to be made between them.

The identity and faith of the first Christians was Jewish. An important part of Judaism, taught in the Tenakh (Old Testament) and preserved in Jewish tradition, is the upholding of food laws. This tradition meant that Jews and non-Jews (Gentiles) could not eat together. When Gentiles became believers in Jesus, some members of the early Church (including St Paul) argued that Gentile-believers and Jewish-believers were equally members, and that divisive rules should be discarded. Others argued that the dietary rules had been given by God and were binding upon all Jews for all time. Acts 10: 9–48 shows St Peter receiving a vision teaching him that the dietary laws no longer applied to Jews who believed in Jesus. This view prevailed, and serves as an example of leaders using their own experience and judgement to depart from scripture and tradition. As a result Christianity has developed as a religion without any food laws at all.

Nicolaus Copernicus (1473–1543) argued on the basis of mathematical calculation that the sun was the centre of the universe and the earth was like all other planets in revolving around it. The Ital-

> **Further study**
>
> How would you respond to the following two assertions?
>
> 'If you think that your belief is based upon reason, you will support it by argument, rather then by persecution, and will abandon it if the argument goes against you. But if your belief is based on faith, you will realise that argument is useless and will therefore resort to force either in the form of persecution or by stunting and distorting the minds of the young in what is called "education".' Bertrand Russell.
>
> '(Faith) maintains that religious doctrines are outside the jurisdiction of reason – are above reason. Their truth must be felt inwardly, and they need not be comprehended... Am I to be obliged to believe every absurdity? And if not, why this one in particular?' Sigmund Freud.

Leaders in conflict with tradition and scripture

See also the conflict and its resolution in Acts 15: 1–35.

Reason in conflict with tradition and scripture

ian scientist **Galileo** (1564–1642) built upon Copernicus' work, looking at the sky through the newly invented telescope and using observation, experimentation, checking and evidence to discern the truth about the solar system. Their conclusions were rejected by both Catholic and Protestant Churches as irreconcilable with Genesis 1's picture of a geocentric universe. In 19th-century Britain **Charles Darwin** (1802–1892) published his theory of evolution by natural selection, which again challenged Genesis 1's account of the creation of all living things. **Samuel Wilberforce** (1805–1873), Bishop of Oxford argued that Darwin's theory was in contradiction with the authority of the Bible and the Church, and an affront to the dignity of humankind.

For more on Darwin, see page 128.

The Roman Catholic Church now officially accepts the bulk of what was taught by Copernicus, Galileo and Darwin, and teaches **Theistic Evolution** (that the universe has indeed evolved, but under the guiding hand of God). However fundamentalist Christians regard the Bible as possessing final authority and embrace various forms of creationism.

For more on Creationism, see pages 121–123.

Religious authority in Buddhism

The Buddha was a teacher whose thoughts and words were conveyed through preaching. His work survived because those who followed him remembered his words and wrote them down. This process took place over many years and led to a number of disputes.

On the Buddha's death in 480 BCE a council of believers met in Bihar in north-eastern India to construct a standardised version of the Buddha's sayings. A century later a dispute emerged over the **Vinaya**, which had been formulated in 480 BCE and contained monastic rules. This early dispute was pretty much confined to the **Sangha** (the monastic orders). This dispute led to the emergence of several groupings during the 3rd century BCE, and these were gradually classified into two movements. The first to emerge, consisting of several conservative groupings, became known as **Theravada Buddhism** (meaning the 'way of the elders'). The later group was **Mahayana Buddhism** (meaning 'great vehicle'); this seems to have formed in opposition to conservative Buddhism around 200 BCE. Today the two schools approach textual authority differently.

Theravadan scriptures

Buddhist tradition holds that Theravadan monks compiled the first Buddhist scriptures at the fourth Buddhist council in Sri Lanka around 50 BCE. The scriptures were written in Pali, the language spoken by the Buddha, and the texts became known as the **Pali Canon**. The fact that Pali was chosen allowed rapid expansion of Buddhism throughout Asia as it was far more accessible to lay people than Sanskrit.

The actual extent of Buddhist literature is vast, far bigger than the Bible. The scriptures are split up into three segments, the *Vinaya Pitaka* (an ethical code), the *Sutra Pitaka* (the sayings of the Buddha) and the *Abhidhamma Pitaka* (Buddhist metaphysics and philosophical writings). The scriptures are sometimes called the *Tripitaka* or 'three baskets' of Buddhist wisdom (they were in fact traditionally kept in three separate baskets).

The *Vinaya* presents a code of conduct, but this applies only to the monastic Sangha and not to lay people. The *Sutras* contain the collected sermons and stories of the Buddha. This method of storytelling, often using metaphor, was the distinctive mark of the Buddha's preaching as he demanded that his disciples adapt their conventional modes of thinking in order to be able to understand his message. The *Sutras* also contain the *Jatakas*, which are tales of the Buddha's former lives and which contain strong ethical and moral teachings. The philosophical writings of the *Abhidhamma* were not produced by the Buddha but by later Buddhists seeking to clarify and expound on earlier texts.

The *Sutras* also contain the *Dhammapada*. This short text consists of 423 verses that are accessible to everyone. They are written in aphorisms and try to express spiritual truth in a succinct way that stimulates reflection by the reader. The teachings often demand a shift in worldview which should be accompanied by a shift in lifestyle. The *Dhammapada* contains the Four Holy Truths and outlines the Eightfold Path of good Buddhist conduct.

The *Dhammapada* is published as an Oxford World's Classic (2000).

For more on the Four Holy Truths, see page 99.

Mahayanan scriptures

Mahayanan Buddhists differ from Theravadan Buddhists in the composition of their scriptures. Whereas Theravadans only accept teachings that can be traced directly to the Buddha himself as authoritative, Mahayanans are happy to accept additional texts that cannot be historically verified as coming from the Buddha yet appear to have a clear intellectual link. For instance the 'teachings on perfect wisdom' (*Prajna Paramita Sutras*) are said to be esoteric teachings of the Buddha that were hidden from mainstream Buddhists incapable of understanding their contents and only brought to light at a later time by the great thinker, Nagarjuna (c.150–250 CE).

Despite there being two schools of textual tradition, the teachings of the Buddha are the primary source of authority for all Buddhists. There is a huge amount of literature to deal with and some Buddhists spend a great deal of time getting to grips with it.

Religious authority in Christianity

The New Testament is a collection of 27 documents recording the life and teaching of Jesus, and describing or reflecting the life and beliefs of the early Church. Although it is unlikely that any of the authors of these documents set out to write scripture, Christians have received these documents as the Word of God.

New Testament

Calling the Tenakh the Old Testament is a judgement that reflects the way the authors of the New Testament view the Jewish tradition. They saw the inherited Jewish tradition as given by God, but as a means to an end rather than as an end in itself. In the New Testament, Jesus is repeatedly referred to as fulfilling the hopes and expectations of Judaism (see Acts 2). But the Transfiguration of Jesus (Mk 9) sums up the New Testament attitude to the Old Testament by showing Moses and Elijah affirming Jesus' status and making clear that they are subservient to him (see page 27).

Like Judaism, Christianity was forced to choose when drawing up its canon of scripture. Early documents which competed for entry included not only the current contents but also the **didache** (teaching)

For more on didache, see page 68.

See www.earlychristianwritings.com for more information on these books.

(c.70 CE), 1 Clement (c.96 CE), the Epistle of Barnabus (c.100 CE), and seven letters of Ignatius of Antioch (c.110 CE). In c.140 CE Marcion, who rejected the Jewish account of an apparently cruel God, produced an anthology which accordingly excluded all Jewish scriptures but included ten letters of Paul and two thirds of Luke's Gospel. This collection forced the Church to choose between the competing Gospels, Acts, epistles and apocalypses, and agree a canon of scripture. Compiled in Rome, the Muratorian Canon (c.200 CE) included the four now-familiar Gospels, Acts, 13 of Paul's letters, 1 John, 2 John and Jude, plus the Apocalypse of Peter. The first surviving list of the New Testament in exactly the form and order that we have it, dates from 367 CE and was written by Athanasius, Bishop of Alexandria. But it was not until 904 CE that Pope Damasus formally recognised the New Testament as canonical, and as late as 1442 it was still felt necessary for the Council of Florence to affirm that the 27 books were fully authoritative.

In a teaching paper *The Gift of Authority* (1999), the Anglican-Roman Catholic International Commission summarised the position thus:

> The formation of the canon of the Scriptures was an integral part of the process of tradition. The Church's recognition of these Scriptures as canonical, after a long period of critical discernment, was at the same time an act of obedience and of authority. It was an act of *obedience* in that the Church discerned and received God's life-giving 'Yes' through the Scriptures, accepting them as the norm of faith. It was an act of *authority* in that the Church, under the guidance of the Holy Spirit, received and handed on these texts, declaring that they were inspired and that others were not to be included in the canon.

Christians of all types call the Bible 'the Word of God' – God's communication or message. The same title is applied in the New Testament to Jesus himself (Jn 1: 14), and the identification of Jesus as the 'Word incarnate' (Word made flesh) implies the belief that Jesus is the means by which God has chosen to make his character, will and purposes clear to humanity. Applying the title to the Bible implies the same for the biblical books in terms of revealing God.

Karl Barth saw three aspects of the Word of God in Christianity: the Word revealed in the life and teaching of Jesus Christ, the witness to this Word in the books of the Bible, and the later proclamation of this Word in and through the Church.

It is important to understand that Christianity came to see the books of the Bible as uniquely important because they were the record of, and the witness to, Christ. In traditional Christian thought, the Old Testament anticipated and set the scene for Christ, and the New Testament recorded and explained the incarnation. The Anglican theologian Hooker summarised this approach to the Bible which is held in common by Protestants, Orthodox and Roman Catholics in his *Laws of Ecclesiastical Polity*:

> The general end of both the Old and the New (Testaments) is one; the difference between them consisting in this, that the Old did make wise by teaching salvation through Christ should come, and that Jesus whom the Jews did crucify, and whom God did raise from the dead, is he.

Three modern approaches to interpreting the Bible have emerged within Christianity (though within these three general categories there will be dozens of different views):

- **Conservative.** The Bible is the Word of God, the historical record kept by the Church of Christ. Its authority is derived from Christ and not the other way round (ie, Christ is not the Son of God because the Bible says so; but because Christ is the Son of God, the Bible is true). This view is held by the Roman Catholic Church and the Catholic Catechism teaches that:

  > God is the author of Sacred Scripture... God inspired the human authors of the sacred books. To compose the sacred books, God chose certain men who... made full use of their own faculties and powers so that, though he acted in them and by them, it was as true authors that they consigned to writing whatever he wanted written, and no more... Still, the Christian faith is not a 'religion on the book'. Christianity is a religion of the 'Word' of God, not a written and mute word, but incarnate and living. If the Scriptures are not to remain a dead letter, Christ must, through the Holy Spirit, open our minds to understand the Scriptures.

  Catechism of the Catholic Church (1993), paragraphs 105–108.

- **Fundamentalist.** The Bible is the direct and inspired Word of God, absolutely and literally true in all respects. Fundamentalists see within the New Testament itself claims for the direct inspiration by God of the Bible (see 2 Tim 3: 16; 2 Pet 1: 21) and hold to the literal truth of the creation of the world by God in six days (Gen 1), the giving of the Law to Moses on Mount Sinai (Ex 19–20), the Virgin Birth (Lk 1–2) and bodily resurrection (Lk 24) of Christ, and the literal future second coming of Christ to the earth as judge (Mt 25). These views are held by some evangelical Protestant Churches.

- **Liberal.** The Bible is a representative and symbolic account of that beauty, truth and goodness which we call God and which was seen most clearly in Jesus. This view is held by many Anglicans and Methodists who see the 'miraculous' events of the Bible as largely symbolic, poetic stories pointing to moral or spiritual truths.

Religious authority in Hinduism

The Hindu scriptures were put together over a long period, the majority being written c.1200 BCE–c.200 BCE. There are two main types of literature, Shruti and Smriti, with Shruti accorded greater status as they are believed to be not simply written by people but divinely inspired.

Shruti

The most well-known examples of the Shruti tradition are the **Vedas**. These texts have supreme authority as they are held to have been 'heard' by the earliest priests and passed down orally through generations of priests who recited them in the temples. There are four Vedas:

Shruti means 'hearing', reflecting the oral transmission of the scriptures. This transmission is held to have preserved intonation as well as the exact words of the revelation.

- The *Rig-Veda* or Veda of Hymns
- The *Sama-Veda* or Veda of Chants
- The *Yajur-Veda* or Veda of Sacrifice
- The *Atharva-Veda* or Veda of Atharvan, which contains magic charms.

The *Atharva-Veda* was written later than the other three. All four were written in Vedic, an old form of Sanskrit. The first three Vedas are used in worship. The *Rig-Veda* is divided into ten *mandalas* (chapters) and collects 1,028 hymns addressed to Hindu deities. All the gods are praised and none is seen as supreme. The *Sama-Veda* repeats many of the hymns in the *Rig-Veda* and organises them for worship. The *Yajur-Veda* is used by priests in worship as it outlines instructions for performing sacrifices.

Each Veda is divided into three levels:

✦ The *Samhita* are the hymns of each section and are the largest and oldest parts of each Veda, and date back to c.1200 BCE

✦ The *Brahmanas* are detailed descriptions of practice for priests and explore in detail the minutiae of the sacrificial rites. Many are thought to have been composed between c.1000 and c.600 BCE

✦ The *Upanishads* were written c.400 BCE–c.200 BCE and contain much of Hindu philosophy; some of it mystical, some esoteric and some essentially teaching. The nature of the writing is speculative, and looks at the nature of the universe and the existential purpose of humankind. The realisation of the full nature of humanity is a matter of primary concern; the texts seek to reconcile the internal aspect of the human being with the external world.

Smriti

The second type of literature that carries great weight in Hinduism is the Smriti, or 'remembered' tradition. These texts were written later than the main body of the Vedas (probably from 500 BCE onwards). The Smriti texts are not seen as divinely inspired and 'heard' like the Vedas, but are taken as being authoritative as long as they do not clash with what is written in the primary Shruti texts. The largest of these texts is the epic poem, the *Mahabharata*, which contains 2,000 verses. It tells of a great war between two families and was composed over an extended period probably between c.400 BCE and c.200 CE. The sixth book of the *Mahabharata* is the *Bhagavad Gita* (c.200 BCE–c.200 CE) which tells the story of Arjuna and his charioteer Krishna, who turns out to be an incarnation of Vishnu. Other Smriti texts include the *Puranas*, dealing with Hindu mythology, and the *Ramayana*, an epic poem telling the story of Rama and Sita. The *Laws of Manu* also emerged around the time of the *Bhagavad Gita* and these outline rules of conduct.

For more on Krishna, Rama and Vishnu see page 108.

Shruti and Smriti texts still tend to be transmitted orally, remembered by believers and said rather than read. The authority of these texts as recorded in the written word lies at the very heart of the spirituality, ethics, ritual and worldview of the Hindu community.

Religious authority in Islam

Muslims have several sources of religious authority that help them shape their understanding of their faith. One important source is the Sunnah of Muhammad, which loosely translates as 'the way of the Prophet'; if a Muslim imitates Muhammad's way of living they are likely to behave according to the modes of ethical and religious conduct most in keeping with the rigorous demands of Islam. Spiritual authority is also found in the collection of sayings attributed to Muhammad, these collections are known as Hadith. The role of Shari'ah (Islamic law) is also very prominent in the Islamic community.

The Qur'an

The basis of all of these sources of authority is the Qur'an. This was compiled as a series of revelations given by God to Muhammad through the medium of the Angel Jibra'il in a cave on Mount Hira. These revelations took place over a period of 22 years and were memorised by Muhammad and written down by his most devoted followers. On Muhammad's death the Islamic community was concerned to try and ensure that Muhammad's teachings did not disappear with him. It became one of the most prestigious positions in the community to learn the Qur'an by heart, thus becoming a **Hafiz**, and so preserving the word of God.

At this time the Qur'an did not exist in a collected written form. Its compilation began under the reign of the second rightly-guided Caliph, Umar. It was not completed until approximately 20 years after Muhammad's death when the third Caliph Uthman, who is praised by Muslims for standardising the Qur'an, was in power. It is written in Quarysh, the dialect of Muhammad's tribe: contemporary Muslims see this as the only appropriate language in which to learn and recite the Qur'an even if a Muslim's mother tongue is not Arabic, because Arabic is considered a sacred language. Muslims hold that the Qur'an is constructed of the most beautiful poetry ever written and that the beauty of the language is held to be evidence of God's hand in its creation. The Qur'an is made up of a combination of rhyming poetry and lyrical verse which is particularly suited for recitation and learning – if not for ease of translation.

> To preserve unity Caliph Uthman burnt all other versions of the Qur'an that existed at the time. The Uthmanic Qur'an is essentially the text that is used today.

The Qur'an is composed of a series of Suras (chapters) subdivided into verses. It is not arranged chronologically; instead the Suras are arranged by order of length from longest (286 verses) to shortest (three verses). Each has a heading (eg Sura 21, 'Al Anbiyah', or 'the Prophets') and ends with either the word 'Makkah' (Mecca) or 'Madinah' (Medina), indicating the place where the revelation was received. The Makkan revelations were earlier and refer to the time prior to the **hijra** in which the Muslims were forced to flee to Madinah to avoid persecution. The Madinan Suras are those written during the time of exile prior to Muhammad's return to conquer Makkah in 630 CE.

> In 622 CE Muhammad led his followers away from Mecca to the city of Medina. This journey is known as the hijra. For more on this see page 110.

Interpretation

The verses are received and interpreted differently by Muslim groups. **Sunni** Muslims generally take the Qur'an literally, believing that the word of God cannot be added to, and is perfect and complete in itself. For a Sunni, searching for the true meaning is potentially to be guilty of the most serious of crimes (shirk), which is to put oneself on the same level as Allah. **Shi'a** and Sufi Muslims believe the Qur'an contains esoteric meanings to be drawn out through serious study and scholarship. For example Surah 76 describes heaven as a garden, in which the blessed are clothed in silk, drink wine and experience unearthly luxury. Some Muslims accept the description as it is written; others believe the language is symbolic as human terms are inadequate in representing the nature of what lies with God beyond the realms of human experience and expression.

> For more on the differences between Sunni and Shi'ite Muslims, and for more on 'shirk', see pages 111–112.

Importance

Despite disagreements over interpretation, all Muslims agree that the Qur'an is the word of God. The Qur'an is the chief source of spiritual authority and ethical guidance, and is used for the formulation of law. The Qur'an contains direct demands on conduct, talks of the nature of Prophethood, gives insights into the nature of God, eschatology, and the meaning and purpose of human existence. It rises above all else in importance as the eternal, immutable word of God.

Religious authority in Judaism

Judaism is an ancient faith and as such has developed a complex series of written forms of authority for the Jewish community. However the tradition of learning, interpreting and seeking to understand the texts has been dynamic throughout Jewish history and is still very much alive today. It is important to be aware that although the written scriptures have ultimate religious authority in the community, the authority of the rabbis, through a process of interpretation, is profoundly important in enabling the Jewish community to deepen its understanding of the faith.

Tenakh

A standard version of the Tenakh developed just after the Babylonian Exile, c.400 BCE. At this point the Torah took on heightened significance for the life of ancient Israel. The reading from the Torah became the central part of the synagogue service and was effectively a working canon by this time. As the synagogue service developed, a second lesson, this time from one of the prophets, was read aloud. Over time, the words of the prophets were granted a high status.

While all Jews accepted the Torah, the five books of Law, there was discussion about which other books should be included in the scriptures. Matters were complicated by the fact that many Jews lived outside Israel and spoke no Hebrew. A Greek version of the Tenakh, the Septuagint, was produced in the 1st or 2nd century BCE to meet the needs of Greek-speaking Jewish communities in Egypt. Other editions were written and these included different books.

'Septuagint' takes its name from the Greek word for 70 because it was reputed to be the work of 70 scholars in Alexandria.

After the destruction of the Temple, Jewish scholars attempted to settle the canon at the Council of Jamnia. They included only those books believed to have been originally written in Hebrew up to the time of Ezra and Nehemiah.

The arithmetic gets confusing at this point. The difference between Christian and Jewish treatments of scriptures comes from differently dividing 1 and 2 Samuel, 1 and 2 Kings, 1 and 2 Chronicles, the 12 minor prophets, and Ezra and Nehemiah.

The resulting scriptures thus comprised 24 books. The first and main part of the Tenakh is the Torah proper, the five books of Moses (Genesis, Exodus, Leviticus, Numbers, Deuteronomy). The text of the Law was fixed at an early stage, and the veracity of the text has been preserved by strict rules on scribal copying, to the extent that the text as we have it today can be relied upon on as an historical record. The prophets were accepted in their entirety, both the earlier (Joshua, Judges, Samuel, Kings) and the later (Isaiah, Jeremiah, Ezekiel, plus The Twelve – Hosea, Joel, Amos, Obadiah, Jonah, Micah, Nahum, Habakuk, Zepheniah, Hagai, Zechariah, Malachi). Ketuvim came to include Psalms, Job, Proverbs, Ruth, Song of Songs, Ecclesiastes, Lamentations, Esther, Daniel, Ezra-Nehemiah and Chronicles. They were accepted primarily on the basis of their harmony with the Torah.

Some 15 documents were not accepted into the Jewish Scriptures, but continued to command interest and respect. Known as the Apocrypha, these are accepted as canonical by the Roman Catholic Church, while the Orthodox Church accepts most of them. For Protestants, as for Jews, they are interesting documents, but do not have the status of scripture.

> **Warning.** Photocopying any part of this book without permission is illegal.

Of the three sections of the Tenakh, the Torah holds particular authority. Its five books provide Jews with their sense of obligation to God as his chosen people and occupy a primary place in worship and study. A strict code of conduct is given in the five books in the shape of 613 commandments (though it is important to remember that many of these refer to Temple worship or other specific situations and so Jews are not expected to strictly adhere to them all).

The Neviim subdivides into two sections. The first is the four earlier prophets (Joshua, Judges, I and II Samuel, and I and II Kings) who look at the past history of the Jewish people and see how that history impacts on its contemporary situation. The second section contains the writings of the major prophets (Isaiah, Jeremiah and Ezekiel) and the 12 minor prophets.

In this context a prophet is not a foreteller but someone who analyses how the community is behaving in relation to divine guidance and then warns of the implications this behaviour may have.

Note that the order of the Tenakh is different from the order in the Old Testament.

The literature in the Ketuvim is more diverse than that in the other two sections of Scripture. Some of the writing, such as in the Psalms and the Song of Songs, is poetical and mystical. Other books have different purposes: I and II Chronicles, for instance, retell Jewish history.

Midrash

While scripture holds primary authority, the extensive interpretive tradition in Judaism is also very important. Jewish scholarship is enormous, and there are many influential interpretations of scripture that challenge and alter the perspectives of the Jewish community. The commentaries written on the Tenakh by rabbis were collected, studied, and added to and so have grown over time. These commentaries are called **Midrash** and those who construct them are called exegetes (meaning textual interpreters). Scholars see some Midrash as fairly fanciful while other parts are more prosaic. The two major collections of Midrashim (c.300 CE–c.500 CE) contain the rabbinical views of how the text should be understood and demonstrate the developing authority of the rabbi. Rabbis have had an enormous impact on the Jewish community as leaders, dispensers of law and interpreters of scripture.

Oral Torah and the Mishnah

This leads to a most important source of authority in Judaism. This is the **Oral Torah**, which was passed down from generation to generation by the leaders of the community. It contains a detailed elaboration of the laws found in the (written) Torah and reputedly comes from Moses himself.

Around the 2nd century CE the oral Torah was written down in the **Mishnah**. The Mishnah contained extended detail on the written Torah that made the written law more easily understood. It was then added to by the **Gemara**, which is an extensive commentary on what is contained in the Mishnah. The Gemara was put together over the 200 years following the writing of the Mishnah. It consisted of the discussions of Jewish scholars and their specific discussions about sections of the Mishnah. The results of these discussions were then published alongside the passage of the Mishnah that had been under discussion. The combination of the Mishnah and Gemara was named the **Talmud**, from the Hebrew word 'to learn' and, along with the Torah, the Talmud has been a significant authority for Jews ever since.

Religion and human experience

Religious authority in Sikhism

Guru Granth Sahib

The Guru Granth Sahib is a collection of hymns that praise God and seek to proclaim his nature. The presence of the word Guru in the name is a reminder that Sikhs treat it as a spiritual teacher, like a living person.

Another name for the Guru Granth Sahib is the **Adi Granth**, which refers to the original collection of writings put together by the fifth Guru, Guru Arjan (1563–1606). This collection of Sikh writings was the first organised compilation by a Sikh Guru and was placed in the then newly constructed Harmandir (House of God) at Amritsar. The writings of the early Sikhs were accepted by the early Sikh community both as authoritative and as central to religious understanding. The name Adi Granth is now used by Sikhs to refer to the Guru Granth Sahib itself.

The Guru Granth Sahib is divided into 31 *ragas* which are musical scores designed to be sung. The divisions are based not on author or subject matter but on the living proclamation of the scripture in public worship. The book also contains readings at the beginning and end that are intended for use in morning and evening worship, and so act as prologue and epilogue to the scriptures themselves. The first section, which is not meant to be sung, contains the Japji poem believed to be written by Guru Nanak himself.

One of the unique features of the Sikh scriptures is that in addition to works by some of the Sikh Gurus, they contain writings from people who are of other faiths. When Guru Nanak met a spiritual person from another faith and recognised the areas of convergence between the two, he demonstrated this by bringing the song or prayer back to the Sikh community. Sikhs respect religious truth in whatever community it exists, indeed one of Guru Nanak's religious aims was to find the universal truth that exists between all men irrespective of social or religious background.

Each copy of the Guru Granth Sahib is identical. They are all written in Gurmukhi, which is Sikhism's holy language, and are constructed in a painstakingly beautiful way. Every copy has the same words in the same place, so the position of words remains constant in all editions. This serves to re-emphasise the authority of the scriptures: as the scriptures are considered to live, they have enormous importance to Sikh spirituality. The words of the Gurus are still alive within the community and so the Gurus themselves are considered to live on through the pages of the Guru Granth Sahib.

Anyone competent to read the Guru Granth Sahib is welcome to do so; a very common Sikh practice is the akhand path, which involves a continuous reading of the entire book by many people who read in relays.

The importance of the Guru Granth Sahib is demonstrated in the way it is looked after in the Gurdwara (Sikh temple) and in the home. In the Gurdwara the book is kept on a raised platform called a **takht**, and under a canopy. A fan or fly whisk is waved over the Guru Granth Sahib to show respect. In the home, many Sikhs set aside a room to keep the scriptures in, and some families will provide a bed in which the book is laid to rest when not in use to symbolise the living word at the centre of the family.

The writing in the Guru Granth Sahib is diverse in nature. The hymns talk of the nature of God and also the relation of human beings to God, most notably in the **Mool Mantra** of Guru Nanak. The nature of meditation is also discussed at great length as it is central to the Sikh spiritual life and so is mentioned in the daily prayers of Sikhs. There is also an ethical aspect to the content of the Guru Granth Sahib as it contains guidelines to good living and desirable moral conduct. Like many scriptures of the world religions there are historical insights into the development of the Sikh community and the lives of its Gurus. The Guru Granth Sahib gives Sikhs guidance for their moral and spiritual development. Sikhs believe that the ultimate aim of a religious life is to be at one with God.

The 'Mool Mantra' means the perfect mantra, a short statement of belief with which the Sikh scriptures open. For more on this, see page 118.

Authority

The authority of the Guru Granth Sahib lies in the fact that it is considered by Sikhs to be the supreme spiritual authority and is thus the leader of the religion as opposed to any human being. There may be other influential writings (such as the Dasam Granth, which are the writings of the last Guru, Gobind Singh, who was too modest to include his own work in the Guru Granth Sahib) and there may be important community figures. However when guidance and understanding is needed Sikhs need look no further than the Guru Granth Sahib.

Test yourself

1. 'The role of religious leaders is to interpret texts for believers so that there is an official interpretation for them to follow, rather than them being reliant upon their own logic or experience.'

    (a) Explain TWO ways in which scriptures may affect the life of a believer.

    (b) With reference to a religion you have studied, explain how religious leaders may provide authoritative teaching.

2. (a) Identify the key features of conversions and mystical experiences. Refer to at least one example of each in your answer.

    (b) 'There is no way of knowing whether religious experiences are truly experiences of God.' Assess this claim.

3. (a) Explain what believers mean when they say their scriptures are 'inspired'.

    (b) Explain and assess the view that 'the teaching of scripture is not binding upon all religious people'.

Old Testament

God and the covenant

Nature of God

The Israelite nation was a comparative latecomer in the ancient Middle East. Sumerian civilisation emerged c.4000 BCE, while Egyptian civilisation was first established c.3000 BCE. Abraham did not emerge until c.1900 BCE while Moses did not lead the Israelites out of Egypt until c.1250 BCE. Moreover the Torah, where the basic principle of **monotheism** (belief in the one-ness of God) is enshrined, did not reach its finished form until after the Babylonian exile (6th century BCE). Two things are important to have in mind when considering this period: the relationship between the emergent Israelite nation-state and the surrounding, often greater, powers; and also Israel's own developing understanding of God.

> Although the Torah is strictly the first five books of Jewish scripture the term is also sometimes more loosely applied to the Jewish Scriptures as a whole. This is better referred to as the Tenakh: see margin note on page 24.

God as one

The Israelite people came to believe that there was only one God and that he was the supreme ruler of all of the universe, including the human world. This view emerged in dialogue with the surrounding pagan **polytheism**, particularly the diverse religious beliefs held by the Babylonian and Egyptian cultures. However Israel, frequently subjected to attacks by foreign aggressors, began to project hopes for its own security on to the heavenly realm by developing belief in its **election** by the one supreme God. Indeed the biblical account of the Israelite God sometimes having to contend with and resist pretenders reflects Israel's frequent conflicts with her neighbours.

> Election means being chosen by God.

Development of monotheism

In the present form of the Tenakh, monotheism is implied everywhere and is sometimes clearly expressed, as in, for instance, Deutero-Isaiah, who wrote during the 6th century BCE. But it is thought that the earlier biblical texts went through a long process of **redaction** (editing), and for that reason it cannot necessarily be assumed that absolute monotheism was a feature of the earliest Israelite theology. In fact parts of the Bible seem to retain traces of an earlier polytheism. For instance in Psalm 82 God is described as presiding over a number of lesser deities in a heavenly court. A recent trend among scholars is to examine the development of monotheism in Israel and to question the extent to which the surrounding polytheism was finally eradicated from the nation-state that David and Solomon founded.

> Deutero-Isaiah is the name given to an anonymous prophet whose words are recorded in Isaiah 40–55. See pages 57–58.

Omnipotent and omnipresent God

The turning point in this theology of dialogue was undoubtedly the exile. This created a crisis of faith in which the very survival of Israelite theology was in doubt. But the Israelite God not only survived the destruction of the Temple and the exile but emerged with his power and kingdom greatly enlarged. The sense that his role was simply the defence of the integrity of Israel and the sanctity of the Temple fell away, and an awareness of God as lord of all the world – and all history – replaced it. God was now viewed by the Jews as omnipotent and omnipresent.

After the exile the Jews also developed the need to find a sense of their own history in which the nation's election by God was the dominant theme. They redacted the different strata of the Torah which had circulated in a variety of forms, and established the writings of the prophets as the second division of the Tenakh. The rise of **prophecy** in Israel refined and channelled the emergent monotheism, making subsequent Judaism rest on the pillars of monotheism, election and covenant.

Abrahamic Covenant

The book of Genesis opens by describing the universal origins of humankind in the creation. Although there are two creation stories in Genesis, their combined effect is to insist that the Israelite God was the creator of the universe and all its inhabitants. This sets the scene for God's election of the Israelite people, which begins with the person called Abraham, the father of the Israelite nation.

Abraham enters the story in Genesis 11. He first appears as a Mesopotamian figure, called by God to journey from the Chaldean city of Ur in the south of modern Iraq through the Fertile Crescent to what God calls 'the land that I will show you' (Gen 12: 1). He set out at the age of 75, taking his wife and family with him.

The biblical portrait of Abraham suggests that he was the leader of a tribal clan with considerable resources. The clan's livelihood depended on sheep and goats, and as a result its members would have been accustomed to a nomadic existence. Perhaps Abraham was an economic migrant and trade was a motivating factor in his journey. But for our purposes we should note that the biblical story of Abraham emphasises the theme of God's promise to bless Abraham, coupled with Abraham's faithful response.

The crucial point in the Abraham story is reached in Genesis 17. Abraham had a vision of God calling upon him to make a covenant. The Hebrew word **berit** originally meant 'shackle' or 'chain'. It subsequently came to designate any form of binding agreement. The Tenakh tells the story of the continuing covenant relationship between God and Israel, which begins with Abraham.

Genesis 17 makes clear the original form of the covenant, and insists that it was God's and not Abraham's initiative that lay behind it. Its origin was in a vision, and the fact that Abraham 'fell on his face' (Gen 17: 3) demonstrates the helpless nature of his response towards this divine self-disclosure. Scholars have often compared this covenant to a vassalage or suzerainty treaty in which the two participants in the treaty are designedly unequal. This is why Abraham appears as a particular named individual; he is in this sense the forerunner of the Israelite monarch.

As a result of the vision God makes a covenant with Abraham (not the other way round). The making of a covenant implies benefits and responsibilities on both sides. God promises Abraham and his descendants land; in response, Abraham and the Israelites are expected to honour God as the only God. This mutual exchange is described in Genesis 17: 7–8:

> And I will establish my covenant between me and you and your descendants throughout their generations for an everlasting covenant,

Abraham

The Fertile Crescent is a strip of land running from the lower Nile Valley, up the eastern Mediterranean coast, curving through Syria to Mesopotamia. It may not all seem fertile today, but its climate was wetter in biblical times.

There is evidence of a westward movement of Semitic people from Mesopotamia from about 2100 BCE. Does this mean that Abraham's journey cannot be seen as exceptional? Or is the truth that the biblical account shows memories of many peoples' migrations being rolled up into a single exemplary story?

The covenant

Note that the Christian title for the Jewish Bible is the Old Testament. The word 'testament' derives from the Latin word for covenant, acknowledging the centrality in these writings of the pact between God and Israel.

See page 53 for more on suzerainty treaties.

Further study

Fear and Trembling by Søren Kierkegaard (Penguin 1985) is one of the most influential of the interpretations of the story of Abraham and his son Isaac. It is a relatively short book and gives an insight into the importance this story has for many believers.

to be God to you and to your descendants after you. And I will give to you, and to your descendants after you, the land of your sojournings, all the land of Canaan, for an everlasting possession; and I will be their God.

Circumcision

Students often conclude that circumcision, the removal of the foreskin of the penis, was originally a hygienic practice. But in the context of your study of covenants, you need to remember its significance in connection with Abraham.

The covenant recorded in Genesis 17 is central to Israelite theology and its external sign is circumcision (Gen 17: 9–14). Abraham is himself shown being circumcised at the age of ninety-nine in what the Torah treats as a fundamental event in the history of the Jewish religion. Jewish male babies are circumcised when they are eight days old as an indication that they belong to God's covenant people. Male converts are also required to accept circumcision.

Mosaic Covenant

Moses

Moses is always referred to in the third person in the Torah. This led the 17th-century philosopher Benedict Spinoza to question whether Moses actually wrote it. Spinoza was labelled a heretic by both Jews and Christians, but despite this doubts have been cast on Moses' authorship ever since.

Moses was a figure of the later 2nd millennium (c.1250 BCE). He is revered as the bringer of the law in Judaism and authorship of the Torah is traditionally ascribed to him. Some scholars have questioned his existence but, although some of the stories about Moses may have been worked up in the long course of transmission and redaction, we need have little doubt about his having been an actual historical figure.

Exodus

Further study

Moses' youth is represented in the 1998 cartoon *The Prince of Egypt* and his life in Cecil B. de Mille's *The Ten Commandments* (1956). Does either film have a religious content?

John Bright, *Authority of the Old Testament* (Paternoster 1998).

The patriarch Joseph had led the Israelites into Egypt. Exodus 1: 8 says ominously of the period after Joseph died that 'there arose a new king over Egypt, who did not know Joseph'. The result of this was that, where once they had been honoured guests, the Israelites became little more than slaves. It fell to Moses to lead the Israelites out of Egypt. The story of how a series of plagues befell the Egyptians, and how the Red Sea parted to facilitate the passage of the Israelites, is well known. Again, its historicity has sometimes been challenged, but as Bright wrote:

> A belief so ancient and so entrenched will admit of no explanation save that Israel actually escaped from Egypt to the accompaniment of events so stupendous as to be ever impressed on her memory.

The wilderness

See the story of God providing manna in the desert in Exodus 16: 2–35.

See Exodus 19–24 for the Mosaic Covenant.

The Israelites may have left Egypt successfully but according to the biblical account they were compelled to spend a period of 40 years in the wilderness before entering the promised land of Canaan. Food and water were scarce, but were provided miraculously. The people nevertheless complained about their God, and the Torah records that God brought them to the mountain of Sinai and entered into a new covenant relationship with them.

This period of history is described in the book of Exodus. Although editorial activity is clear in the present form of the narrative, it appears that the covenant was concluded in a common meal in which, at least on the evidence of Exodus 24: 10, God himself was a participant and was seen by the leaders of Israel. As the Torah developed, various other elements were incorporated within the Sinai revelation; but it is likely that this period of history has an historical core that centres around the Decalogue, or Ten Commandments.

The Ten Commandments

The concept of God as lawgiver and judge is central to Jewish Scriptures, and Law is not only a key term of the Jewish Scriptures, it can even be used as the name for the whole of scripture. The Ten Commandments (Ex 20: 1–17) are central to the defining of the new covenant. Scholars usually call them **apodictic**, which means they are based in absolute law, as opposed to conditional law, which is expressed with a protasis and an apodasis. The following regulations are enshrined within them:

1. You shall have no other gods before the Israelite God
2. You shall not make any graven images or likeness of God
3. You shall not invoke God's name in vain
4. Keep the Sabbath
5. Honour your father and mother
6. Do not murder
7. Do not commit adultery
8. Do not steal
9. Do not bear false witness against your neighbour
10. Do not covet your neighbour's property.

Eight out of ten of these are prohibitive: they are negative, not positive commandments. But it should not be assumed that negativity is a general feature of the Mosaic Covenant. The Decalogue loosely defines behaviour that is deemed impermissible in order to encourage ethical and virtuous living.

One of the most exciting features of recent research has been the comparison between the Ten Commandments and other legal codes from the Ancient Middle East. Scholars have distinguished two types of covenants in the culture of the surrounding worlds:

✦ The reciprocal or parity covenant
✦ The suzerainty treaty.

The former is a treaty between approximate social equals, while the latter is designed to demonstrate the absolute subjection of one party to the other. This enshrines the benefit of protection but brings with it the duty of obedience. It is clear that the Mosaic Covenant is a suzerainty treaty.

Covenant in Jeremiah

From Moses in c.1250 BCE we leap forward to Jeremiah in the period of the Babylonian exile (586–538 BCE). Although we have yet to consider the rise of prophecy in Israel, which occurred during the 8th century BCE, the leap is an appropriate one in terms of the history of the covenant in Israel. The prophets are dominated by the theme that Israel either failed to keep the covenant or else adhered to the letter of the covenant while ignoring its obvious spirit. Some prophets imply or even state that the exile was a direct punishment for Israel's covenant infidelity. Thus we find Jeremiah announcing that the Day of the Lord, which earlier prophets had presented as a matter of hope, was a day of doom and despondency. This is because the Israelite God was finally punishing his people for their disobedience.

The book of Jeremiah is made up of four different sections:

Protasis and apodosis are Greek words used by philosophers and grammarians. The former is a conditional clause to which the latter is the answering clause, as in the sentence *If you buy the fish and chips* (protasis), *we'll buy the drinks* (apodosis). Laws framed with a protasis and an apodasis are easily imagined.

By the time of Jesus, the Ten Commandments had been summarised in the twofold demand to love God and to love one's neighbour (see Mk 12: 28–31). Indeed, this not a bad summary of the Commandments' original spirit.

Other legal codes from the Ancient Near East include those of: Ur-Nammu, which survives on clay tablets from c.2050 BCE; Hammurabi, who ruled Babylonia 1792–1750 BCE; Lipit-Ishtar, a Sumerian ruler; and Eshunna of the Amorite kingdom.

Further study

Read the whole story of Moses in Exodus. Is the story of Moses in the scriptures dominated by his personality, or does his personality serve the religious needs of narrative?

For more on the development of prophecy, see pages 55–61.

Warning. Photocopying any part of this book without permission is illegal.

- Chapters 1–25: a discrete section composed mainly of prophetic oracles
- 26–45: biographical material interspersed with prophecies of judgement and hope
- 46–51: prophecies against the surrounding nations; some of this material comes from later writers
- 52: an historical conclusion describing the fall of Jerusalem.

Jeremiah became a prominent figure at the start of King Jehoiakim's reign, when he made an impassioned speech against the Temple cult in Jerusalem, which is recorded in Jeremiah 7 and 26. Jeremiah criticised abominations which included child-sacrifice and social oppression. According to Jeremiah 26, this speech caused great consternation among its audience.

Worse was to come. Jeremiah lamented his people's failure to keep to their side of the covenant agreement, and called the people of the southern kingdom the owners of 'a stubborn and rebellious heart'. This stubbornness had resulted in an institutional form of religion in which people trusted only in externals such as the Ark (Jer 3: 16), circumcision (Jer 4: 4), the Torah (Jer 8: 8) and the Temple (Jer 7: 4). Jeremiah alleged that this formalism was combined with a blatant failure to keep to the demands of the covenant. People coveted their neighbours' wives (Jer 5: 8) and showed no concern for those without resources (Jer 5: 28). In a famous passage, Jeremiah lamented that 'the heart is deceitful above all things and desperately corrupt' (Jer 17: 9).

Jeremiah saw God's judgement in the historical process. He spoke eloquently of 'the foe from the north' (notably in Jer 4), a reference to the advance of Babylonia. In a particularly passionate section (Jer 8: 18 to Jer 9: 3), Jeremiah weeps over the destruction of Jerusalem. His identification with the fate of the Israelites in terms of his personal anguish was in every sense a complete one. Later, in the reign of Zedekiah, Jeremiah was imprisoned for his prophecies.

A new covenant

The most pertinent passage in Jeremiah is Chapter 31. This anticipates the formation of a renewed covenant community in the period following the restoration of Jerusalem. Jeremiah speaks with the first-person voice of God, asserting that:

> The days are coming... when I will make a new covenant with the house of Israel and the house of Judah, not like the covenant which I made with their fathers when I took them by the hand to bring them out of the land of Egypt, my covenant which they broke (Jer 31: 31–32).

Like the old covenant, this new covenant was to rest on the gracious initiative of God. However it was not to be the precise equivalent of the Mosaic Covenant. The Mosaic Covenant had failed, as Jeremiah understood things, because of Israel's inability to keep to the covenantal agreement. Nevertheless Jeremiah believed that the new covenant would fulfil the intention of the Mosaic Covenant in the sense that it was to be essentially a matter of inward perception. This would bring a new community into being, one characterised by honest intention and the provision of divine forgiveness.

Jehoiakim's son Jehoiachim reigned for only three months before being defeated by Nebuchadnezzar and carried off into Babylonian exile (2 Kings 24).

For more on the split between the northern kingdom of Israel and the southern kingdom of Judah, see pages 61–62.

Warning. Photocopying any part of this book without permission is illegal.

Jeremiah's conviction that the time was ripe for the formation of a new covenant between God and Israel depended upon the crisis that had led to the exile in 587 BCE. He saw this as the opportunity for a fresh divine initiative in which God would make his people faithful once again.

Development of prophecy

The prophetic books

The prophetic books form part of the second section of the Tenakh, the Neviim (prophets). They are subordinate in status to the Torah but are nonetheless of great significance in their own right. However the organisation of the prophetic books in English translations of the Bible differs from that of the Hebrew text in two important ways. First, in English versions the books are not arranged in chronological order. Second, English translations include two books – Daniel and Lamentations – as part of the second section, while the Tenakh groups them with the third section, Ketuvim (writings). Furthermore in English translations the prophetic books of Isaiah, Jeremiah and Ezekiel are referred to as the major prophets, while the twelve shorter prophetic books, including Lamentations and Daniel, are often called the minor prophets. In order to avoid confusion over chronology and status, these differences need to be kept in mind.

Lamentations more closely resembles part of the Psalms and, as its name implies, laments the Babylonian destruction of Jerusalem. Daniel includes an apocalypse, a genre of writing associated with literature composed between the Old and the New Testaments, and is the latest of the books of the Hebrew Bible, having been written c.165 BCE.

Types of prophets in the 10th and 9th centuries BCE

There is a little uncertainty as to what the Hebrew word which is translated as prophet actually means. It might have an active sense, 'one who calls', or a passive sense, 'one who is called'. Despite this uncertainty, it is clear that the prophets communicated the divine will to Israel. They were people who were called by God, and they in turn called the people of Israel and Judah to consider their religious position. That prophets were called by God, and not the other way round, needs emphasising: prophets are chosen, they do not choose themselves. Some of them don't even seem obvious candidates for the job (Moses may even have had a speech impediment) but the task is given, not earned. Thus their authority is not personal: it comes entirely from God. Deutero-Isaiah implied this when he declared 'The spirit of the Lord is upon me' (Is 61: 1).

Declaration of the divine will

The term 'prophet' is often loosely understood to mean a diviner, or forecaster. For example Saul visited Samuel in search of advice on where to find his father's lost donkeys (1 Sam 9: 6–20). But while the Israelite prophets did occasionally predict the future, that was not the essence of their role. Their real function was to declare the divine will to the nation. A whole variety of passages (for example Amos 1: 3–5) begins with the phrase, 'Thus says the Lord'. This is an indication of what the prophets actually did. They offered a form of direct divine pronouncement that differed in this respect from the exegesis of the Torah (although it sometimes included that).

'Exegesis' is another word for explanation or interpretation.

The origin of prophecy

Israelite prophecy originated with Moses and the exodus: Moses is called a prophet in Deuteronomy 18: 18. In the period of the monarchy, we read of 'a band of prophets' in 1 Samuel 10: 5. It is clear from this passage that the earliest form of Israelite prophecy involved ecstatic possession. Thus Saul, in a prophetic rapture,

Warning. Photocopying any part of this book without permission is illegal.

removed all his clothing and lay in a trance for a day and a night (1 Sam 19: 19–24).

Ecstatic prophecy existed in a variety of ancient cultures, including in Canaan and in Asia Minor. The difference between Israelite prophets and others was that the message and activity of the former was determined by the divine covenant with Israel and was always related to that theme. The prophets would thus confront departures from Judaism, such as a move towards idolatry.

Prophetic guilds

1 Kings 20: 35–42 describes an anonymous member of a guild of prophets denouncing King Ahab's actions to his face.

The early prophets belonged to guilds, such as the 'band of prophets' already mentioned. They lived together in communities, under the leadership of a senior figure such as Elijah and tended to be nomadic. They travelled from place to place as occasion demanded; and, on the evidence of 2 Kings 4: 1–7, they included women among their number.

Other prophets were more closely tied with the great cultic centres of Israel, such as Bethel and Jerusalem. These prophets had great liturgical significance. They presented the prayers of the people and then communicated God's response to individual requests. They probably played a large part in the annual festivals that determined Israelite religious life in this period.

Regard for the prophets

1 Samuel 28: 6–15 mentions three means of discerning God's will in this period of history:

Further study

Find out more about the importance of Samuel: is he the last of the judges or the first of the prophets? George E. Mendenhall has said of him: 'The Israelite religion survived largely because of Samuel.' Try looking at Mendenhall's *Ancient Israel's Faith and History* (Westminster John Knox Press 2001).

◆ Dreams (as throughout ancient culture)

◆ The Urim and the Thummim (a set of stones)

◆ Prophecy.

The Urim and the Thummin were perhaps used like lots or dice, with their way of falling being interpreted by a priest. But they were limited to 'yes' and 'no' answers, whereas the prophets were believed to communicate the divine will directly and to make it relevant to particular situations. As a result of their ability to address a wide range of issues, the prophets were highly regarded.

Rise of prophecy

See 1 Kings 13 for the circumstances in which two unnamed prophets meet.

The rise of prophecy is characterised by the appearance of specific, named prophets. These individuals, most notably Elijah and Elisha, act as a bridge between the 10th- and 9th-century BCE companies of largely amorphous (and sometimes anonymous) prophets and the writing prophets of 8th century BCE and beyond. The individual prophets served to guide Israelite religion through the social crises of the 8th century BCE through the political crisis of the exile in the 6th century BCE and beyond to the prophecies of Haggai and Zechariah in the 4th century BCE.

Elijah

Elijah's elevated status within Judaism is indicated by the tradition that he attends every circumcision. A special chair is always set out for the prophet to sit on at the ceremony.

The Elijah cycle is told in 1 Kings 17–19 and 21. He is described as being strangely dressed and as having the ability to appear and disappear largely at will. His first action (in 1 Kings 17) is to announce a drought. This challenges the prowess of the Canaanite god of fertility, Baal, and effectively wrests away control of this particular province from Baal and transfers it to the Israelite God.

1 Kings 18 contains the story of Elijah and the prophets of Baal. This passage begins with the famous phrase, 'If the Lord is God, follow him; but if Baal, then follow him' (1 Kings 18: 21). Elijah thus confronts the people with a stark choice. Either they follow the Israelite God or they follow Baal: between the two there can be no compromise. When there is no reaction from the people, he challenges the prophets of Baal to prove the power of their deity. They are unable to do so, and are taunted by Elijah. The power of the Israelite God is then demonstrated by the appearance of fire from heaven, and the people recognise that the Lord is God. The prophets of Baal are exposed as impostors.

This story forms the basis of an oratorio by Mendelssohn, *Elijah*. Try the version with Bryn Terfel in the title role (Decca 4556882).

> 'Wherever Elijah appears, there is an eruption like the outbreak of a volcano. No other prophet of the early period of the monarchy approaches him in effectiveness, or in his readiness for complete involvement in Yahweh's (God's) cause.' Klaus Koch *The Prophets* (SCM Press 1982).

Elijah was followed by Elisha, of whom it was said 'the word of the Lord is with him' (2 Kings 3: 12). Elisha's name means 'God is salvation'. He is credited with a series of miracles and presented as a faithful follower of the Israelite God. He continued Elijah's struggle against Ahab by sending a messenger to anoint Jehu as king.

Elisha

Elijah's mantle literally passed to Elisha: see 1 Kings 19: 19; see also 2 Kings 2: 8 and 2: 13–14.

Development of the prophetic tradition

The prophetic tradition as we know it spanned five crucial centuries. This period begins following the division of the monarchy between Israel in the north and Judah in the south after the death of Solomon. It concludes with the return from the Babylonian exile under the Persian ruler Cyrus the Great in 538 BCE and the reconstruction of the Temple. The prophetic tradition is divided into two groups: the major prophets and the minor prophets.

Isaiah, Jeremiah and Ezekiel are called the major prophets because their writings are longer than those of the other prophets. All three underwent a process of composition and redaction which especially affected Isaiah. Scholars now believe that **Isaiah** was written by three distinct authors at three different times. The original Isaiah wrote in the 8th century BCE. His oracles are Chapters 1–39. Chapters 40–55 come from a writer known as Deutero-Isaiah or Second Isaiah. He wrote his famous prophecy of exile and restoration during the period of the Babylonian exile. Third Isaiah (sometimes called Trito-Isaiah) comes from the last twenty years of the 6th century BCE, when some of the exiles had begun to return home. This last part of Isaiah takes a special interest in the Temple and its worship.

The major prophets

Jeremiah contains a wealth of biographical material that helps us reconstruct the tragic life of the author, who was imprisoned for a considerable period. Jeremiah taught that the disaster which befell Jerusalem in 586 BCE was God's punishment for repeated breaches of the covenant. He anticipated disaster in the period leading up to the exile and his prophecies won him few friends. Jeremiah initially stayed in Jerusalem after the exile. Against his will, he was eventually taken to Egypt, where he died, it is reported, with words of judgement on his lips (Jer 44).

For more on Jeremiah and his prophecies, see pages 53–55 and 60–61.

Ezekiel was a strange character, prone to what have often been described as abnormal psychological experiences. He criticised the persistent obstinacy of people, comparing Jerusalem (Ezek 16) to an illegitimate child, and suggesting that her wickedness exceeded that of Samaria and even Sodom. Ezekiel is remarkable for his

Warning. Photocopying any part of this book without permission is illegal.

For more on Ezekiel's vision, see page 25.

visionary experience, in the course of which he saw the divine glory depart from the Temple and hover over it (Ezek 9–11).

The minor prophets

The minor prophets are Hosea, Joel, Amos, Obadiah, Jonah, Micah, Nahum, Habakkuk, Zephaniah, Haggai, Zechariah and Malachi. The last three (and probably also Jonah) come from the period after the exile; Haggai and Zechariah comment especially on the lethargy that characterised attempts to restore the Temple in Jerusalem during that period.

Hosea is unique among the corpus of prophets because its author came from the northern kingdom of Israel in the period following the division of the monarchy. The book was compiled after Hosea's death and passed through more than one editorial stage. Hosea describes tragic personal circumstances in which his wife Gomer becomes a prostitute: this may be genuinely autobiographical or it may be that the figure of Gomer is an allegorical one which Hosea uses as a metaphor for Israel's infidelity to God. Hosea is thus able to praise God's faithfulness to the covenant in wooing the wife (Gomer/Israel) who had deserted him. Certainly the naming of the three children of this marriage as Jezreel (the place both of Naboth's disputed vineyard and where Jezebel was murdered at the time of Jehu's triumph over Ahab's son), Not My People and No Pity suggests that the story of Gomer is largely metaphorical. Some commentators have suggested that Gomer was actually a cultic prostitute in the service of Baal (perhaps Hos 2: 8 retains a hint of this).

1 Kings 21: 1–23 and 2 Kings 9: 30–37 for Jezreel; Hosea 1: 4–9 for the naming of the three children.

But biblical children are given symbolic names: see 1 Samuel 4: 21 for the naming of Ichabod, 'where is the glory'.

Micah, on the other hand, was an 8th-century BCE prophet based in the southern kingdom of Judah. Although Micah criticised the depravity of both the northern and the southern kingdoms, and he mentions socio-economic abuses in particular, Jeremiah 26: 18–19 states that he commanded the king's respect. A famous passage at the beginning of Chapter 6 sets up a lawsuit between God and Israel, stating that the heart of Israelite religion was 'to do justice and to love kindness' (Mic 6: 8).

Prophecy and established religion

Not all of the prophets took the same view of established religion. For example some of the early classical prophets, such as Amos, Hosea and Micah, were opposed to the central religious establishment, including the Temple, but other prophets supported it. It is therefore incorrect to speak of a single and determinative prophetic attitude with regard to organised religion.

The reasons for the variations in the stance of the prophets are complicated. It is not simply that some prophets were more religious than others, or that some found a greater use for established forms of religion than others. Instead, prophets responded to what they perceived to be God's direct word to them. When that word addressed breaches of the covenant by Israel, some sort of conflict with the Temple was often inevitable. This was exacerbated by the traditional divide between the prophet and the priest in Israel, and by the way in which priests tended to be regarded as cultic functionaries rather than as spokesmen of the divine will.

Conflict and criticism

Conflict with national religious understanding is evident in the prophetic corpus from Amos onwards. Amos opens with a series of denunciations of the nations surrounding Israel, in what must originally have been regarded as a form of national tub-thumping. As Amos unfolds, however, it becomes clear that this is merely a rhetorical device and not at all the complete picture. In the second half of Chapter 2 Amos denounces the abominations of Judah and Israel. He speaks of punishment for Judah for rejecting the divine law (2: 4); and for Israel for social oppression (2: 6). This leads to the famous prophecy of judgement: 'Flight shall perish from the swift, and the strong shall not retain his strength' (2: 14).

Amos explicitly denounces established religion, recollecting the experience of apostasy in the desert before the settlement in Canaan: 'I hate, I despise your feasts, and I take no delight in your solemn assemblies. Even though you offer me your burnt offerings and cereal offerings, I will not accept them' (5: 21–22). This must be set within a context where feasts and offerings were associated with the Temple in Jerusalem and with the work of the priests in particular. Amos goes on to criticise the ruling authorities in 6: 1–3.

In fact there is criticism of the temple as early as Nathan in King David's day (c.1100 BCE; 2 Sam 7), as God says that he does not need a Temple in which to dwell. The significance of this view of the Temple for the development of later prophecy should not be neglected. The biblical scholar de Vaux comments that the 'school of thought which disliked the Temple continued in existence, though it is rarely mentioned'. De Vaux points to the example of the Rechabites, who always lived in tents. There is also important material in Isaiah 66: 1 where God asks rhetorically: 'Heaven is my throne and earth my footstool; what is the house which you would build for me, and what is the place of my rest?'

The chapter includes a pun on the word 'house', which God promises to build for David (2 Sam 7: 11), when in fact the meaning is a metaphorical one which refers to the Davidic dynasty.

The Early History of Israel by Roland de Vaux (Darton, Longman and Todd 1978).

Having said all this about conflict between the prophets and organised religion, it is important to note that Ezekiel came from a priestly family. Clearly, then, not all the prophets were against established religion. In any case, religion rapidly centralised during this period. In Judges and even during the early monarchy there were numerous sanctuaries in Palestine, including the notorious 'high places' (eg 2 Kings 17: 21) where polytheistic worship often occurred. But David transferred the Ark of the Covenant to Jerusalem, and his son Solomon built and dedicated the first Temple in Jerusalem. The books of Kings praise Hezekiah and Josiah for reforming the religion of Israel, which they did by removing foreign religious customs, and thereby contributing to establishing and centralising Israelite religious practices.

Ezekiel 1 makes clear that Ezekiel was originally a priest, and that he did not become a prophet until he was 30 years old when he had a vision of God.

Prophecy and politics

The prophets were never political innocents, not even in the days before the emergence of classical prophecy. They regularly engaged in such debate as they believed was mandated by the revelation to them of the divine will, and this led to as great a variety of political positions as it did religious positions.

The earliest 'band' is mentioned in connection with activity against the Philistines. Elijah appears more than once in conflict with national opponents; notably in the conflict with the prophets of Baal in 1 Kings 18.

However pre-classical prophets were by no means always mouthpieces for the king and state. For instance Elijah himself famously opposed Ahab's marriage to the Phoenician princess Jezebel and the consequent introduction of the cult of Baal, for which the king built a temple and erected an altar (1 Kings 16: 29–33). Other prophets – probably including the settled prophets in Jerusalem – were more conciliatory to royal demands. But the ambivalent political position of the wandering prophets lay at the root of an anarchic tradition that we meet again in Amos.

For Amos, see pages 62–64.

Anti-establishment?

So was Israelite prophecy essentially against the political establishment? There is insufficient evidence to address this question in full because there is no record of the views of the prophetic bands or of those of the prophets who were allied to the national sanctuaries. However the evidence of Elijah and Amos indicates that named prophets – although certainly exceptional figures – were prepared to speak against the ruling authorities out of the conviction that God had mandated them to do so. Nowhere is this more obvious than in Jeremiah.

Jeremiah's conflicts

For more on Jeremiah, see pages 53–55.

Jeremiah's prophetic activity spanned 40 years. During this time he was frequently in conflict with the political establishment, largely because of his willingness to speak of the overrunning of Jerusalem by the Babylonians (which, of course, happened in 597 BCE and then again much more seriously ten years later), behaviour that the authorities regarded as treason.

The Babylonians led by King Nebuchadnezzar (605–562 BCE) defeated the Assyrians and Egyptians at Carchemish. The victory established the Babylonians as the dominant power in the Middle East until defeated by Cyrus and the Persians.

The battle of Carchemish (605 BCE) highlighted the fact that the Babylonians were a serious threat to the Israelite nation. Jeremiah took the opportunity to publish his oracles and had his secretary, Baruch, write down the material. Baruch was sent to read the resulting scroll in the temple, because Jeremiah was banned from there at the time. King Jehoiakim reacted by having the scroll burned. But Jeremiah was so convinced by the divine authentication of his message that he simply started working on a more lengthy second version (Jer 36: 32).

Jeremiah's most famous polemic is the so-called Temple Sermon. It is preserved in two different versions in Jeremiah 7 and 26. King Jehoiakim had revived the paganism which his father Josiah had tried to eliminate. In Jeremiah 7: 8–10, the prophet responds by accusing the people of committing abominations that go against the spirit of the Torah, such as theft, murder and adultery. Notably, he refers to Mosaic and covenantal traditions to strengthen his criticism of the nation. Jeremiah rejects the dominant view of the king and his courtiers by appealing to an older tradition which made essentially ethical demands. The following passage is typical of Jeremiah and indicates some of the issues at stake:

> But this command I gave them, 'Obey my voice, and I will be your God, and you shall be my people; and walk in all the way that I command you, that it may be well with you.' But they did not obey or incline their ear, but walked in their own counsels and the stubbornness of their evil hearts, and went backward and not forward. From the day that your fathers came out of the land of Egypt to this day, I have persistently sent all my servants the prophets to them, day after day; yet they did not listen to me, or incline their ear, but stiffened their neck. They did worse than their fathers (Jer 7: 23–26).

The interplay of religious traditions with contemporary politics is complicated, but it does demonstrate the extent to which Jeremiah believed himself mandated by God to act in accordance with the Mosaic Covenant. He criticised breaches of that covenant, in particular what he saw as ethical and religious abominations. Inevitably, Jeremiah's belligerent approach brought him into conflict with the ruling authorities.

> **Further study**
>
> Find out whether the Tenakh contains women prophets. You might find the following book useful: Tamar Frankiel *The Voice of Sarah: Feminine Spirituality and Traditional Judaism* (Harper San Francisco 1990).

Prophecy in the 8th century BCE

Understanding the 8th century BCE

Following the reign of Solomon (961–922 BCE), the original Israelite settlement in Canaan was divided in two: the north was the kingdom of Israel and the south the kingdom of Judah. The second half of the 9th century BCE had proved disastrous for the northern kingdom and had inaugurated what Bright calls 'a period of calamitous weakness in which the northern state almost lost independent existence', as internal weakness was compounded by the increasing power of the Assyrians. Although the southern kingdom of Judah was not so threatened by external opposition and was internally more stable, it too remained weak.

The division of the kingdom

See *A History of Israel* by John Bright (Westminster John Knox Press 2000).

However the 8th century, by contrast, brought about a reversal of fortune for both kingdoms. This was due both to able leadership and also to more favourable regional conditions.

Israel and Judah revive

Assyrian power was crushed in 802 by the Arameans. Thereafter the Arameans concentrated their efforts east of the Euphrates, while Assyria was racked by internal conflict and threatened by the kingdom of Urartu. King Jehoash (802–786 BCE) of Israel took the opportunity to expand his territory and also managed to reduce Judean strength. In 786 BCE Jeroboam II acceded to the Israelite throne. Jeroboam recovered some of the territory plundered by the Assyrians and succeeded in extending Israel's southern borders.

Uzziah became king of Judah in 783 BCE and sought to emulate the expansion achieved by his Israelite counterpart. He repaired the defences of Jerusalem, re-equipped the army and then used his revitalised forces to snatch some territory from the Edomites. However Uzziah's aggressive designs were brought to a premature end when he was struck by leprosy and forced to appoint his son Jotham as co-regent.

It is held that Uzziah was struck by leprosy as a punishment for his attempt to offer incense at the altar, an activity which was traditionally carried out only by the High Priest (2 Chron 26: 16–21).

The territorial expansion of the two kingdoms meant that, by the middle of the 8th century BCE, their combined dimensions rivalled those possessed by the Israelite settlement in King Solomon's day. Israel and Judah controlled the area's major trade routes, and this brought considerable income from tolls. Bright comments of this period that:

> All this resulted in a prosperity such as no living Israelite could remember. The splendid buildings and costly ivory inlays of Phoenician or Damascene origin unearthed at Samaria show that Amos did not exaggerate the luxury that Israel's upper classes enjoyed. Judah was equally prosperous… It was, superficially at least, a time of great optimism, and of great confidence in the promises of God for the future.

See *A History of Israel* by John Bright (Westminster John Knox Press 2000).

> **Warning.** Photocopying any part of this book without permission is illegal.

A useful website for Amos is www.bible.gen.nz/amos/frametext.htm.

Very little is known about Amos. He is not mentioned in any other book of the Bible or in any other source, so all that we know about him comes from the book of Amos itself.

Prophecy in a nutshell

> **Further study**
>
> Amos says clearly that he is neither a prophet nor a prophet's son (Amos 7: 14). Think about what this tells us about the concept of what a prophet was in the 8th century BCE. Can you distinguish between prophets and priests?

Amos 7: 7 has a vision of God with a plumbline in his hand. A plumbline was a string with a weight attached to it and was usually used for checking whether a wall was vertically true. This is a metaphor for God checking whether the city of Jerusalem itself was true.

> **Warning.** Photocopying any part of this book without permission is illegal.

Amos

Amos 1: 1 states that the prophet was active in the reign of Uzziah, 'two years before the earthquake'. This is not a particularly accurate indicator since we do not know when this earthquake took place, but it does suggest that Amos began his prophetic activity c.760–750 BCE. A crucial passage in Chapter 7 explains his prophetic vocation. When denounced by the priest Amaziah before Jeroboam, Amos replies: 'I am no prophet, nor a prophet's son; but I am a herdsman, and a dresser of sycamore trees, and the Lord took me from following the flock, and the Lord said to me, 'Go, prophesy to my people Israel.' Amos here distances himself from the prophetic guilds, and places the emphasis on God's peculiar and unexpected choice of him as a prophet.

In fact Chapter 7 gives a good idea of the whole of Amos. Amaziah complains to Jeroboam that Amos had 'conspired against you in the midst of the land of Israel', and further alleges that Amos had declared that 'Jeroboam shall die by the sword, and Israel must go into exile away from his land' (Amos 7: 10–11). This is prophecy in a nutshell: Amos, believing himself inspired by God, preaches an unpopular message, which goes against the political grain. Consequently he is denounced by representatives of the Jerusalem establishment (note the fact that Amaziah is a priest). Amos responds with the significant rejoinder, mentioned in the preceding paragraph, that he is not a prophet at all but a herdsman and landowner.

This gives a new meaning to the term prophecy. It tends away from the cultic or official sense and towards a dynamic sense in which a prophet is identified as anyone who is inspired by God to preach a particular message.

Amos on God

The emphasis thus falls, as in the original covenant with Abraham, on the phenomenon of divine choice and election. This is indicated by the way that Amos opens: 'The Lord roars from Zion, and utters his voice from Jerusalem' (Amos 1: 2). This introductory theme is picked up in Chapter 3 in what is rightly regarded as almost the birth charter for classical Israelite prophecy: 'Does the lion roar in the forest when he has no prey?... Surely the Lord God does nothing, without revealing his secret to his servants the prophets' (Amos 3: 4, 7).

God's position with regard to Israel is declared by Amos 3: 2: 'You only have I known of all the families of the earth; therefore I will punish you for all your iniquities.' This threat of judgement is a familiar theme in the book. It is repeated in Amos 5: 2: 'Fallen, no more to rise is the virgin Israel; forsaken on her land, with none to raise her up.' It is further repeated in the dramatic visions of Chapter 7 when Amos sees locusts, fire and a plumbline. But the most famous image occurs at the beginning of Chapter 8. Amos sees a basket of summer-fruit, which in Hebrew is very similar to the word for end or destruction. The basket is held to mean that 'the end has come upon my people Israel'.

Amos on the covenant

Permanence of the covenant

The basis of these condemnations lies in Amos' belief in the permanence of the covenant that God made with Israel, first with Abraham and then with Moses. The transgressions mentioned in Chapters 1 and 2 are all those condemned by the Mosaic legislation. Thus it is said of Judah that 'they have rejected the law of the Lord, and have not kept his statutes' (Amos 2: 4); and of Israel that 'a man and his father go in to the same maiden, so that my holy name is profaned' (Amos 2: 7).

Declaration of the divine will

As a result, Amos, without ever saying so himself, puts himself in the position of Abraham and Moses as the person who declares the divine word to Israel. This is the point of his recital of Israelite history in Chapter 7. In the period of the divided monarchy, different traditions were circulating, and Amos offers a different reading of Israelite history from the creation in reverse chronological order. In effect he interprets the present in the light of a corporate past whose authority is denied to those who breached the covenant, including in this instance the royal establishment and Temple cults in Jerusalem. He reiterates the nation's sacred tradition in order to deny the authority of the dominant people in Judah.

It is the covenantal relationship that gives a structure to all Amos' criticisms and threats. For instance Amos 3: 2 is a clear appeal to this relationship whereby God had freely chosen Israel. The Judeans had interpreted this to mean that God would give them prosperity by the very fact of the covenant having been created. Hence the force of the criticism in 6: 1, 'Woe to those who are at ease in Zion'; the irony of 6: 8, 'I abhor the pride of Jacob'; and the threat of 6: 14, 'For behold, I will raise up against you a nation, O house of Israel'.

> Amos' threats are similar in nature to the punishments detailed in Leviticus 26: 14–33 for those who fail to keep to the Commandments.

Amos and judgment

The background to this disputed understanding of covenantal traditions was the social prosperity of the 8th century BCE, which had created the belief that all would be well in Israel and Judah no matter how people behaved. But Amos taught that the persistent breaches of the covenant would lead God to punish his people. He echoes in this the original mutuality of the covenant agreement in which Israel was offered election in return for covenant obedience. Starting with Amos, the prophets begin to declare that the people's behaviour had led them to turn their backs on the covenant. The prophets then taught that God would abandon his people because they had failed to be obedient to him.

This is the rationale behind Amos' preaching of judgment. He picks up the notion of the Day of the Lord, which was an early eschatological view linked to Messianism, and interprets it in a sinister fashion:

> Woe to you who desire the day of the Lord! Why would you have the day of the Lord? It is darkness, and not light; as if a man fled from a lion, and a bear met him (Amos 5: 18–19).

Amos insists that the Day of the Lord is imminent but that it will be a time of disaster and not deliverance. This is vividly expressed in a passage at the beginning of Amos 9:

> 'In making his heavy emphasis upon doom, Amos leaned over backward to counteract the false optimism of his time. Later on, when the desperate political situation drove people to fanaticism or despair, the prophets were to proclaim a message of hope. But the age of Jeroboam II did not need to hear the divine promise, for the people already believed that 'God is with us' (Amos 5: 14). What they needed to hear was the word of divine judgment that would shatter their complacency and false security. Then, perhaps, they would understand that the promise rests, not on political and economic factors, but on the gracious dealings of God with his people.' Bernard W. Anderson *Understanding the Old Testament* (Longman 1978).

> I saw the Lord standing beside the altar, and he said: 'Smite the capitals until the thresholds shake, and shatter them on the heads of all the people; and what are left of them I will slay with the sword; not one of them shall flee away, not one of them shall escape. Though they dig into Sheol, from there shall my hand take them; though they climb up to heaven, from there I will bring them down' (Amos 9: 1–2).

The nature of this threat is specified in 6: 14: '"For behold, I will raise up against you a nation, O house of Israel," says the Lord the God of hosts.' The die is cast by this passage. Amos declared his hand against his people in God's own name. He thereby distanced himself from the establishment in Jerusalem and determined the course that subsequent prophecy would take.

Repentance

But the purpose of Amos' preaching, as he understood it, was not simply to be a prophet of doom but to give his people the chance to repent. This is made clear by a passage in Chapter 5:

> Seek good, and not evil, that you may live; and so the Lord, the God of hosts, will be with you, as you have said. Hate evil, and love good, and establish justice in the gate; it may be that the Lord, the God of hosts, will be gracious to the remnant of Joseph (Amos 5: 14–15).

Test yourself

1. Outline the early development of prophecy.
2. What do Jeremiah's conflicts with King Jehoiakim show about the nature of prophecy?
3. 'The Book of Amos offers a vision of punishment and despair: it entirely forgets forgiveness and hope.' Outline the evidence for this claim and assess how far it is true.
4. (a) What are the main features of the Mosaic Covenant as it is presented in Exodus 19–20?
   (b) 'Patriarchs and prophets re-emphasise the Covenant, but they never revise it.' To what extent do you agree with this statement?

New Testament

Biblical criticism

In studying the New Testament, you need to be aware of and able to draw on four types of biblical criticism. These are the tools of the trade for understanding the text.

Form criticism

This method of biblical criticism has its origins in German theology. Originally called Formgeschichte (literally, 'form history'), it was first applied to the New Testament by Dibelius, Schmidt and Bultmann. Their starting point was that all ancient literature assumed a certain literary form, just as the traditional folk literature of Europe could be categorised as fairy tales, biography, history etc by observing the way it was written. By looking at the literary form of Gospel writing, form critics claimed to be able to tell a great deal about the situation of the writer and first readers.

See, for example, Martin Dibelius, *From Tradition to Gospel* (Nicholson and Watson 1934).

Form criticism set out to uncover the meaning of the text as intended by the author and as originally understood. The period between the death and resurrection of Jesus, and the writing of Mark (c.65–70 CE) was called the oral period and form critics were interested in how the story had developed during that time. Where common strands of thought were found with other similar literature of the time (for example Dead Sea Scrolls, Old Testament, Hellenistic literature) then the writings were considered true to the thought patterns of the time, and more likely to be authentic.

The situation in which the early Church communities existed is often referred to by the German term 'sitz im leben', which means 'life situation'.

The forms identified by Dibelius were:

- **Paradigms** – brief stories culminating in a striking statement made by, or about, Jesus, eg Mark 2: 23–28
- **Tales** – stories that were probably exaggerated over the oral period, perhaps by a story-teller who deliberately recast the Jesus tradition to be more like the stories associated with Greek gods, eg the miracle stories
- **Legends** – stories, usually with no basis in fact, intended to justify honouring Jesus
- **Myths** – stories involving the supernatural, eg Luke 4: 1–13
- **Exhortations** – teachings used to instruct new converts to Christianity, eg Matthew 5–7.

Form critics demonstrated that the reason for the survival and development of the Jesus tradition was the early Church. However that tradition was not preserved unaltered but was developed by communities with their own needs, and the text in part reflects this. The work of form critics has not always been welcomed by Christians, partly because form critics tend to be extremely sceptical about the truth of miracle stories and other supernatural events in the Gospel. Some Christian scholars accuse form critics of bias in automatically assuming that miracle stories had no basis in fact. These scholars suggest that form critics assumed that the Gospel writers were unconcerned with historical fact, whereas the

> **Further study**
>
> Look at the way scholars approach the New Testament, taking the example of Mark. You may find the following helpful:
>
> *The Gospel of St Mark: The Penguin New Testament Commentaries* by D. E. Nineham (Penguin 1992). Mark had a variety of concerns in writing the Gospel and these would have affected his approach to history as we see that subject today.
>
> 'Galilee and Jerusalem: History and Literature in Marcan Interpretation' by Elizabeth Struthers Malbon in *The Interpretation of Mark* ed. William R. Telford (T&T Clark 1995). Mark's Gospel is better understood as literature rather than as history.
>
> *I Believe in the Historical Jesus* by I. H. Marshall (Hodder and Stoughton 1977). The Gospels were meant to be seen as historically correct and can be read as being so.

writers themselves are often insistent that what they wrote was indeed historically accurate (eg Lk 1: 1–4; Jn 19: 35).

Source criticism

This attempts to identify the sources that the Evangelists had used to write the Gospels, as well as examining the interrelationship between them. Central to it is the hope of getting back to the authentic sayings of Jesus.

The most significant development occured when the scholar Griesbach placed the Synoptic Gospels into three columns side by side with one another. He identified a connection between them and sought to find out what it was.

> Johann Jakob Griesbach (1745–1812) published *A Synopsis of the Gospels of Matthew, Mark and Luke* in 1776. This effectively founded modern Gospel studies and since that time these three Gospels have been referred to as the Synoptics.

Following Griesbach, several theories about the relationship between the Synoptic Gospels have been advanced, for example one-source theory, two-source theory and four-source theory.

One-source theory

The one-source theory maintained that the Synoptic Gospels shared a (now lost) common source, and are similar in both content and order. However this theory does not explain the variations in the content, wording and order of the Gospels.

Two-source theory

Much of Mark's Gospel is reproduced (in a shortened or edited form – compare Mk 9: 14–32 with Mt 17: 14–23) in the other two Synoptic Gospels (90 per cent of it appears in Matthew and 50 per cent in Luke). Matthew's knowledge of Mark, and Mark's apparent ignorance of much of Matthew, suggest that Mark was written first. Furthermore Mark's literary style is the most basic of the three, which might suggest that his is the earliest account. However Matthew and Luke also share material that is not found in Mark, including the Beatitudes (Mt 5: 1–12; Lk 6: 20–23), the Lord's Prayer (Mt 6: 5–15; Lk 11: 2–4) and the Parable of the Great Feast (Mt 22: 1–14; Lk 14: 12–24). Scholars have suggested that this material was drawn from a second written source. This hypothetical and unknown source is referred to as 'Q'.

> A beatitude is a declaration of blessedness.

> The name 'Q' is from the German *Quelle*, 'source'.

Four-source theory

> B. H. Streeter, *The Four Gospels: A Study of Origins* (Macmillan 1924).

Building upon the two-source theory, scholars such as Streeter noticed that both Matthew and Luke each has material particular to his own Gospel. In Matthew's case this included the visit of the Magi, and the Parable of the Sheep and Goats; in Luke it included the Good Samaritan parable. It was proposed that, in addition to Mark and Q, there were two further hypothetical and unknown sources: 'M' (used by Matthew) and 'L' (used by Luke).

Source critics maintain that material that appears in more than one source is more likely to be authentic. In studying the Gospels scholars try to find parallel material in other Gospels. According to source criticism, this (where it can be found) is the most reliable material in the text.

> **Further study**
> There are a number of further theories about the relationship between the Synoptic Gospels: www.mindspring.com/~scarlson/synopt provides a comprehensive, illustrated summary of them.

Redaction criticism

> Redactor means editor.

Redaction critics try to understand why the editors of the Gospels shaped the traditions as they did. Why did they select some material and exclude other material? Why did they arrange it as they did? How did their editing make the material directly relevant to the needs of the communities for which they originally wrote? What emphases did each writer put on the traditions and why?

The assumption is again made that the writers of the Gospels were more concerned with presenting their own portrait of Jesus than they were with historical fact, but redaction criticism does acknowledge the importance of the writers/editors, and sees them as creative and capable of shaping the Jesus tradition to the needs of their readers. It must be remembered that none of the writers of the Gospels would ever have known that their writing would one day come to be regarded as holy scripture. They wrote what they did to communicate with a group of people whom they knew and who were in a particular situation. Redaction criticism helps us to understand the text better as we gain insights into the authors/editors and their original purposes.

> A notable redaction critic is John Drury. See his *The Parables in the Gospels* (SPCK 1985).

> Look at John 3: 1–21 for an example of a passage that may have been heavily redacted. It would appear that a number of phrases have been added later by an editor to aid comprehension of Jesus' message. Verses 16–21 may have been added later for this reason.

Narrative criticism

Narrative critics see the Gospels as narratives which the writer shaped in order to create a rounded whole. The reader is intended to play an active part in reading the Gospel and must adapt to the author's viewpoint in order to understand the text fully. Matthew 13: 34–35 is an example of the author breaking in to the text to offer the reader a commentary on what's happening and for narrative critics this is a reflection of Matthew's intention to encourage the reader to adopt a particular view of events.

Story and discourse

Narrative critics identify two levels in the Gospel: story and discourse. The story is the content of the narrative: plot, events, characters and settings. The discourse is the way in which the story is told, the meaning given to the story. Mark, for example, makes clear in Mark 1: 1–13 that Jesus is the Son of God. The reader can grasp this immediately and is then able to judge whether the characters in the narrative are right or wrong in their assessment of Jesus. However while the reader is aware of Jesus' true status Mark develops the plot of the Gospel in such a way that the first human being (as opposed to the demons) to recognise Jesus as the Son of God is the centurion at the cross in 15: 39.

Symbol and irony

Symbol and irony are of interest to narrative critics. You may have looked at such issues in the study of, say, Shakespeare, and the Evangelists can be just as stylish in their use of these devices. The crown of thorns is ironic: Jesus is mocked as king, when in fact the soldiers are unknowingly right to call him king. The readers are in a position to appreciate the irony of the mockery.

Places

Places are important for the narrative critic. Jerusalem may be a place of rejection and Galilee of acceptance, or vice versa. Jerusalem is the centre of activity in Luke's Gospel and is the place from which the Church will expand, whereas Mark and Matthew see Galilee as the gathering place for the post-resurrection community.

Characters

Characters too are important. There are flat characters that do not develop during the narrative, and rounded characters that change and grow. The Jewish authorities are examples of flat characters that remain hard of heart and hypocritical, whereas the disciples develop – the 11 in Acts 2 are very different to the two disillusioned

> This observation assumes that Acts is the sequel to Luke's Gospel and the work of the same author.

men on the Emmaus Road (Lk 24). Readers are encouraged to use the disciples as characters against which they can judge their own responses.

Jesus and the early Church

Jesus in the Kerygma

Set texts: Acts 2: 14–39; 13: 13–48.

Kerygma is a Greek word which means 'proclamation, announcement, preaching', and in New Testament studies it refers to the basic message of the early Church, which was designed to introduce a person to Christ and to bring about their conversion.

Kerygma differs from didache (doctrine, teaching), which refers to the doctrinal and ethical teaching of the Church in which a person was nurtured once they were converted.

C. H. Dodd, *The Apostolic preaching and its developments* (Hodder and Stoughton 1936).

Dodd attempted to decipher the Kerygma by examining sermons in the book of Acts and in certain other significant New Testament texts. He identified six main messages within them:

A new age has dawned

The 'last days' promised by the prophets have come; all God's purposes are being fulfilled, and history has reached its climax. God's promises were made to the Jewish people through the Old Testament prophets, and anticipated a time of peace and justice when God would reign over the whole world. The early Church modified this message, seeing the Age of Fulfilment in spiritual, rather than earthly, terms (Acts 2: 16–21; 13: 16–23).

Jesus brought this new age

The Age of Fulfilment has come through Jesus Christ. In him God has intervened decisively and finally in human history. His teaching, miracles and in particular his death reveal the nature, will and purpose of God. His death was the fault of the Jews, not only for calling upon Pilate to crucify him, but also for continually rebelling against God and thus necessitating the need for Jesus to die to save them (Acts 2: 22–23; 13: 24–29). The speeches in Acts have no clear idea of how Jesus' death is important in terms of atonement or sacrifice, but do see his death as part of God's design to redeem humanity (Acts 3: 18; 4: 28).

Notice how the Kerygma preaching in Acts blames listeners for the death of Jesus – this is a key element leading to response (see 'Call to respond' *below*).

Jesus now exalted

Jesus has conquered death through the power of God, and is therefore vindicated and exalted as God's Messiah, and as the leader of the new Israel, the Church. This is seen as the decisive proof that God is acting through Jesus. It places Jesus at the heart of the early Church's preaching and his resurrection as the most important aspect of his life (Acts 2: 24–32; 13: 30–37). The title **Messiah** (or in Greek, **Christ**) has not yet become part of Jesus' name but is still used as a title in Acts, reflecting the primitive nature of the book's ideas about the identity of Jesus.

The theological study of ideas about Jesus' person and deeds is called Christology.

Holy Spirit is a sign

Jesus' glory is demonstrated by the power of the Holy Spirit in the Church. For instance, the Speaking in Tongues of Acts 2 and later miracles and preaching in the book of Acts demonstrate Jesus' ongoing miraculous work (Acts 2: 33; 13: 38).

Future promise

The conclusion of the Messianic Age will be reached when Jesus returns in glory to judge all humanity. Everyone should prepare themselves for this time (Acts 2: 14–26; 13: 40).

Call to respond

Therefore people everywhere should repent and believe, and God will forgive their sins and impart to them the Holy Spirit and so enable them to live a moral life (Acts 2: 37–41; 13: 46–48).

Warning. Photocopying any part of this book without permission is illegal.

Vermes, a contemporary Jewish scholar, maintains that the Kerygma of Acts is essential to uncovering what the early Church believed about Jesus. It was only later that Paul and John developed the idea of a new, divine Jesus, a Jesus that the early Church would not have recognised.

Jesus in Paul

Paul represents a radical departure from the Synoptic Gospels in his treatment of the Jesus tradition. Although Paul wrote approximately a third of the New Testament, the name Jesus appears on its own only ten times or so in his writing, and even then is only mentioned in association with the aspects of Jesus which were most important to Paul – his death and resurrection. Moreover Paul did not concern himself with the Jewish title Messiah and its kingly associations, other than to say that Jesus was a descendent of King David. With Paul the title Messiah evolves into its Greek version – Christ – and instead of a kingly title it becomes almost a double-barrelled name, Jesus-Christ. Paul wrote in part for Gentiles who had little or no prior understanding of Jewish Messianic hope, and he sought therefore to present Jesus as a saviour figure for all humanity rather than as a specifically Jewish Messiah-king. Perhaps because of his reworking of the Jesus tradition, Paul had much more success in his missionary work among Gentiles than with Jews.

> Set texts: 1 Cor 1: 1–9, 22–25, 30–31; 5: 1–8; 15: 1–28; Gal 2: 16–21; 5: 1–11.

> 'The Acts of the Apostles contains nothing that could possibly be interpreted as pointing to a divine Jesus. It contains no prefiguration ... of Paul's Christ/Son of God, let alone of John's eternal Logos.' Geza Vermes, *The Changing Faces of Jesus* (Penguin 2001).

Some of the ways of referring to Jesus found in the Synoptics are alien to Paul. He never uses the title prophet for Jesus, which would make him out to be only one among many. The title Son of Man is also absent. Instead, Paul uses four key designations for Jesus.

Son of God

There are two elements to Paul's use of the title Son of God: status and mission. In terms of status, it is difficult to determine whether Paul meant that the Son and Father are co-equal, but Philippians 2: 6–11 and Romans 9: 5 might imply that he did. On the other hand, in his prayers Paul usually distinguishes Christ from the Father (for example, Rom 15: 30; 1 Cor 1: 4; 15: 57). It seems likely, then, that Paul did not see the Son as co-equal with the Father. In his Prologue John specified the moment at which the pre-existent Word became incarnate in the historical Jesus (Jn 1: 1–18). Paul suggests that Jesus became the Son of God at the moment of his resurrection (Rom 1: 4).

> See pages 70–71 for more on John's Prologue.

Jesus' mission for Paul depends upon what he achieved for humanity through his death and resurrection: atonement. By dying for the sins of humanity, and by being raised from the dead by God who vindicated him with his divine power, Jesus has reconciled God with rebellious humanity and become the Son of God, the central figure of the human race.

Lord

Lord in the Synoptic Gospels is often used as a polite term of reference, akin to saying Sir. In Paul it is a designation of status, referring to the fact that Jesus is the route to salvation (Rom 10: 9; 1 Cor 8: 6), and denoting his primacy over all humanity (2 Cor 4: 5), over all the created order, and even over heaven and hell (Phil 2: 10). Paul uses the title some 250 times in his writings to refer to Jesus.

Christ Crucified

Paul insists that his preaching is of nothing more or less than Christ Crucified (1 Cor 1: 23; 2: 2). Paul places the crucifixion at the heart of human history, and his writings seek to amplify not why he was killed in historical terms, but what his death means for those who will believe in him. Christ died for all sinners (Rom 5: 8–12), redeeming them and making it possible for them to be saved if only they will place their faith in him and him alone. Paul speaks of a blood sacrifice, following the train of Jewish thought from the Cain and Abel episode in Genesis through the Passover in Exodus and the establishment of sacrificial imagery and ritual in Judaism (1 Cor 5: 7). For Paul, Christ offers salvation to Jew and Gentile alike and all one needs for this salvation is faith (1 Cor 1: 22–31).

Last Adam

Paul contrasts the Adam of Genesis, who was held responsible for the introduction of sin and death into human experience, with Jesus – a new Adam – who brings salvation and eternal life to humanity (1 Cor 15: 20–22). Life after death was a concept which developed late in Judaism. The Torah does not refer to it and in the 1st century CE many Jews still didn't believe in it. Jesus is the first to rise from the dead, thus opening the way for a new creation. The only way to salvation is not through making repeated efforts to obey all the commandments of the Jewish Law (Gal 2: 16), but to place one's faith in Christ-Crucified, the last Adam (Gal 5: 1–11).

> Sadducees refused to believe anything that was not in the Torah, whereas Pharisees (the group to which Paul, in his pre-converted life as Saul of Tarsus, belonged) did believe in an afterlife.

Jesus and the Evangelists

The Prologue to John's Gospel

> Set text: Jn 1: 1–18.

Unique to John, and found in the poetic hymn which begins his Gospel, the Prologue (1: 1–18) is the identification of the title Logos with Jesus. John's Prologue traces the unfolding of God's word through the creation, Judaism and the prophets, to the climax of its revelation when the Logos became a man in Jesus.

> Logos is the Greek for 'word', 'reason' or 'meaning'. Read the Prologue several times over, substituting for 'word' the different possible English words – reason, meaning, revelation.

Origin of the Logos concept

The concept of Logos has a long history. In Judaism, God's word:

- Has its own creative power (Gen 1: 1; Ps 33: 6)
- Brings salvation (Ps 107: 20; Isa 40: 8; Ezek 37: 4–5)
- Has a semi-personal independent existence (Isa 55: 11)
- Is linked with the idea of 'personified wisdom' (rather like we may speak of Lady Luck or Mother Nature, Jews thought of Lady Wisdom) (Prov 8: 1)
- Is linked with prophecy (Jer 1: 4)
- Provides guidance and law (Ps 105: 19).

All of this must, to a degree, have been in the mind of the author of the Prologue. Some scholars also believe that the author drew upon Greek philosophy. In the 6th century BC, the Greek thinker **Heraclitus** used the concept of Logos to describe the principle of eternal order in an ever-changing universe. In 1st-century CE Alexandria, the scholar **Philo** merged Greek philosophy with Jewish thought. Dodd saw Philo as a major influence on the Prologue, but other scholars see a much greater dependence upon the Jewish tradition of the Logos as described above.

> Don't forget that Israel was occupied by the Greeks and the population became partly Hellenised ('made Greek') until Antiochus IV Epiphanes' campaign against Temple Judaism sparked a revolt: the two OT Apocrypha books of Maccabees tell some of the story.

Because the Logos is not identified with Jesus until John 1: 14, not every reference to it is a reference to Jesus. Hence the Logos:

The Logos in John's Prologue

✦ Is pre-existent (compare with Gen 1: 1; Ex 3: 14)

✦ Is equal with God (but not the same as God) (compare with Jn 5: 17 and Jn 14: 28)

✦ Is the agent (not the source) of creation

✦ Becomes incarnate in Jesus

✦ Is the revealer of God (Jn 1: 18).

There are, in the Prologue, three phases through which the Logos reveals God:

✦ **Creation** (Jn 1: 3–5). Simply by looking at creation people can realise that God exists and that he is good

✦ **Judaism** (Jn 1: 10–13). The message of the Law and the Prophets, the traditions and rituals of Judaism all point to the truth of God. By following Judaism with a sincere heart, people can find God, according to John

✦ **Jesus** (Jn 1: 14). The Logos in human form, the clearest and plainest revelation of the character, will and purpose of God, the climax of revelation in history, superior to the created order and even (according to John) to Judaism itself.

The Prologue develops the themes of light and darkness, truth and error, acceptance and rejection, and the superiority of Jesus as the Logos-made-flesh over Moses who simply spoke of the Logos (the revelation of God) in giving the commandments on Mount Sinai.

References to John the Baptist in the Prologue are problematic. Some redaction critics think they were added later to underline Jesus' superiority over John the Baptist, and certainly they break up the flow of poetry and concepts in the Prologue.

Birth narratives

Luke describes how Joseph and Mary journeyed from Nazareth, in the region of Galilee, into Judea, and to Bethlehem. Scholars speculate that Luke tells of Bethlehem as Jesus' birthplace because it was the city of King David; thus Luke draws a direct parallel between the greatest king of Israel and the new king, Jesus.

Luke

Set Texts: Lk 1: 5–2: 40; Mt 1: 18–2: 23.

Luke also places a great deal of emphasis on the miraculous nature of the birth:

✦ Mary is described as a virgin (Lk 1: 27)

✦ An angel appears to Mary to invite her to become the mother of Jesus, who will reign over an eternal kingdom and who will be called 'Son of the Most High' (Lk 1: 30)

✦ The miraculous mode of conception is then introduced to the story: Mary will conceive 'by the Holy Spirit' (Lk 1: 35).

Some **evangelical scholars** defend this account on the grounds that Luke states in the first verses of his Gospel that he has investigated the matters he writes about fully. They are eager to

Warning. Photocopying any part of this book without permission is illegal.

defend the tradition because otherwise some doubt is cast on the divine inspiration of the Gospel and of the Bible as a whole.

Catholic doctrine defends the tradition on Christological grounds: it is important that Jesus was conceived by the Holy Spirit and born of a virgin to emphasise his divine origins, the God-Man sent from heaven. He is truly God and truly man, his nature drawn both from the Holy Spirit and the Virgin Mary.

Liberal scholars (see page 73) cast doubt upon the historicity of the narratives, seeing them as reflections of early-Church belief in the unique quality of Christ and his message.

The picture of Jesus Luke presents is simpler and more human than those of the other Synoptic writers. The genealogy (Lk 3: 23–38) which traces Jesus' lineage back to Adam, the first human being, underlines Luke's eagerness to present Jesus as the perfect human being.

Luke includes some very human touches in the story perhaps because he wrote for a Gentile audience. For instance Mary is presented as a normal woman, whose initial reaction to the angel's message is fear. Jesus is an ordinary baby, with earthly relatives, and he is visited by lowly shepherds who do not bear the expensive gifts of Matthew's wise men. Later, there is even brief mention of his childhood (Lk 2: 41–52). So, apart from the miraculous nature of his virginal birth, it is essentially a normal, human Jesus who emerges from Luke's birth narrative.

Matthew

Matthew's birth account is unrelated to Luke's. No dependence has been proved between the two.

- Mary was found to be pregnant 'of the Holy Spirit' (Mt 1: 18)
- Joseph sees an angel in a dream who instructs him not to hesitate to marry Mary because the child is 'of the Holy Spirit' (Mt 1: 20)
- Joseph did not have sexual intercourse with Mary at all before Jesus was born (Mt 1: 25).

Throughout his Gospel, Matthew portrays a Jesus whose Jewishness is beyond doubt. He begins by tracing Jesus' genealogy all the way back to Abraham. He does this largely because his main concern is to present Jesus as a Jewish teacher even greater than Moses.

Matthew uses a word for virgin ('parthenos') that is a quotation from a prophecy of Isaiah. However in the original Hebrew version of Isaiah, this means a young woman and does not refer to sexual inexperience. Matthew's birth narrative draws greatly upon Old Testament analogy, presenting Jesus as the fulfilment of Jewish aspiration and prophecy. Jesus' birth is royal – wise men (astrologers) from the east see portents in the stars of a royal birth and seek the new-born king. They present gifts that are both extravagant and symbolic: gold for kingship, incense for worship, myrrh foretelling an early grave.

Mark and John

John was written after Matthew and Luke.

If Jesus truly was born from a virginal birth, does Mark's and John's silence indicate:

- Ignorance of the virgin-birth tradition?
- Rejection of the virgin-birth tradition?
- An assumption that awareness of the virgin-birth was so widespread that it was not worth mentioning?

John 8: 41 reflects rumour that cast doubt upon Jesus' parentage: he was called illegitimate.

John omits all reference to Jesus' birth and concentrates instead (Jn 1: 14) on a theological summary of the significance of Jesus as God's message in human form. John wanted to make a theological point about Jesus' significance and divine origins that is not irreconcilable with a virgin birth.

Warning. Photocopying any part of this book without permission is illegal.

Belief in the birth narratives is dependent upon a philosophical assumption that God can and does intervene in human affairs, breaking the established laws of nature (an issue on which Christians are divided). Theologians who have not taken the birth narratives at face value have developed a number of different interpretations:

The **Mythical interpretation** sees the birth narratives as myths based upon the virgin-birth prophecy of Isaiah 7: 14 and the Son of God prophecy of Psalm 2: 7. Matthew and Luke built a mythical interpretation of these prophecies which served to illustrate their belief that Jesus was uniquely the revealer of God.

The **History of Religions** school of theology sees the birth narratives as Christian adaptations of pagan myths. It points to the virgin births of central characters in Buddhist, Hindu, Assyrio-Babylonian, Zoroastrian and Mithraic myths. Certainly in the 1st century CE stories and legends about people having been born to a virgin mother and a divine father were not unknown. Officially sanctioned legend held that the Emperor Augustus was the son of a mortal mother and the sun god Apollo. Some scholars argue that early Christian writers adopted the virgin-birth story in order that Jesus' story would directly challenge Roman authority by paralleling the legends surrounding Augustus (and other Roman heroes).

Redaction critics see the birth narratives as developing the themes of Isaiah and Psalms, with the writers/editors of Matthew's and Luke's Gospels expressing in contemporary modes of thought the central conviction that Jesus was the Messiah and Son of God.

Form criticism sees the birth narratives as following the same pattern as **Midrashic Haggadah**, the Jewish teachers' method of commenting upon text which took a central ethical ideal, and built upon it rules and myths which illustrated the importance of the ideal. A modern example of this is telling children to be good before Christmas so Santa Claus will bring them presents. The Santa Claus tradition is mythical but useful when attached to the moral imperative to be good. Similarly, Matthew and Luke have attached a virgin birth myth to the central themes of Christ's message – the sanctity of life and of sex, and the universality of Christ's salvation. Moreover form critics tend to see the birth narratives as reflections of the early Church's creativity in communicating its core message rather than as history of the real Jesus.

Parables of Jesus

The Parable of the Sower and an interpretation of it is present in all three Synoptic Gospels. Matthew and Luke probably used Mark as their source for the parable, so Mark's version is the most important of the three.

The parable, like nearly all of Jesus' parables, concerns the establishment of the kingdom of God. For Jesus, the kingdom of God will right all wrongs and bring about true justice, peace and mercy. Jesus' teaching about the coming kingdom deals with both the present and the future. People must accept the rule of God in their lives in the present, in order to be ready for the final fulfilment of the kingdom of God in the future. Emphasising the present response

Significance of the birth narratives

See the section on miracles in the Religion and science chapter, pages 132–135.

'In the 1st century, there are dozens of stories like that. They're all over Greek and Roman mythology. So, what do I do? Do I believe all of those stories, or do I say all of those stories are lies except for our Christian story?' John Dominic Crossan, Emeritus Professor of Religious Studies, DePaul University Chicago.

The Sower

Set texts: Mk 4: 1–20; Mt 13: 1–23; Lk 8: 4–15.

Warning. Photocopying any part of this book without permission is illegal.

Joachim Jeremias, *The Parables of Jesus* (SCM Press 1972); C. H. Dodd, *The Parables of the Kingdom* (James Nisbet 1935).

A notable feature of Mark's Gospel is that Jesus' true identity remains a mystery. He is only recognised by those on the margins of acceptability (women and demons): even the disciples don't fully understand who he is. This is the 'Messianic secret'.

The Great Feast

Set texts: Mt 22: 1–14; Lk 14: 12–

Further study

Look at Jesus' teaching through parables in Matthew and their importance today. You may find the following helpful:

Out of the Treasure: Parables in the Gospel of Matthew by Jan Lambrecht (Peeters Press 1992). Detailed analysis of all the Matthean Parables.

The Gospel according to Matthew by Leon Morris (IVP 1992). See the commentary on Mt 13 and 25. Includes comments on how the parables apply to daily life.

The Gospel of St Matthew: Penguin New Testament Commentaries by John Fenton (Penguin 1991). Follow through the references to Parables in the subject index.

The evidence suggests that Matthew wrote c.80–90 CE and addressed his work to Jewish Christians who were being pushed out of the larger Jewish groups located in northern Galilee.

The Greek word used by the Synoptic writers for miracles is 'dunameis' and refers to mighty acts.

and experience is **realised eschatology**; emphasising the future fulfilment is **futurist eschatology**.

Jeremias and Dodd, examining Mark's version of the parable, both attribute verses 3–9 to Jesus, and link them with his apparent failure to get his message across and to elicit faith – even from his disciples. But verses 10–12 presented major problems. These verses imply that the real message is deliberately hidden in parables, whereas form critics generally viewed parables as being designed to clarify Jesus' message. Jeremias and Dodd therefore saw Mark 4: 10–12 as being later additions by the early Church. For Jeremias, their purpose for the early Church was to explain why the Jews of Jesus' time had not been persuaded by Jesus' messages, while Dodd saw in the verses a change of style and emphasis away from the harvest to people's responses to the message.

On the other hand, Drury, a redaction critic, believes that Mark's version must be considered as a whole, and sees verses 10–12 as the key to understanding the purpose of the parable. Taken from Isaiah 6: 9–10, they are part of an Old Testament tradition that insiders will understand the things of God which are, by their nature, obscure to those outside God's will. This, Drury suggests, is compatible with Mark's theme of a secret Messiah.

This parable describes an invitation to a banquet by a wealthy and powerful host, and a rejection of that invitation by his guests. This theme is developed in different ways in the two Gospels, and Matthew's version has what appears to be an addition about a guest who does appear at the feast, but is inappropriately dressed.

Jesus' main teaching point, according to Dodd, is that those righteous Jews who have been invited to the (Messianic) banquet will see the places they refused being taken by those whom they consider to be religious outcasts (the Gentiles, and perhaps Jews who believed in Jesus). Thus the whole parable can be seen as a metaphor for God's plan of salvation for the human race through the Jewish people.

Dodd and Jeremias both think that Matthew and Luke adapted the parable for the needs of their own communities. Luke, for example, has an additional invitation. This perhaps refers to the Church's appeal to the Gentiles: redaction critics observe that outreach to the Gentiles is crucial in Luke's Gospel. Dodd argues that Matthew adapted the parable to make Christological points: the feast is a marriage for a king's son because Matthew wants to present Jesus as King of the Jews. The sack of the city refers to the sack of Jerusalem, which Matthew's Jewish community perhaps interpreted as a judgement on the Jews for rejecting their Messiah. Finally, Dodd believes that the incident of the man without the wedding garment was originally a separate parable – after all, it does not appear in Luke's version – and is a warning from the community not to accept Gentiles into the Church too easily.

Miracles of Jesus

The Synoptic tradition sees miracles as mighty acts which display God's power at work. Old Testament miracles, such as the parting of the waters of the Red Sea, were understood in a similar way.

The purposes of the miracles in the Synoptic Gospels are:

✦ To respond to faith, to bring about faith, or to expose a lack of faith (Mt 12: 39; Mk 4: 40; Lk 7: 9–10, 8: 48)

✦ To point to the nature and imminence of the coming kingdom of God (Lk 7: 22; 11: 20)

✦ To illustrate the true nature of Jesus (Mk 4: 41; 2: 2–12)

✦ To demonstrate the compassion of God through Jesus (Mk 6: 34; Mt 9: 35–36; 14: 14; 20: 34)

✦ To add to early-Church understanding of the sacraments (for example, the Feeding of the Five Thousand as a commentary on the Eucharist, the Walking on Water for teaching about Baptism)

✦ As encouragement in times of persecution (for example, the Calming of the Storm as symbolic of troubled times)

✦ As anticipation of the greatest miracle, the Resurrection.

Form critics mainly concentrate on Mark's version of the Calming of the Storm, because it is probably the earliest. Bultmann and Dibelius see the miracle as an invention by the early Church, created from Old Testament texts such as Psalm 104: 6–7, which have similar vocabulary. The early Church may have used the miracle to demonstrate Jesus' lordship over nature and to show his superiority over other miracle workers. Indeed, Dibelius sees the story as a demonstration of the power of God.

Nineham holds that the storm represents demonic forces, and that the miracle therefore is about Jesus'/God's victory over evil. He also holds that the miracle exhorts persecuted Christians not to be downhearted but to put their trust in God: Jesus' sleep represents the perfect trust in God that believers should have.

Redaction critics such as Günther Bornkamm saw Matthew as making the following key changes:

✦ Sharpening the focus of the relationship between Jesus and his disciples

✦ Softening the rebuke to the disciples

✦ Revealing the divinity of Jesus

✦ Demonstrating the necessity of faith for salvation.

Thus Matthew's story becomes a commentary on discipleship.

This story is a good example of the difficulty that exists in attempting to authenticate Jesus' miracles. Because this miracle story is found in John as well as in Matthew and Luke, some scholars argue that it reports a historical event. But analysis undermines this by revealing the differences in the accounts:

✦ The illness is uncertain: paralysis in Matthew, fever in John, unspecified in Luke

✦ There is no direct encounter between Jesus and the sick boy nor any description of Jesus' healing technique

Calming the Storm

Set texts: Mt 8: 23–27; Mk 4: 35–41; Lk 8: 22–25.

Mark depicts Jesus as performing an incredible range of healing miracles. He seems to rush from one miracle to the next: in Mark, the word 'immediately' appears 39 times.

The Gospel of St Mark (Penguin 1963) by D. E. Nineham.

Günther Bornkamm, *Tradition and Interpretation in Matthew* (SCM 1982).

Matthew's concern about the state of the Church is reflected in the way he tells the story of Jesus calming the storm. According to some interpreters, this story is really a metaphor: the disciples represent the Christian community and the boat is the Church. In the face of upheaval and uncertainty that challenges faith and threatens disaster for the Church Jesus promises: 'Behold, I am with you always.'

Centurion's Slave

Set texts: Mt 8: 5–13; Lk 7: 1–10.

Warning. Photocopying any part of this book without permission is illegal.

✦ Neither the centurion nor the boy confirms that a healing occurred, instead it is reported only by others (servants or friends or the narrator).

What lies behind the story is a religious confession based on the model of the Roman patronage system. Jesus is acclaimed as a healer because he, like the centurion, is viewed as a broker of a higher authority. By asking Jesus to heal his boy (Lk 7: 7) and then describing the patronage system in Roman Palestine (Lk 7: 8), the centurion reveals his belief that Jesus occupies a similar mediating function with God as he does with Caesar. Jesus is amazed that the centurion has such a sophisticated insight (Lk 7: 9). But such analysis of the theological significance of the action suggests that the story developed from a simple narrative to a later reflection on the meaning of the miracle. As a result, other scholars have concluded in the light of the saying in Luke 7: 9 ('I tell you, not even in Israel have I found such faith'), that the miracle was created by the early Church to justify its mission to the Gentiles.

As Jesus seems to have seen his mission only in terms of Jews (Mt 10: 5–6; 15: 24), some form critics doubt that the event dates back to Jesus. Matthew's version includes the passage about the exclusion of the Jews from the Messianic banquet, and Luke has a parallel passage but in a different context, suggesting that the comment in both Gospels is artificial, and was placed to suit the needs of the Churches. Furthermore, redaction critics point to the additional praise in Luke for the centurion from the Jewish leaders, which emphasises the universality of Jesus' appeal.

Passion narratives

The Passion narratives, the parts of the Gospels that deal with the trial and death of Jesus, were of great importance to the early Church and its message. This is reflected in the fact that Mark, for instance, devotes a third of his Gospel to the Passion.

Historical accuracy

Form critics argue, for the most part, that the Gospel writers were not worried about historical accuracy. But the Passion narratives demonstrate that the writers were concerned with what they took to be the facts: they are full of historical and geographical details that aren't theologically symbolic. Luke's account is less geographically accurate, but where he is unsure he generalises instead of making things up.

Blame

Both Mark and Luke place the blame for Jesus' death firmly on the Jewish authorities and not on the Romans. Furthermore they dissociate Jesus and his followers from any connection with the Jewish independence movement that led to the defeated First Jewish Revolt (66–70 CE). Political factors were at play here: the early-Church communities did not wish to be linked with a failed rebellion or branded as troublemakers by the Roman authorities in whose regions they were seeking to spread the message of the Gospel.

Supernatural events

Mark's crucifixion scene is highly supernatural (Mk 15: 33–37). Darkness descends as Jesus dies, bitterly abandoned, and the curtain to the most holy place in the Temple is torn by an invisible hand. The tearing of the curtain, according to most scholars,

---

Further study

Think about the NT understanding of 'miracle'. You may find the following helpful:

The Puzzle of God by Peter Vardy (Fount 1995). Includes a chapter specifically on miracles, and much of the book is concerned with the philosophical problems presented by the idea of God acting in the world.

Set texts: Mk 15: 21–47; Lk 23: 26–56.

John's Gospel is the bitterest where relationships with the Church's Jewish roots are concerned.

represents the removal of the barrier between God and humanity. Some also see in it a foretelling of the destruction of the Temple, a punishment for the Jews for their rejection of Jesus. Luke adopts a different approach to Mark (Lk 23: 44–46): the darkness is ascribed to the failure of the sun itself (rather than to a cloud) and the Temple curtain is torn before the death of Jesus, thus adding to the drama of the actual moment of death.

In Mark Jesus' death is tragic: he dies abandoned by all, even by God. But in Luke Jesus dies with an affirmation of his trust in God and submission to him, which emphasises his noble character, and the durability of his faith. Mark's is the more human account, Luke's the more heroic.

Death

Mark's text anticipates the death of Jesus very early and sees that death as the most crucial part of his mission. Mark 2: 19–20 hints at the coming plot against Jesus. The theme of the plot is developed (in Mk 3: 6; 11: 18 and 12: 12). Jesus himself predicts his death (Mk 8: 31; 9: 12; 10: 32–34, 45). Mark's Messianic secret is revealed at the cross, when the centurion (a Gentile) is the first outside the group of the disciples to realise and proclaim that Jesus was the Son of God (Mk 15: 39).

'Mark tells us that Jesus died being mocked and in agony and I think Mark is writing for the experience of people in the 70s who are dying like that and who need the consolation that Jesus had died that way before, feeling abandoned by God.' John Dominic Crossan.

Wright argues that in Mark's account Jesus saw his own death as necessary:

✦ He is the representative of Israel, the Suffering Servant (Is 52 and 53)

Mark for Everyone by Tom Wright (SPCK 2001).

✦ His death accomplishes the will of God and enables the Gentiles to be part of God's 'New Israel'

✦ Jesus quotes Zechariah 13: 7.

Thus Mark sees Jesus' death as a fulfilment of Old Testament prophecy.

Every year at **Yom Kippur** (the Day of Atonement) one young goat was presented as a sin offering in the Holy of Holies. A second was symbolically invested with the sins of the people by the High Priest and was then abandoned in the wilderness – the scapegoat. This was representative of two things. The first was the need for the nation to approach God with a repentant attitude and the second was a recognition of the fatality of sin to the soul.

Atonement for sin

Jesus takes on all the roles in the atonement for sin:

✦ The High Priest, because he is the representative of Israel at the sacrifice

✦ The sin-offering whose life is given so that repentant sinners can be forgiven

✦ The scapegoat carrying the sins of the world.

Luke draws on two independent stories of the Passion, one of which he shares with Mark and Matthew, and another, source 'L'. In Luke Jesus is:

The differences in Luke

✦ An innocent victim of injustice

✦ In control of his fate, accepting it and triumphing in it as the means through which he will bring salvation.

Warning. Photocopying any part of this book without permission is illegal.

Only Luke mentions:

✦ The sweating of blood in Gethsemane

✦ The trial before Herod Antipas

✦ The exchange with the women of Jerusalem

✦ The words of forgiveness from the cross.

Luke attempts to demonstrate that neither Jesus nor, by implication, his followers, were enemies of the Roman state. For instance, Luke largely avoids the question of whether Jesus is the Messiah, with its possible political overtones. He also ignores much of the trial before Caiaphas, particularly the threats against the Temple, which concentrate on the question of whether Jesus was the Messiah. Luke's Jesus accepts the title 'Son of God' which may well be seen as blasphemous by Jews but which was of little concern to the Romans. Moreover, Luke was keen to underline Jesus' innocence:

✦ Pilate states three times that Jesus has done nothing wrong

✦ The thief on the cross declares that Jesus has done nothing wrong

✦ The centurion at the foot of the cross declares that Jesus is innocent (as opposed to being the Son of God, as in Mark and Matthew).

Luke accuses the **Sanhedrin**, the great council of the Jews. It is the Sanhedrin that presents Jesus before Pilate on a charge of subverting the nation (Lk 23: 2) and stirring up rebellion (Lk 23: 5). But Pilate realises that there is no substance to the charges and is prepared to release Jesus. However the Jewish leaders request that Barabbas, who ironically *is* guilty of insurrection and rebellion (Lk 23: 19) be released instead. Thus the Sanhedrin become the guilty body, while Pilate appears innocent.

Jesus' death brings about a reaction from some of the bystanders that only Luke reports. Some leave the scene of his death 'beating their breasts', a classic symbol of admission of guilt and a show of repentance (Lk 23: 48). Women are also important in Luke's version of the Passion: Jesus predicts to them the judgement of Jerusalem as they wait to mourn him.

Resurrection narratives

Set texts: Mt 28: 1–20; Lk 24: 1–53.

The earliest documentary evidence for the Resurrection occurs not in the Gospels but in the writings of Paul (1 Cor: 15). Paul quotes a piece of primitive tradition which he had received (presumably from the oral tradition or from the apostles in Jerusalem whom he met after his conversion). Next come the references to the Resurrection in the Kerygma speeches of Acts, which again rely upon early sources. When it comes to the Gospels, there is wide disagreement over the nature and circumstances of the Resurrection and the appearances of the risen Christ. The form critic Dodd believed that the stories of the Resurrection in the Gospels are of the same type as other stories about Jesus, and ought to be judged on the same basis, not classified into their own group.

Warning. Photocopying any part of this book without permission is illegal.

After describing the empty tomb, Matthew builds upon Mark's ending. Matthew speaks of the risen Christ appearing to the women (unique in his text are references to the guard at the tomb, and to the descending angel and an earthquake) Also, Matthew, probably writing for a community in northern Galilee, has Jesus appearing to the 11 remaining disciples in his locality, and it is there that Jesus commands them to spread his message to all humanity and promises to be with them always. Moreover Matthew's Jesus began his preaching (Sermon on the Mount, Mt 5–7) in northern Galilee, and therefore it is appropriate that Jesus should end it there.

For Matthew the key themes developed in the Resurrection narratives are the power of God at work in, around and through Jesus; the comparison of Jesus with Moses; the mission of the Church to all nations and peoples; the role of each Christian in spreading the good news; and the promise of Jesus to be with his followers always, thus fulfilling prophecy.

Luke describes the women, having found the empty tomb, bringing the news to the perplexed remaining disciples. He goes on to record three appearances:

- To Cleopas and another disciple on the Emmaus Road (this underlines the importance in the early Church of the Eucharist)
- To Peter (Lk 24: 34)
- To the 11 and others in Jerusalem before 'departing from them' at Bethany.

Luke's Jesus only appears in Jerusalem.

Luke emphasises the continuing importance of the Eucharist as a means of connecting with Jesus; the authority of the apostles' teaching in that Jesus spends 40 days between Resurrection and Ascension teaching them; the promise of the Holy Spirit and its vital role in the Church; and the mission to all people.

Matthew

Further study

Look at the New Testament evidence concerning the Resurrection. You may find the following helpful:

Who Moved the Stone? by Frank Morison (STL 1983). A conservative-evangelical defence of the historical reliability of the Gospel account of what happened to the body of Jesus.

Gospel Fictions by Randel Helms (Prometheus Books 1988). The Gospels contradict each other and Paul in turn contradicts the Gospels.

Luke

'The stories about the Resurrection in the Gospels make two very clear points. First of all, that Jesus really, really was dead. And secondly, that his disciples really and with absolute conviction saw him again afterwards. The Gospels are equally clear that it's not a ghost... Now, as an historian, this doesn't tell me anything about whether Jesus himself was actually raised. But what it does give me an amazing insight into is his followers, and therefore, indirectly, into the leader who had forged these people into such a committed community.' Paula Fredriksen, William Goodwin Aurelio Professor of the Appreciation of Scripture, Boston University.

Test yourself

1. 'The stories about Jesus in the New Testament exist not to record history, but to present to the reader the core beliefs of the early Church. They are more an insight into the feelings of his first followers than a record of what actually happened.'

    (a) With reference to the birth narratives in Matthew and Luke, explain the above claim.

    (b) What similarities exist between accounts of the resurrection of Jesus in the Synoptic Gospels?

2. (a) Using TWO examples from the parables/miracles of Jesus, explain how critical approaches may help the reader to understand the text more fully.

    (b) 'Studying the New Testament using critical approaches takes away the value of the text.' Assess this claim.

3. 'Paul developed a god-like Jesus far beyond anything the Synoptic Gospels would recognise.' Explain and assess this view.

Religion and ethics

Note that this module is called 'religion and ethics'. The exam board is clear that it wants you to be familiar with religious perspectives on all the issues you're studying. Make sure that you are able to examine issues from the point of view of the ethical principles within one religious tradition. The issues specified are medical and environmental, and the philosophical perspectives offered are Utilitarian and Kantian. Let's start by examining these ways of approaching ethical questions, and then see how to apply them to a few actual problems.

Utilitarianism

The founder of Utilitarianism was the lawyer **Jeremy Bentham** (1748–1832). Bentham's most important work is the *Introduction to the Principles of Morals and Legislation* (1789), in which he describes much of his moral theory.

The principle of utility

Greatest happiness for the greatest number

The basis of Bentham's moral philosophy is what he calls 'the principle of utility'. By this Bentham did not mean just the usefulness of things or actions, but the extent to which these things or actions promote the happiness of everyone. Specifically, the morally correct thing to do is the one that produces the greatest amount of happiness for the greatest number of people. Bentham defines happiness as the presence of pleasure and the absence of pain. He writes that:

> By the principle of utility is meant that principle which approves or disapproves of every action whatsoever, according to the tendency which it appears to have to augment or diminish the happiness of the party whose interest is in question: or, what is the same thing in other words, to promote or to oppose that happiness.

Bentham emphasises that this applies to 'every action whatsoever'. Anything that does not maximise happiness (eg, an act of self-sacrifice like giving up chocolate for Lent) must be morally wrong.

Consequences

Teleology refers to the belief that all things have a natural end or final purpose. For instance the purpose of an acorn is to become an oak tree.

Bentham's theory is **teleological** or **consequentialist**: hence it is not based (like Kant's) on the nature of the action itself, but on the results of the action. To put this another way, if honesty is to be regarded as a good thing, then it must be because it is *instrumentally good* (it brings about a good end or result), and not because it is *intrinsically good* (good in itself).

Bentham emphasises that individuals must be able to choose their actions freely. This is because the whole idea of moral responsibility depends on the person concerned having a real choice of whether to perform the action or not.

How, then, does an individual choose the morally correct action? Imagine that you have a choice of two actions – between, say, eating ice cream and revising for an exam. According to Bentham, you ought to act in a way that will bring you greater happiness: in this case you should probably eat the ice cream. However Bentham would also say that you must factor in the possible resulting amount of unhappiness. Eating ice cream may bring you more happiness, but also some possible unhappiness (such as feeling sick if you eat too much, or toothache). On the other hand, revising may initially make you unhappy, but this unhappiness will be counter-balanced by feelings of self-satisfaction and achievement.

Bentham also says that the *net amount* of happiness should be calculated, and that one should act to bring about the greatest balance of happiness. So, if there is a choice between greater happiness for myself, and less happiness for myself but more happiness for other people then I should certainly choose the latter because personal happiness cannot equate to the happiness of all those involved. It may well be, of course, that there is no conflict between my happiness and the happiness of other people. Where there is a conflict, however, Bentham states that the individual must give way.

Hedonism

Bentham was a hedonist, that is to say someone who believed that pleasure is the only good thing and pain the only evil thing. For Bentham, these 'two sovereign masters' determine all actions equally, both causes and effects. Concepts of what is right and wrong are tied to the amount of pain or pleasure they produce.

These two experiences – pleasure and pain – determine how the principle of utility works. Thus the morally good action is the action that brings about the maximum amount of pleasure and the minimum amount of pain for all those involved.

Bentham believed that pleasure and pain could be quantified, so that a net amount of happiness could be calculated. The method he uses to do this is called the **hedonic calculus**. This examines seven factors when weighing up the amount of pleasure or pain:

1. Intensity
2. Duration
3. Certainty or uncertainty
4. Propinquity or remoteness (the closeness in time to pleasure/pain being experienced)
5. Fecundity (the chance it has of being followed by sensations of the same kind: that is, pleasures, if it is a pleasure: pains, if it is a pain)
6. Purity (the chance it has of not being followed by sensations of the opposite kind: that is, pains, if it is a pleasure; pleasures, if it is a pain)
7. Extent (the number of people to whom it extends, or who are affected by it).

The balance of pleasure and pain is compared with that of other options and the best result is then determined. The action that will bring about the best (pleasurable) consequences is the morally correct one.

Mill and Utilitarianism

John Stuart Mill (1806–1873) was greatly impressed by Bentham's ethical theory and believed that in his work 'all previous moralists were superseded'. He later made a contribution to utilitarian theory with a short book, *Utilitarianism*, published in 1863. Like Bentham, Mill puts forward a teleological or consequentialist system of ethics. For Mill, motives (like kindness) are not morally important unless the presence of those motives within people tends to produce good consequences.

Hedonic calculus

> 'Nature has placed mankind under the governance of two sovereign masters, pain and pleasure. It is for them alone to point out what we ought to do, as well as to determine what we shall do. On the one hand the standard of right and wrong, on the other the chain of causes and effects, are fastened to their throne. They govern us in all we do, in all we say, in all we think: every effort we can make to throw off our subjection, will serve but to demonstrate and confirm it. In words a man may pretend to abjure their empire: but in reality he will remain subject to it all the while.'
> Jeremy Bentham *Introduction to the Principles of Morals and Legislation*.

Mill

Further study

Mill wrote a vivid autobiography entitled simply *Autobiography* (Penguin 1989). It's a short and very interesting book.

Mill accepts the principle of utility and agrees that any action is to be judged by its tendency to produce happiness. He made clear that it was not the moral agent's *own* greatest happiness, but the greatest amount of happiness altogether which should be the guiding principle in decisions. However Mill never wanted the brutish majority to crush the needs of the individual.

Mill writes about the importance of **law** as a set of principles developed and tested by history which normally ensure the greatest happiness for the greatest number. This was a response to critics who claimed that there was not enough time to consider the consequences of every action in terms of pleasure and pain.

Qualitative adaptation of Bentham

'It is better to be a human being dissatisfied than a pig satisfied; better to be Socrates dissatisfied than a fool satisfied.' John Stuart Mill, *Utilitarianism*.

Mill differs from Bentham in one very important respect: he came to reject Bentham's quantitative account of pleasure and replaced it with a qualitative one. Hence Mill's definition of happiness distinguishes between what he calls the **higher** and **lower** pleasures. He says that human beings have a sense of dignity that predisposes them to favour the higher pleasures over the lower ones. The higher pleasures are intellectual and are of greater value than the lower pleasures, which are sensual or bodily. For Mill it is the distinction between higher and lower pleasures that makes human beings unique in being able to make moral decisions. The higher pleasures are not accessible to any other creatures in the world.

Mill suggests how to distinguish between the higher and lower pleasures. He states that only those who have experienced both kinds of pleasure are capable of deciding which are morally better. He calls these people the **competent judges**. If these competent judges consistently choose one pleasure over another, then this pleasure must be morally better. Mill believed that the competent judges would always choose the higher, intellectual pleasures over the lower, sensual ones.

Evaluation of Utilitarianism

Advantages

Bentham's utilitarian theory has several useful-looking aspects:

+ It seems reasonable to link morality with happiness and the avoidance of unhappiness

+ Many people naturally think of the consequences of actions when considering whether or not those actions are moral

+ It provides a balanced method for promoting the happiness of the majority of people

+ It shows a commonsense approach to morality which could easily be put into practice in many situations.

Disadvantages

However there are a number of difficulties associated with Utilitarianism.

+ **The accurate prediction of the future.** While some consequences may be seen immediately, some may not become apparent for a very long time. At what point should we make our calculations and decide whether our actions are morally correct?

+ **The evaluation of pleasure.** Bentham's hedonic calculus cannot distinguish between different kinds of pleasure or pain.

How can we compare, for example, the pleasure of eating ice cream with the pleasure of a parent seeing their child take its first steps? Mill's theory of the higher and lower pleasures does not necessarily help here either. Who is to say who the competent judges are and how will they be selected?

- **Justice.** We may try to ensure that the majority of people will be happy, but how is that happiness to be distributed? What happens to minority groups? It is possible for a Utilitarian to punish an innocent person for the greater happiness of the majority, or for a number of sadistic people to torture a child. The problem is that while actions like these may maximise the sum total of happiness, they may do this by an unequal distribution of justice.

Kantian ethics

Immanuel Kant (1724–1804) is generally regarded as one of the most influential thinkers in the history of western philosophy. He needs to be understood in the context of the **Enlightenment**, the 18th-century intellectual movement in Europe and North America that emphasised the value of scientific experiment and human reason, rather than religious faith and tradition. Indeed Kant held that it is this ability which constitutes a human's intrinsic dignity. Moreover he maintained that reason binds person to person – we can solve disagreements through the use of reason because it leads us to the one right, rational answer.

Kant

The Enlightenment is also known as the Age of Reason. Kant is usually referred to as one of the last, and greatest, voices of the Enlightenment.

Kant's moral philosophy operates on these two premises:

- There is one correct answer to any moral problem
- This answer may be found by humans through their use of reason.

Kant also suggests that human beings are dualistic – ie made up of two parts. These are the **phenomenal** – the physical, instinctive, animalistic self – and the **noumenal** – the rational higher self. If a person is to act morally, they must act in accordance with their noumenal self, because this is universal and rational. Acting according to reason is autonomous behaviour, whereas acting according to the phenomenal self is the opposite of freedom, because of the influence of non-rational, non-universal forces.

Dualism

Kant set out the essential features of his moral philosophy in the *Groundwork of the Metaphysics of Morals* (1785). In this book, Kant says that moral laws must be universal: they must be applicable to everyone at all times. In order for this to be the case, moral laws must contain something that is unconditionally and universally good. Kant calls this the 'good in itself' or the 'highest good'. In order to define it, Kant examines various possibilities:

Highest good

The 'highest good' is also referred to by the Latin term 'summum bonum'.

- 'Talents of the mind' (eg intelligence, good judgement)
- Character traits (eg courage, loyalty)
- 'Gifts of fortune' (eg wealth, power).

But Kant rejects these because they are all capable of making a situation morally worse. For example loyalty to a friend may lead someone to do something illegal. For this reason Kant says that these qualities cannot be called intrinsically good, or, in Kant's phrase, 'good without qualification'. Only something which is intrinsically good can be moral. He says that:

> It is impossible to conceive of anything at all in the world, or even out of it, which can be taken as good without qualification, except a good will.

The good will

Having a good will is what makes a good person. Without a good will, a person cannot be morally good. The first thing Kant says about the good will is that it is not good because of the *results* it brings about – it is good because it is intrinsically good, not instrumentally good. Kant was a **deontological** thinker, concerned with the duties, rights and motives behind actions, and not their consequences. For example the murder of an evil dictator might bring some important benefits (freedom for thousands of people, an end to oppression), but it would still be an act of murder. For Kant, murder would always be wrong, whatever the consequences. He believed that the consequences of an action were of no relevance when making a moral decision, and that only the intrinsic rightness or wrongness of the action itself should be considered. If we were to take consequences or effects into consideration, the good will would no longer be universal. It would become an instrumental good, dependent, that is, on certain results being achieved. It would not be the 'good without qualification'.

Think about how Kant's deontological ideas compare with the teleological, or consequentialist theories of the Utilitarians, Bentham and Mill.

The good will and duty

The second thing Kant says about the good will is that it is *the right intention* that makes it good: the only motive of good will is to act *for the sake of duty*. When we do our duty, we are being moral.

> 'It certainly accords with duty that a grocer should not overcharge his inexperienced customer; and where there is much competition a sensible shop-keeper refrains from so doing and keeps to a fixed and general price for everybody so that a child can buy from him just as well as anyone else. Thus people are served honestly; but this is not nearly enough to justify us in believing that the shopkeeper has acted in this way from duty or from principles of fair dealing; his interest required him to do so. We cannot assume him to have in addition an immediate inclination towards his customers, leading him, as it were out of love, to give no man preference over another in the matter of price. Thus the action was done neither from duty nor from immediate inclination, but solely from purposes of self-interest.'
> Immanuel Kant *Groundwork of the Metaphysics of Morals*.

Kant tells us a great deal about what doing our duty does not involve. In particular, it is clear that looking after your own interests is not acting for the sake of duty. Kant uses the example of a grocer who keeps his prices fair and the same for everybody, not through a sense of duty or good will towards his customers, but through economic self-interest (see *left*). The grocer is honest not because it is his duty to be honest, but because it is good for business. By not cheating his customers, he will make greater profits. He is therefore being self-interested. This is not the good will. The grocer may also be personally inclined to be honest towards his customers. Being honest may be a natural thing for him to do. But for Kant, this does not count as doing his duty. His purpose in this would then be to do what he enjoys, rather than simply do his duty. It is possible that, if he no longer enjoyed being honest, he might change his mind and do something different. There would then be an ulterior motive, and he would not be guided by the good will.

So, acting for the sake of duty involves being free from all personal motives. This allows one to act in accordance with reason, so that the noumenal self is in control: the good person's only reason for doing the right thing is the awareness that it is the right thing to do.

Imperatives

We now know that according to Kant right action is universal (because reason is universal) and that it is in accordance with duty, and done with good will. Because it comes from the good will, it is good in itself rather than because of any other good emotion or beneficial consequences it might bring.

84 Religion and ethics

It is at this point in Kant's reasoning that he introduces the idea of the imperative. An imperative is a command, telling us what we ought to do. One form of imperative is the hypothetical imperative. A hypothetical imperative is normally in the form of 'If x, then y'. For example, 'If you want to gain an A grade at A level, then you must work hard'. Here the result (gaining an A grade) is dependent upon the means (hard work). If, however, you do not want to gain an A grade, the command is not relevant to you. Therefore hypothetical imperatives are not universal.

The other kind of imperative is the categorical imperative. This takes the form 'Do x', or 'Do not x'. The categorical imperative is universal (it applies to everyone) and unconditional (it does not depend upon situations, circumstances, or consequences). For Kant, the categorical imperative is good by reason of its virtue alone, and is the 'imperative of morality'.

There are two particularly important formulations of the categorical imperative. The first is:

> So act that the maxim of your will could always hold at the same time as a principle establishing universal law.

Kant here puts forward a very simple test to show whether or not a contemplated action is moral. If it were acceptable for everyone to act that way, then it is moral; if it were not, it is immoral. Kant gives the example of keeping to promises. Imagine someone is in need of a loan, and promises to repay the money. However the person knows that actually they will never be able to repay it, but they promise to do so nevertheless. If the categorical imperative is applied to this it is obviously immoral. This is because if everyone broke promises they would become worthless and society would be undermined.

The second formulation of the categorical imperative is:

> So act that you treat humanity, whether in your own person or in the person of any other, never simply as a means, but always at the same time as an end.

This is consistent with Kant's deontological theory: people are 'ends in themselves', and cannot simply be used as instruments for something, no matter how worthy that aim might be. This makes clear that everyone has certain basic rights that cannot be ignored.

Kant ends his discussion of the categorical imperative with an explanation of the contradictory nature of immoral actions. He mentions two kinds of contradiction – 'contradictions in the law of nature' and 'contradictions in the will':

- A contradiction in the law of nature is where a maxim becomes self-contradictory if it is universalised. An example would be: 'Never speak until spoken to'
- A contradiction in the will is where, although the maxim could be universalised, we could not possibly want it to be. An example of this would be: 'Never help other people'.

Evaluation of Kant

Kant's theory provides a very strong set of moral principles because it applies to everyone at all times. Other advantages are:

Hypothetical imperative

See page 53 for discussion of the framing of the Decalogue.

Categorical imperative

'Do not commit murder' is an example of a categorical imperative.

A 'maxim' is a general principle or rule which governs the actions of rational people.

This is the exact opposite of any form of Utilitarianism, where the consequences are the grounds for moral choice.

Immoral actions

Advantages

- The high value placed on human life and dignity

- That the morality of an action is based on its intrinsic rightness or wrongness, thus promoting an impartiality of justice

- That individuals can receive justice specifically because of the universal nature of the categorical imperative

- The clear distinction between duty and inclination. This helps to correct our individual inclination to do what is best for us and demonstrates that morality is far more than mere personal preference.

Disadvantages

However there are crucial difficulties with Kant's theory. First, it is not always able to deal satisfactorily with a conflict between two duties. When a hospital manager has to make decisions about how to allocate limited resources, then the categorical imperative may not prove very helpful because it is the manager's duty to look after all patients. Second, Kant's insistence that there can be no exceptions to a principle can lead to major problems. If it is always correct to tell the truth, what happens when telling the truth will get a friend into trouble? Kant does not make allowances for difficult decisions where we may have to weigh up right and wrong, and where the course of action is not obvious.

Christian ethics

> You are expected to study the ethical principles expressed within one religious tradition. We use Christian ethics as our exemplar.

There is a wide range of Christian ethical perspectives. However the major areas are: Natural Law, the Bible, Tradition and Situation Ethics. Let's take these one at a time.

Natural Law

> Aristotle's ethical theory can be found in his *Nicomachean Ethics* (Oxford University Press 1998). He suggests that the ultimate end of all human action is happiness.

The idea that there is a Natural Law running through the universe goes back at least as far as Aristotle (384–322 BCE), from whom it was later taken over by Christian theologians, notably **St Thomas Aquinas** (1225–1274 CE) in his *Summa Theologica*.

In his *Treatise on Law*, Aquinas makes a distinction between four kinds of law: eternal, divine, natural and human. For Aquinas, Natural Law is contained in the essence of all created things. He believed in a God who created humans with a particular nature and a capacity to know through their conscience what is in accordance with that nature. Human beings should follow moral principles laid down by God which allow them to express this human nature. Aquinas conceived the Christian concept of sin as being the result of failing to do this.

Teleology

> This is a complicated point. It is perhaps worth thinking again of the acorn and its end of developing into an oak tree (see page 80). Humans also have their own end: to be united with God. But while an acorn will simply develop into an oak tree if given the right conditions, humans need to use their reason and will to move towards their end.

Aquinas follows Aristotle in presenting an account of human nature which is 'actualising potentiality', that is, aiming at goals or objectives which are often unclear, even to the person who strives for them. Ultimately, the only objective that will satisfy human beings – their 'true end' – is, for Aquinas, to be united with God. But which actions are genuinely in accordance with that objective? Because if we can identify them, we will observe ourselves being 'as we are meant to be' – following our true purpose and developing our God-given potential as rational creatures. In other words, the goodness of our actions should be measured by how closely they adhere to and reflect our ultimate end. This dynamic process from potential to actual is found throughout the universe, but it takes a distinctive form in human nature because humans possess consciousness and will.

Aquinas believed that the purpose of human beings was self-preservation. With this in mind, Aquinas suggested four **primary precepts**. These state that we are intended to:

1. Continue the species through reproduction
2. Acquire knowledge
3. Live harmoniously in society
4. Worship God.

These primary precepts do not change. Any action that will uphold them is good, while any action that does not is bad. Aquinas defined as **secondary precepts** more specific rules governing actions that either uphold or fail to uphold the primary precepts. Thus the Roman Catholic Church has ruled against contraception and homosexual activity: these rulings are secondary precepts based on the fact that both allow sexual acts with no connection to reproduction (the first primary precept).

The Bible

Some Christians believe that the Bible, as the Word of God, is the ultimate authority in all matters, while all agree that it is an important source of moral guidance. However it is often difficult to interpret or understand what the intended outcome of this guidance might be, particularly as many issues, such as transplantation, abortion and pollution, are not specifically mentioned.

Equally not all Christians agree on how specific teachings or passages from the Bible should be applied. Some Literalist or **Fundamentalist** Christians believe that the Bible contains the *actual words* of God, and thus argue that it must be accepted at face value and has a straightforward meaning. This approach provides absolute authority, and offers a definite and simple solution to problems. The difficulty, however, is that Literalists are invariably selective when it comes to choosing appropriate biblical teaching.

Other Christians will look for general principles in the Bible and apply them to moral issues. These general principles would include, for example, the concept of God as the creator of everything in the universe. Within this is the specific idea that human beings are made in the image of God. This means that humans are responsible beings, answerable to God for their actions. Another important general principle in the Bible is that God has established a covenant between himself and humankind. This is a two-sided agreement, where God promises to bless and look after his people, while they in turn promise to honour God and obey his laws. It is in the Bible, and particularly in sections such as the Ten Commandments and in the life and teaching of Jesus, that we can see the standards that God has set for people.

Tradition

Traditional established ways of behaviour reflect the actual historical experiences of the Church and of past Christians, and as

Self-preservation

A precept is a rule which suggests a particular course of action.

Interpretation

For more on covenant, see pages 50–55.

For more on the Ten Commandments, see pages 52–53.

Warning. Photocopying any part of this book without permission is illegal.

such are important to many Christians today. This is because they believe that what Christians have tended to practise and believe is a reliable guide to what is morally right and wrong. Christians can look at how issues have been dealt with in the past to guide them in the present. Looking to tradition depends on a belief in a common God-given rationality, ie that people have tried to do what they felt to be right just as we try to do the right thing now.

Tradition is often linked to a Natural Law approach to ethics and is followed mostly by Roman Catholics, who call tradition the 'ordinary magisterium' of the Church. It is important to note that the lessons to be learned from tradition can be negative as well as positive – tradition shows Christians the errors to avoid as well as actions to follow.

For more on tradition, see page 36.

Situation Ethics

Situation Ethics is a radical form of Christian ethics, developed in the 1960s by the Protestant theologian, **Joseph Fletcher** (1905–1991). Fletcher believed that an approach to ethics based on law did not work because it was overloaded with rules and regulations. However he thought that to have no ethical principles whatsoever was wrong. So he proposed an ethical system that recognised one principle of moral behaviour, that of love, and which would apply this principle in every individual situation. By love Fletcher meant the Christian quality of **agape**, which is the Christian love revealed by Jesus and which desires the best for others irrespective of their personal qualities. He argued that 'justice is love distributed' so that doing the most loving thing is to act in a just way.

Joseph Fletcher, *Situation Ethics: The New Morality* (Westminster John Knox Press 2nd rev. ed. 1997).

Agape is a three-syllable Greek word (A-gap-e) for spiritual love.

Fletcher was keen to avoid any suggestion that Situation Ethics had a sentimental approach to ethics. He insisted that love was a demanding principle of action.

Fletcher based his ethics on four presumptions:

+ **Pragmatism.** Concern with that which works for the best, and only the end of love justifies the means
+ **Relativism.** Love is the only absolute; all other rules depend on the situation
+ **Positivism.** It is important to act, and to act in accordance with love
+ **Personalism.** Human beings should be put first.

Medical issues

Abortion

Abortion is the deliberate and artificial termination of the life of a foetus. It has been legal in Britain since 1967. Approximately 180,000 abortions are carried out each year in England and Wales.

Utilitarian perspectives

Neither Bentham, Mill nor Kant had anything *directly* to say about abortion, but later philosophers have taken their principles and applied them to the issue.

After 14 days the primitive streak is formed and with it the basic capacity to register pain.

There are no absolute rules within Bentham's or Mill's system, not even on the sanctity of human life. Thus it is always possible to justify an abortion if it can be shown via Bentham's hedonic calculus or by Mill's concept of higher and lower pleasures that more pleasure and less pain will result if it is carried out.

But Bentham and Mill both include all sentient beings in their theories. Therefore after the foetus has been alive for 14 days it should be considered in any decision and it will be afforded progressively greater rights as it develops. However, given Mill's

88 Religion and ethics

emphasis on the higher pleasures, we might expect him to give more weight to the interests of the adults involved, as long as these interests did not violate their sense of dignity.

Turning to Kant, let us consider this proposal: 'I plan to abort this foetus so that it will not make my life less agreeable.'

- ✦ If we use the first formulation of the categorical imperative, then this type of reasoning could not be universalised because it would be contradictory. The desire for self-preservation, which is here reduced to the desire to lead an agreeable life, would actually lead to the ending of a life
- ✦ The crucial question with the second formulation is whether the foetus has the status of a rational being who should be treated as an end. In one sense the foetus does not have the power of reason and could be treated as a non-person. Accordingly, an abortion would be reasonable
- ✦ But we can look at the second formulation in a different way. A human foetus is clearly in a different category to, say, a banana or a developing moth in that it has the potential to become a fully rational agent worthy of being treated as an end. Some Kantians would argue on the basis of this potentiality that the foetus should be accorded the rights of a fully rational being.

Christian Natural Law theories have almost always come down on the side of the sanctity of life. According to such theories, God has imbued the natural world, including humans, with a biological desire to live. The embryo and foetus are unconsciously obeying this natural instinct. Disrupting this built-in tendency artificially is tantamount to contradicting God.

The Church's teaching has always maintained the absolute sanctity of all human life and essentially has always been against abortion. The only exception is where the life of the mother is threatened by the pregnancy. Even in this extremely rare situation, however, some Christians suggest that the woman should follow the example of Jesus, and sacrifice her life for that of her child.

Situation Ethics has had a significant impact on the way in which some Christians approach abortion. For Fletcher, even the principle of the sanctity of life could be set aside if love was best served by an abortion. For instance, an abortion might be sanctioned if a girl became pregnant as a result of rape. More controversially, some situation ethicists permit the termination of unwanted teenage pregnancies. They argue that the mental well-being of the mother might be adversely affected and an unloved child may result if an abortion is not carried out. But situation ethicists would certainly insist that decisions about abortion should not be made lightly and that all factors need to be weighed up.

Euthanasia

Most doctors and ethicists agree on the following definition: 'Euthanasia is the intentional killing by act or omission of a person whose life is not thought to be worth living. It is done for the patient's own sake.'

Kantian perspectives

> **Further study**
>
> Look at the moral and religious issues raised by abortion. You may find the following books helpful.
>
> 'An Almost Absolute Value in History' by John T. Noonan in *The Morality of Abortion. Legal and Historical Perspectives* ed. John T. Noonan (Harvard University Press 1970).
>
> 'An Argument that Abortion is Wrong' by Don Marquis and 'A Defence of Abortion' by Judith Jarvis Thomson in *Contemporary Moral Problems* ed. J. White (Wadsworth 2000).
>
> 'On the Moral and Legal Status of Abortion' by Mary Ann Warren in *The Problem of Abortion* ed. J. Feinberg (Wadsworth 1997) pages 111–112.

Christian perspectives

An embryo is a developing fertilised egg. It is called a foetus once it is 14 days old.

Situation Ethics

See *Matters of Life and Death* by John Wyatt (Inter-Varsity Press 1998).

Utilitarian perspectives

There are various types of euthanasia including voluntary, involuntary, passive, active and assisted suicide. The differences between them are often incredibly subtle.

Utilitarian pro-euthanasia arguments are:

Pain. If a patient was near death, in intense pain and experiencing little happiness, euthanasia might be justified. In terms of the hedonic calculus, the pain suffered is certain, intense and fecund (ie, it leads to more pain). Therefore, since there is no balancing pleasure, euthanasia would be ethically justified.

Resources. Performing voluntary euthanasia on one terminally ill patient would release resources for other patients who may experience more collective happiness and have a greater quality of life.

Dignity. Some Utilitarians argue that voluntary euthanasia gives people the right to die with dignity, because it allows them the autonomy to make decisions about the means and moment of their death. The idea of autonomy might well come into Mill's category of a 'higher pleasure'.

However there is also a range of anti-euthanasia arguments. In particular some Utilitarians argue that the laws banning euthanasia are justified for the sake of the happiness of the majority, even if this means that some individuals have to suffer. Furthermore, permitting voluntary euthanasia might lead to other problems such as:

Pressure. Patients who are dying slowly may be coerced into asking for euthanasia by their relatives or heirs. This would be a severe hedonic loss to the patient involved and also to society at large which would be condoning such behaviour.

Misdiagnosis. If a doctor diagnoses a terminal disease and the patient then decides on euthanasia, any discovery in the future that the disease was not actually terminal (revealed for example by the post-mortem) will be irreversible. This would cause the family great pain and would be of concern to the wider population.

Distrust. Patients might feel suspicious and afraid of medical staff.

The policies of Nazi Germany in the 1930s and 1940s demonstrated that a government could use involuntary euthanasia as a means of social selection.

The slippery slope. As soon as the taboo on taking adult human life goes, it might not just be elderly, terminally-ill patients who lose their lives.

Value and use of embryo and foetus

An embryo is a developing fertilised ovum (egg) of up to 14 days after conception, before the formation of the primitive streak. After this point, the embryo becomes a foetus. The following are the main ways in which embryos are used:

In vitro is Latin and means 'in glass', a reference to the test tubes and other laboratory equipment involved.

IVF. In vitro fertilisation therapy is the process by which a woman's egg, removed by laparoscopy, is fertilised with sperm in a laboratory. Usually the woman's ovaries are stimulated by a fertility drug and then several eggs are removed and fertilised. The most promising fertilised egg (by now a developing embryo) is placed in the woman's uterus and, if it implants, will be born in the normal way.

Medical research. The 1990 Human Fertilisation and Embryology Act allows research on two types of embryos: spare embryos left over from IVF treatment, or embryos created for the specific purpose of research. Sperm and egg donors must give their consent for both

Warning. Photocopying any part of this book without permission is illegal.

types of research, which can only be conducted for up to 14 days after conception. The Act did not allow the cloning of human embryos for research purposes or modification of the genetic structure of the human embryo, but more recent legislation has allowed this.

PGD. Pre-implantation genetic diagnosis can be used when a couple are at very high risk of having a child with a serious genetic disorder. IVF techniques are used to produce several embryos and one free from genetic disorders is then implanted into the mother's uterus. The other embryos are discarded. This treatment was first used successfully in 1988.

The Masterton family in Scotland attempted to use PGD to select a female baby, but were prevented from doing so because the law states that PGD should only be used for pressing medical reasons.

How can we apply Bentham and Mill's consequentialist views to these areas?

Utilitarian perspectives

✦ Use of the embryo up to the point of sentience (14 days) would probably be permitted by Benthamite philosophy, because embryos cannot feel pleasure or pain and thus would not be included in the hedonic calculus

✦ The hedonic gains possible from research are considerable: for instance, IVF and PGD can be greatly beneficial to humans

✦ Currently embryos can only be used for research with the donors' consent. Nevertheless some donors could still be caused anguish by the thought that embryos they had helped to create were being used for research. Such pain would have to be entered into any hedonic calculus

✦ Mill would have emphasised the importance of the donors' consent because he was concerned that their interests should not be overridden by the majority.

Mill might well have expressed unease at the purposes of some forms of research on embryos. He might have felt that some of this research could be seen to undermine the dignity which lay at the heart of his distinction between higher and lower pleasures.

Most medical attempts to defend the use of embryo and foetus in research point to the hypothetical benefits to be gained. Doctors point out that embryo research may eventually allow them to treat genetic diseases such as Tay Sachs Disease.

Kantian perspectives

Tay Sachs is a fatal genetic disorder that mainly affects children. If both parents are carriers of the disease then the child has a 25% chance of having it. Children with the disorder usually die by the time they are five years old.

Kant is highly critical of hypothetical imperatives (Do x if you want y). In simple terms, this kind of medical defence is not a moral defence because it does not have universal relevance. In fact whenever a defence of a particular action (eg abortion, euthanasia, destruction of natural resources) is made in terms of probable consequences, Kant's view of hypothetical imperatives becomes relevant.

Instead, Kant applies the categorical imperative. The first formulation can certainly be applied to embryo research. Consider the proposal: 'I plan to experiment on embryos (leading to their death) in order to prolong an agreeable life for the living who have certain diseases.' There seems to be a logical contradiction here: the ending of one life in order to save, or extend, another. Consequently Kant would probably argue against experimentation on embryos.

Following the second formulation the important question with regard to embryo research would be whether embryos have the status of rational beings. This leads to two possibilities:

✦ Embryos do not have the power of reason. Therefore it would be logical to use them in research, so that they could be used as a means to medical advance

✦ Embryos have the potential to become fully rational agents. Some Kantians would argue on the basis of this potentiality that the embryo should be accorded the status of an adult.

Christian perspectives

> 'For you created my inmost being; you knit me together in my mother's womb... All the days ordained for me were written in your book before one of them came to be.' Psalm 139.

Christian views on the value and use of embryos and foetuses are rooted in Genesis 1: 26–27. This passage says that humans are made in the image of God, and that their task is to care for and rule over creation on behalf of God. Moreover this status as the bearers of God's image does not depend on humans developing certain qualities and attributes. Rather it is conferred on every human simply by the act of creation. It is this elevated view of human nature that leads to the important Christian idea of the sanctity of every human life. Several biblical passages, such as Genesis 9: 6 and Proverbs 14: 31, make reference to the fundamental value of all human beings because they are created by God and therefore reflect God in many ways.

See *Bioethics* by Gilbert Meilaender (Paternoster 1997).

Equally many Christians do not accept the argument that an embryo only becomes sentient or 'human' 14 days after conception. Modern genetics informs us that, from conception, a person's physical characteristics (and many mental/intellectual ones) are already established in the genetic code of the foetus. Roman Catholics often cite this as a key argument against the use of embryos and emergency contraception. Some Christians, such as the bioethicist **Meilaender**, define implantation in the uterine wall (at 14 days) as the start of human life, but not all of them condone research on embryos. They point out that it is not God's intention that embryos be brought into existence simply to be used for research and then discarded.

Further study

Find out about the following stages in foetal development: conception, implantation, quickening, ensoulment or animation, and the point of viability. Consider how they may be relevant to different ethical perspectives on abortion, IVF, and medical research using embryos left over from IVF and PGD.

Transplantation

There are essentially three different types of organ transplantation which raise important ethical issues:

Live donor transplantation. When a healthy person voluntarily donates an organ (e.g. one of their kidneys) to help another person, the (live) donor is able to continue with a more or less normal life after the transplant has taken place. Some religious groups argue against this type of transplantation because it interferes with the wholeness of a person created by God.

Cadaver donor transplantation. When a person dies, their major organs (e.g. heart, liver, kidneys, lungs, eyes) may be donated to other needy patients. Permission may have previously been given by the deceased person (perhaps with a Donor Card) or by their relatives, and ethical debate revolves around the issue of permission.

Xenotransplantation. When an organ of one species is transplanted into a different species (e.g. a pig's heart in a human being), the ethical issues involve the autonomy of the creatures involved and the rearing of them specifically for transplantation.

Utilitarian perspectives

There are a number of Utilitarian arguments that favour transplantation. For instance:

- Many Utilitarians would argue that the health benefits to the recipient of the transplanted organ justify the action
- The British Transplantation Society (BTS) has noted the possible psychological benefits accrued by the donor of an organ. Donors' sense of purpose and well-being increases because they know they have contributed to someone else's health
- In the case of cadaver transplant the individual donating their organ(s) is no longer sentient and therefore need not be considered in any Utilitarian calculation.

But equally there are a number of Utilitarian perspectives which argue against various forms of transplantation:

- In a global situation in which health resources are very limited, particularly in developing countries, the expensive and uncertain process of transplantation does not constitute the best use of those limited resources. Resources should be allocated to more basic, cheaper treatments that could save millions rather than just a few
- The well-being of the family of the deceased person must be considered, and often they wish to bury (or cremate) the whole body, rather that the shell of a body left after the usable organs have been removed

  The risks to the stability and well-being of society at large of not respecting the interests of the family are clear, and were demonstrated by the Alder Hey Children's Hospital scandal.

- The wishes of people while they are alive about what should happen to their bodies after their death should be considered
- Some utilitarians emphasise that the welfare of the animal must be taken into account when considering xenotransplantation.

  See *Writings on an Ethical Life* by Peter Singer (Fourth Estate 2002).

Kantian perspectives

Most decisions on transplantation are made on a consequentialist basis. Therefore they are hypothetical imperatives. From a Kantian perspective, many attempts to defend transplantation (and also many attempts to criticise it) are thus fundamentally flawed.

The key issue for most Kantians is consent. This is particularly true for live donor transplants, but it could also apply to cadaver transplants if the dead person had expressed a wish concerning what should (or should not) be done with their organs. Can the dead be treated as a means to an end? Some Kantians would say that they can, but others maintain that decisions made by people when alive have validity for the future.

Christian perspectives

There are few Christian objections to the concept of cadaver donor transplantation; indeed, with few exceptions religious groups worldwide have accepted the worth of such transplants. More problematic for Christians is the issue of live donor transplantation. Those against transplanting organs from live donors point to the many references to the sanctity of the body in the Bible: God created our bodies in his own image (Gen 1: 27), they are not our own, but temples for God (1 Cor 6: 19). They will eventually be offered to God as 'a living sacrifice, holy, acceptable unto God' (Rom 12: 1), and those who 'sin against' their bodies by damaging their own health will be called to account for their stewardship (1 Cor 6: 18–19). Many Christians have inferred from

This is because the Bible doesn't recognise a dualism between body and mind: the idea that the two could be separate was introduced to the Christian tradition by St Augustine.

this that to donate an organ is wrong on the grounds that the body must be physically complete at the resurrection.

Most Christians accept however that the resurrection has more to do with one's soul than physical body and it is true that, on the whole, the Bible seems less concerned with the body itself than the actions we carry out with it. Many justify support for live donor transplantation on grounds of love and charity. Perhaps the predominant theme of the New Testament is that the Christian has to be Christ-like in his behaviour and attitude towards others. Jesus' prime directive to humankind was that we should love one another as he loved us, and this has determined many Christian approaches to the issue of transplantation. Jesus stated: 'Greater love has no man than this, that he lay down his life for his friends' (Jn 15: 13), a claim that has motivated many Christians to become organ donors. Situation ethicists would justify live donor transplantation in the same way. As long as donation is altruistic, unreserved and devoid of pressure; and as long as the decision is motivated by love alone, then it is entirely ethical. There is even a biblical reference to transplantation to advocate this view: Paul commends the Galatians for their response to the painful illness of the eyes that brought him there, reminding them 'You would have plucked out your own eyes and given them to me' (Gal 4: 19).

Christian attitudes to xenotransplantation are varied. Many oppose the process on three major grounds:

✦ Some biblical texts (Lev 19, Deut 22) document how the intermingling of species, seeds or yarns is forbidden. God created animals and plants 'after their kinds' (Gen 1): species were created as distinct from one another and thus ought not to mix

✦ By transplanting the organs of an animal into the body of a human, one is rearranging God's created order. In manipulating life in this way, human beings misappropriate something that really belongs to God

✦ Genesis establishes humankind as the stewards of the natural world. Christians recognise that this entails responsibility for the welfare of animals, rather than the right to mistreat them. Some Christians object to xenotransplantation on the grounds that its development requires massive experimentation on laboratory animals, as well as the breeding of pigs in specific pathogen-free environments.

However this is not to imply that Christians have reached a consensus on this matter. For many, the considerations based on love and charity overwhelm all other objections to xenotransplantation.

Allocation of resources

With a National Health Service that offers more and more treatments to an ageing population, issues of resource allocation are crucial.

An important method currently used by hospitals to decide how to allocate resources is QALYs: Quality Adjusted Life Years. This aims to calculate the relative benefits of different treatments for individuals by asking how many years of good-quality life would result if the patient were to receive a particular treatment.

Utilitarian perspectives

The hedonic calculus seems ideal for use in QALYs. It can be applied to a wide range of issues, and most people agree that the avoidance of pain and the increase of pleasure are good things. Furthermore by assessing the interests of everyone, in a more or less objective fashion, the calculus offers the possibility of fairness.

Kantian perspectives

The second formulation of the categorical imperative is usually applied to resource allocation issues, because the decisions made can often lead to situations which seem to be using a number of patients as a means to the end of someone else's welfare. For example a doctor may have to decide between treating a person who smokes and one who does not. If the doctor goes to the smoker and involves him in the decision, then he is recognising him as a human being with the power of reason who should therefore be treated as an end. However such decisions are normally taken without reference to the patients concerned.

Christian perspectives

John Wyatt argues for the following Christian principles to be applied to issues of healthcare resource allocation:

Matters of Life and Death by John Wyatt (IVP 1998). Wyatt examines fertility treatment, abortion and euthanasia among other topics.

+ **Transparency.** Wyatt argues that too many decisions about the allocation of resources and the scale of public spending on health are taken 'behind the back' of patients and the electorate. These decisions should be 'open to public debate and democratic challenge'

+ **Defence of the rights of the poor and vulnerable.** Old Testament law was particularly concerned with the widows, orphans and foreigners in Israelite society. Wyatt argues that resources should be targeted at their modern equivalents, 'the dying, the chronically disabled, the genetically stigmatised, the elderly, the immigrant, the abused child, the chronic psychiatric patient and the malformed foetus'

+ **Equality.** Irrespective of 'racial, social or geographical divides... the most painful and inescapable inequalities lie in the gulf in health resources between rich and poor nations'

+ **Impartiality.** Wyatt points to the teaching of Jesus in the Sermon on the Mount (Mt 5: 43–45). According to this, God loves us all and treats us all impartially, irrespective of our faults. Humans should do likewise and should not deny certain groups access to medical resources on the basis of their lifestyles.

Environmental issues

The world is faced by increasing levels of pollution and by the rapid depletion of natural resources.

Utilitarian perspectives

Bentham's hedonic calculus explicitly takes into account the interests of all sentient beings. This has clear implications for our use of environmental resources. For instance, the destruction of natural habitats (such as rainforests) results in reduced biodiversity and even in the extinction of some animals. Pollution, moreover, has caused massive loss of animal life.

Later Utilitarian thinkers, notably Peter Singer, have placed particular emphasis on the fact that we cannot ignore animals in our decision making.

Mill's insistence that the decision maker must treat equally all those who could be affected by a decision has a bearing on the use of natural resources. The intensive use of carbon-based fuels, for example, is almost certainly causing global warming and, as a

> Warning. Photocopying any part of this book without permission is illegal.

result, the rise of sea levels. Many places are at risk of being submerged and some of these, such as southern Bangladesh, are densely occupied by poverty-stricken people who are unable to move to less hazardous areas.

Mill's distinction between higher and lower pleasures can easily be applied to the modern consumer lifestyle. Our pursuit of physical comfort beyond what is purely necessary would clearly be seen as a lower pleasure. This sort of lifestyle is ultimately unsustainable because it places massive demands upon natural resources and results in pollution.

Kantian perspectives

'Wonder' and other essays by R. W. Hepburn (Edinburgh University Press 1984).

R. W. Hepburn builds on Kant's formula of the end in itself (the second formulation of the categorical imperative), arguing that it can legitimately be made to relate to the proper human response to the natural environment. This, according to Hepburn, is one of wonder. This attitude is non-exploitative – ie, not looking at the natural environment in terms of how it can be exploited for human needs – and is characterised by respect, compassion, gentleness and humility. Hepburn's argument runs as follows:

✦ Kant admired the natural world and this would have made him uneasy with simply giving it an instrumental value in relation to human needs

✦ The spirit behind the second formulation permits a broader application to many parts of the natural world than Kant explicitly gives it.

Hepburn argues that Kant would have wanted the greedy exploitation of natural resources and the resultant pollution to be stopped.

Paul Taylor also develops Kant's ethical system to argue that we should respect and care for the natural world. His theory is based on two concepts closely related to Kantian philosophy:

> 'We can think of the good of an individual non-human organism as consisting in the full development of its biological powers. Its good is realised to the extent that it is strong and healthy. It possesses whatever capacities it needs for successfully coping with its environment and so preserving its existence throughout the various stages of the normal lifecycle of its species.' *Respect for Nature: a theory of environmental ethics* by Paul Taylor (Princeton University Press 1986).

✦ **Inherent worth.** Taylor explains that: 'To have the attitude of respect for nature is to regard the wild plants and animals of the Earth's ecosystems as possessing inherent worth'

✦ **Good of its own.** Taylor comments that: 'To say that an entity has a good of its own is simply to say that, without reference to any other entity, it can be benefited or harmed.'

Thus Taylor extends Kant's idea of the respect due to humans as rational agents with their own ends to every living organism, sentient or non-sentient. In fact, recent discoveries about the rational and reflective capacities of particular animals (chimpanzees and dolphins would be the most obvious examples) might in any case have led Kant to extend the range of sentient beings which should be treated as ends.

Further study

Look at the moral and religious issues raised by conservation issues. You may find the following books helpful:

'Re-valuing Nature' by Lori Gruen in *Ethics. The Big Questions* ed. J. Sterba (Blackwell 1998).

'The Land Ethic' by Aldo Leopold in *Ethics in Practice* ed. H. LaFollette (Blackwell 2001).

The Environment and Christian Ethics by Michael S. Northcott (Cambridge University Press 1996).

Furthermore the distinction between humans and animals has been blurred by the increase of our knowledge of genetics. For example, we now know that chimps and humans share 98% of the same DNA (and that even tree bark shares 50% of its genetic material with humans). Some philosophers argue that this blurring is sufficient to extend the second form of the categorical imperative to cover the interests of all sentient beings.

The first formulation of the categorical imperative could also be applied to environmental issues. In particular, the logic behind Kant's prohibition on suicide might well seem to rule out the current rate of use of environmental resources, which threatens the welfare of future human generations.

The Bible teaches that humans should have a caring, responsible and respectful attitude to nature and the environment:

Christian perspectives

God's creation. Many passages in the Old Testament make it clear that the existence of the world depends upon God and that the natural environment should illustrate and reflect his goodness and glory. Of course pollution, the destruction of natural habitats for industrial farming, skin cancers from ozone depletion and so on do little to declare God's glory.

See for instance Psalm 19: 1–4 and Psalm 104.

Stewardship. God is the rightful owner of the world, but he has delegated control over it to humankind. Yet humans do not have the authority to do what they like with God's creation, because we are only stewards. Our task is to preserve the beauty and order of the world.

Subdue and rule. Humans are instructed by God in Genesis 1: 28 to: 'Be fruitful and increase in number; fill the earth and subdue it. Rule over the fish of the sea and the birds of the air and over every living creature that moves on the ground.' Some have seen 'subdue' and 'rule' as suggesting that humans may dominate the world for their own ends. However, in the wider context of Genesis and the rest of the Old Testament, this is an untenable interpretation.

The fact that Adam and Eve were instructed to be vegetarians (Gen 1–2) indicates that the emphasis was on care and not on exploitation.

Jesus' teaching. Christians today often look to the commentary of Jesus and the practices of the early Church when arguing about the dangers of greed and the modern consumer lifestyle. A lifestyle which relies heavily on the continued exploitation and overuse of the natural environment is, they argue, inconsistent with Jesus' teaching. He repeatedly criticised greed. He said, for example, that 'No one can serve two masters. Either he will hate the one and love the other, or he will be devoted to one and despise the other. You cannot serve both God and money' (Mt 6: 24).

Jesus also emphasised the importance of the simple life. He said in Matthew 6: 28–30, 'why do you worry about clothes? See how the lilies of the field grow. They do not labour or spin. Yet I tell you that not even Solomon dressed in all his splendour was dressed like one of these. If that is how God clothes the grass of the field… will he not much more clothe you'. The early Christians followed Jesus' example and lived quite frugally, sharing their houses and possession according to need (Acts 2: 44–45).

Test yourself

1. Identify and explain the central differences between a Kantian and Utilitarian approach to ethics.
2. 'From both a religious and a Kantian perspective, abortion could never be permitted.' Assess this claim.
3. Describe the approach of Christian ethics to the care and conservation of the environment.
4. (a) Outline how Utilitarianism could be used to defend euthanasia.

    (b) Assess this attempt to defend euthanasia.

World faiths

This module gives you the opportunity to make an introductory study of **one** of the major world faiths: Buddhism, Christianity, Hinduism, Islam, Judaism or Sikhism. Although you have to study just one of these religions, you may well be interested to read about several of the other ones and this might improve your understanding of your chosen religion.

Buddhism

Buddhism uses two languages: Pali (pronounced Parl'ie) and Sanskrit. In this chapter the Pali terms are used, but where Sanskrit spellings are better known, we add these in brackets.

Unlike Christianity, Islam and Judaism, Buddhism has no formal creed and no essential belief in a personal god. It offers the possibility of transcending the material world and, through this, of gaining enlightenment. It emphasises spiritual progress through teaching while recognising that such teaching is ultimately dispensable.

The emergence of Buddhism in India

The social and religious context

Northern India in the 6th century BCE was divided into a number of tribal groups ruled over by an assembly of elders. However the traditional structures of local government, controlled by the heads of leading tribal families, were being replaced by a system dependent on a distant king and an impersonal bureaucratic regime.

The dominant religion in India was **Brahmanism**. This involved sacrifice to a range of gods and was controlled by the priestly Brahmins. They, as the only people qualified to make the necessary sacrifices, were the focus of religious life.

The new monarchical system meant that many had lost the local social, moral and religious structures they had known and depended on. An increased interest in matters of personal belief and morality resulted in dissatisfaction with Brahmanism. **Samanas** (wandering philosophers) rejected the old beliefs and had begun to look for answers to questions about the meaning and purpose of life.

It was within this social and religious context that Buddhism emerged.

Concepts and practices

The Three Refuges

Buddhism is founded on three refuges or 'jewels'. The Three Refuges are repeated each day by Buddhists. The words are:

'The notion of a "refuge" here is not that of a place to hide, but of a place the mind can go to be purified and strengthened.' *An Introduction to Buddhism* by Peter Harvey (Cambridge University Press 1990).

>   I take refuge in the Buddha
>   I take refuge in the Dhamma
>   I take refuge in the Sangha

These phrases are repeated three times.

✦ **Buddha** represents the possibility of finding truth and contentment in life

✦ **Dhamma** (or Dharma) is the Buddha's teachings; following these teachings can set one on the path to enlightenment

✦ **Sangha** is the word for those who follow the Buddha's teaching in monasteries.

Buddha

Gotama, later to be known as the Buddha (the Enlightened or Awakened One) was born in the Terai lowlands near the foothills of the Himalayas, either in 563 or 448 BCE. The old tribal structures had survived most strongly here despite the threat of the monarchies, and Gotama, whose father Suddhodama was a tribal chieftain, was initially largely isolated from the developing discontent of the surrounding areas.

In Buddhist legend it is held that Gotama's privileged and secluded life was turned upside down in a single day, when he saw an old man, an ill man and a corpse. These sights made him think about the meaning of human life. Then he saw a **sadhu**, a religious man who had given up all his wealth to seek the truth about life and its meaning, and became convinced of the supreme value of religious life. As a result he became a wandering mendicant.

Gotama learned meditation and practised extreme **asceticism**, aimed at control over the body, which led to him becoming very thin and weak, but this did not bring the release and insight he was seeking. Finally Gotama sat and meditated beneath a tree, determined not to move until he found what he was seeking. He entered into a deep meditative state and attained supreme enlightenment, waking up to the truth about how to live in a way that was free of suffering. He spent a further four weeks beneath the sacred tree, hereafter known as the **bodhi** (enlightenment) tree and then decided to spread to others the enlightenment that he had achieved.

Buddhists believe that Gotama saw four truths at the moment of his enlightenment. These are known as the **Four Holy (or 'Noble') Truths**, and are at the centre of the Dhamma:

- **First Holy Truth.** Life is suffering and it is impossible to be completely satisfied
- **Second Holy Truth.** The cause of the suffering and evil in the world is desire, which springs from ignorance
- **Third Holy Truth.** It is possible to eliminate desire and suffering; the state of non-suffering is called **nibbana** (or 'nirvana')
- **Fourth Holy Truth.** In order to achieve nibbana, follow the Eightfold Path laid out by the Buddha.

Gotama gathered round him a group of disciples and converts, and these formed the core of the Sangha or Buddhist order of monks, which has remained at the heart of Buddhist life. Its function is to provide the best possible conditions for individual spiritual development and to teach the Dhamma to others.

The Buddha taught that every individual is reborn many times. Buddhists believe that one life follows another as a result of kamma (or 'karma') a doctrine of cause and effect. The key aspect of this teaching is the effect that it has on helping us to decide how we should act in our lifetime. If we act with an unselfish attitude and aim to help others then we get good kamma and our next life will bring us closer to nibbana. If we act selfishly then we will get bad kamma and our next life will take us further away from nibbana.

Following the example set by the Buddha, meditation is the central religious practice in Buddhism. Meditation is the purposeful training of the mind and the emotions, and is necessary in order to follow the mind development aspects of the Eightfold Path. The three

There is some scholarly debate over Gotama's dates. Tradition holds that he lived from 563–483 BCE, while modern research has tended to suggest that his dates were 448–368 BCE.

Although Buddhists believe Gotama was a historical figure, it would make no difference to their faith if his life was mythical and exemplary rather than absolutely historical.

In his years of asceticism (accepting a harsh life for religious purposes) Gotama was following the practice of others at that time.

One of the most common representations of the Buddha shows him touching the earth so that it might bear witness to the moment of his enlightenment.

Dhamma

See *What the Buddha Taught* by Walpola Sri Rahula (Oneworld 1997) for a more extensive explanation of the Buddha's teachings.

The Eightfold Path is a guide to wisdom, morals and the development of consciousness. See *An Introduction to Buddhism: Teaching, History and Practice* by Peter Harvey (Cambridge University Press 2002).

Sangha

Kamma and rebirth

Meditation

Warning. Photocopying any part of this book without permission is illegal.

World faiths 99

most important forms of meditation are Samatha, Vipassana and Zen.

Samatha ('calm') meditation involves awareness of the body, the mind, one's mental state and one's feelings. It aims to bring about physical and mental calm, progressing towards increased detachment from the sensory world. There are four levels of **jhana** (detachment), varying from the elimination of sensory desire to complete detachment and absolute peace.

> Vipassana meditation on the idea of 'I', say, might discover that 'I' is a collection of constantly changing thoughts, feelings and bodily states, so that ultimately it can be seen that there is no 'I' that can suffer.

Vipassana ('single-pointed') is a more advanced, analytical form of Samatha meditation. The aim of this sort of meditation is to focus on something that seems ordinary, and, by reflecting on it, to discover that it is something more than it at first appears. Vipassana plays a vital role in the quest for freedom from suffering for the Buddhists who practise it.

Zen is the Japanese translation for 'jhana'. Zen meditation practices have been known in Japan since the 7th century CE but did not become firmly established until the 12th century CE. Zen takes the view that enlightenment comes in spontaneous flashes of insight, which cannot be achieved through intellectual study, but rather through complete clarity of mind. Artistic expression (such as poetry) and martial arts can aid the search for enlightenment which, according to Zen, is possible in the here and now.

> **Further study**
> Find out more about Zen in the West. The following books may be helpful:
> *The Penguin Book of Zen Poetry* ed. Lucien Stryk (Penguin 1987)
> *An Introduction to Zen Buddhism* by D. T. Suzuki (Rider 1991).

Buddhist schools

There are two great schools of Buddhism. They are geographically distinct and each has its own history.

> 'Theravada' means the 'Doctrine of the Elders'.

Theravada Buddhism is the oldest form of Buddhism. It has about 100 million adherents, most of whom live in south-east Asia. Theravada Buddhists lay great emphasis on the importance of the monastic life and discipline, and on preserving the original form of the Dhamma. They also believe that nibbana can only be achieved after many rebirths. If a good life is led then the next rebirth will bring one closer to the state of nibbana.

> 'Mahayana' means the 'Great Vehicle'.

Mahayana Buddhism developed at the beginning of the first millennium CE, having split from Theravada Buddhism on doctrinal grounds. Today there are some 25 million followers of the pure school of Mahayana Buddhism and another 365 million 'Buddhists of the Eastern tradition' who can also loosely be classified as Mahayana Buddhists. The claim to be the 'Great Vehicle' was not based upon the large number of adherents but on the belief that this form of Buddhism could be more popular because of the greater laxity that was permitted in the interpretation of monastic rules. The Mahayanans entered into scholarly dialogue with Brahmins, and adopted Sanskrit as the language for their scriptures and commentaries, while the Theravadans stuck to Pali.

There are many points upon which the two schools agree. They both follow the Buddha as their only master, and both believe in the Three Refuges, the Four Holy Truths and the Eightfold Path.

Lay and monastic relations in Theravada Buddhism

Theravadan societies accept that those who are closer to the state of nibbana would want to join the Sangha and become monks or nuns. The division of Theravadan Buddhist societies into Sangha and laity established a social structure that has endured for some 2,500 years. But the Sangha has never been separated from the rest of society. The monasteries are often important social centres. Medicine is practised in them, children are still sent to them to be educated and they are used as advice centres. The laity is expected to support the Sangha with gifts of food, robes and other necessities, but doing this is seen as a way of earning spiritual merit. The Sangha does not beg for food, as it is accepted that the person giving benefits as much as the person who receives.

The major difference between monastic and lay life is the emphasis placed on morality and on keeping to strict precepts. Although moral teaching lies at the heart of all forms of Buddhism, monastic morality is far stricter than that imposed upon lay believers. Lay Buddhists undertake to keep the five principles of Buddhist morality, or the **Five Precepts**. These say that all Buddhists should abstain from killing, stealing, misuse of sensual pleasure, false speech, and drugs and alcohol. Monks on the other hand, follow the 227 precepts of the **Vinaya** (discipline), which cover moral, organisational and disciplinary issues. Many of the precepts are practical and are concerned with upholding the good name of the Sangha. All breaches of the Five Precepts are serious breaches of the Vinaya and result in immediate expulsion from the Sangha. The 227 precepts are recited by the monks once every fortnight in a process known as **Uposatha**. Any monk who has broken one of the precepts is expected to confess at these recitations.

> **Further study**
>
> The importance of morality is exemplified by the famous saying, attributed to the Buddha, that religious life is concerned with 'giving, morality, heavens and detachment'. You might find the following book of interest: *An Introduction to Buddhist Ethics* by Peter Harvey (Cambridge University Press 2000).

Christianity

The development of the early Church

The followers of Jesus did not immediately split from Judaism to found a separate religion. But quite quickly the distinctive worship of God *and* of Jesus made such a break inevitable. Bruce identifies the following features of this first Christian group:

- ✦ **Church.** The group quickly referred to itself by the word that in the Old Testament is used to describe the whole of Israel. In Greek this is ecclesia, usually translated as Church

- ✦ **Apostles.** The leaders were the 12 apostles chosen by Jesus, with Judas Iscariot replaced by Matthias. Some authorities believe that the number was recorded as 12 because of the Gospel authors' awareness of the 12 tribes of Israel

- ✦ **Community of goods.** There was no individual wealth or property

- ✦ **Growth.** The new group grew quickly

- ✦ **Early Divisions.** There was already a division between Hebrews (Jews who became Christians from a strictly Jewish background) and Hellenists (Greek-speaking Jews who became Christians from a background more sympathetic to Greek culture).

The apostles were the leaders of the early Church. They were able to give the Holy Spirit to others by laying their hands upon them

Organisation

See *New Testament History* by F. F. Bruce (Nelson 1969).

Apostles and deacons

'Deacon' comes from the Greek word for servant.

(Acts 8: 14–24), and were capable of miraculous acts (Acts 5: 12). In Acts 6: 1–6 it is reported that seven deacons were appointed to look after the practical distribution of food to release the apostles from that duty. The role of deacon eventually became an important one in the Church, but it is hard for us to tell quite what this role was at this early stage.

The divisions of the Church

The Christian Church is now divided into three groupings, separated by doctrinal disagreements, which have led to different liturgical practices.

Orthodox Church

The early Church had five patriarchates, all within the Roman Empire: Alexandria, Antioch, Byzantium, Jerusalem and Rome. Barbarian invasions separated the Greek-speaking east from the Latin-speaking west and later three patriarchates passed out of Christendom as the Muslim armies swept out of Arabia.

The sacramental functions of a Christian priest are usually: baptism, confirmation, consecrating bread and wine at Mass/Eucharist, marrying couples, forgiving sins, ordaining people to the priesthood and healing.

The Orthodox Churches developed from the churches of the east Mediterranean at the time of the Roman and then Byzantine empires, and remain strongest in south-eastern and eastern Europe, including Russia. They are characterised by the following:

- Orthodox bishops must be unmarried
- Priests may marry, but only before ordination
- Monasticism is central to the life of the Church
- Both bread and wine are given at Communion
- Worship is **sacramental** and centred on the Eucharist
- Icons are venerated
- Statues are forbidden
- Easter is the main feast
- Continuity and tradition are emphasised
- The Church year follows the Julian calendar.

Roman Catholic Church

It was the Roman Church's view of a papal monarchy and its change to the wording of the Creed that eventually resulted in the Great Schism (separation) of 1054 CE between the Orthodox east and the Catholic west. The Byzantines were critical of the Roman rewrite of the Creed, both because it was the common possession of the whole Church and changes to it should be made by an Ecumenical Council and not by the Roman Church alone, and because they held that it was simply untrue: the Holy Spirit proceeded from the Father alone.

The Roman Catholic Church claims continuity of practice and thought since apostolic times, and regards St Peter as the first Pope. It distinguishes itself from other Churches by its:

- Acknowledgement of the Pope as its head
- Creed containing the extra Latin word Filioque so that it states that the Holy Spirit 'proceeds from the Father *and from the Son*'
- Emphasis on tradition and ritual
- Eucharistic doctrine of transubstantiation (see page 105)
- Celibate male priesthood
- Emphasis on confession
- Doctrine of the seven sacraments
- Veneration of the Virgin Mary and other saints
- Laity receive only the bread at Mass, only the priesthood receives both the bread and the wine
- Importance of monastic tradition for both men and women.

After the Second Vatican Council (1962–1965) Roman Catholicism:

- Began using vernacular languages in the liturgy

Warning. Photocopying any part of this book without permission is illegal.

- Participated more in the ecumenical movement
- Felt the increasing effect of liberation theology.

At the same time it maintained:

- Hostility to divorce
- Hostility to abortion
- Hostility to artificial contraception
- Condemnation of homosexuality
- Status quo on the position of women
- Celibacy of priests.

Protestantism began as a movement for reform of the Roman Catholic Church. Protestant Churches include:

- Anglicans
- Lutheran Churches
- Methodist Church
- Baptist Churches
- Presbyterian or 'Free' Churches
- Pentecostalists
- Reformed (Calvinist) Church.

Protestantism
Protestants take their name from a 'protestatio' (declaration) of Reformation leader Martin Luther.

Most Protestant Churches agree on the following:

- Rejecting the authority of the papacy
- Accepting authority of scripture
- Use of vernacular translations of the Bible
- The laity receiving Eucharist or Communion in both kinds
- Clergy may marry
- Monasticism is either rejected outright or (as in the Anglican community) is practised but is marginal to most believers' experience of the Church
- Women can become priests in several but not all Protestant Churches
- The status of tradition and ritual varies from the Anglo-Catholics of the Church of England (very important) to the Quakers (not important at all).

In the Church of England women can become priests but not bishops, though this is being debated at the time of writing.

The nature of God

Christian theology has its origin in the reformulation of Jewish monotheism that took place in the wake of the resurrection of Jesus. Monotheism is the fundamental principle of Hebrew Scriptures (Old Testament). St Paul summarised the Christian account of this inheritance: 'For us there is one God... and one Lord, Jesus Christ' (1 Cor 8: 5–6). This **Binitarian** formula acknowledges belief in two divine powers: God and Jesus Christ. Within the 1st century CE the fundamental belief in three divine beings – the Father, the

'Binitarian' comes from the Latin word for 'two' and refers to God as experienced in two forms; 'Trinitarian' comes from the Latin word for 'three'.

Son and the Holy Spirit – had been articulated. This **Trinitarian** belief was articulated into the classical doctrine of 'one God in three persons' by the Nicene Creed.

The Nicene Creed

Disputes about the divine significance of Jesus dominated the Christian Church in its earliest centuries:

- **Arius** (c.250–336 CE) taught that Christ was not fully divine
- **Apollinarius** (c.310–390 CE) taught that Christ was not fully human.

The Council of Nicaea (325 CE), convened by the first Christian emperor, Constantine, drew up the Nicene Creed. It resolved that Jesus is 'of one being' with the Father, not deficient in terms of his divinity or lacking in his humanity. The subsequent Council of Chalcedon (451 CE) ratified this understanding, as a response to fresh debates about the nature of Jesus.

The Nicene Creed is a formula of belief whose origins reputedly lie in the 1st century CE but which in reality reflects a baptismal creed of this somewhat later period. It is sometimes (more strictly) called the Niceno-Constantinopolitan Creed.

Orthodox Christianity from this point on has adhered to belief in one God who subsists in the three persons acting and being perceived in three uniquely different but complementary ways:

- God the Father is the creator of the physical universe
- God the Son redeemed the created order by sacrificing himself on the cross
- God the Holy Spirit mediates the divine presence in the world and brings things towards their eventual conclusion by means of his guiding presence.

Sin and salvation

The Nicene Creed also sums up teaching on sin. Sin separates human beings from God, but the death of Jesus on the cross liberates human beings from the effects of sin. By becoming a human being, God the Son made salvation possible for humans, allowing them to share the divine nature and transcend the effects of death.

Religious practices

These theological understandings are expressed in the distinctive ritual practices of Baptism and Eucharist. Both of these trace their origins back to the New Testament, but have slightly different significances in the different branches of the Christian religion.

Baptism

Jesus was baptised by John in the river Jordan (Mk 1: 9–11).

The origins of Christian Baptism lie in the ritual activity of John the Baptist, the leader of a Jewish sectarian movement whose early adherents included Jesus himself. Despite Jesus not being recorded as administering any baptisms himself, Christians adopted the practice early on. Baptism was a universal Christian rite by the 2nd century CE. Christians were baptised once a year before Easter after a lengthy period of preparation and baptism constituted an important rite of passage.

In the Roman Catholic and Anglican Churches children are baptised by a priest at an early age without an extensive period of preparation. Promises are undertaken on the child's behalf by the parents and by sponsors called **godparents**. When baptised children are older, generally about 13, they make those promises for themselves in another ceremony known as **confirmation**, which is performed by a bishop. Only after confirmation do members receive communion.

Baptists dispense with confirmation by reserving baptism itself until children are ready to profess the Christian religion for themselves.

The Baptist Church dates back to 1609 CE but has its roots in the earlier German Anabaptist movement.

Eucharist

Participants in the Eucharist share wine and bread in a symbolic partial recreation of the Last Supper. In the Gospels' account of the original meal, Jesus is recorded as linking his own death with the coming of God's kingdom, evidently anticipating his resurrection within that eschatological context.

The Roman Catholic, Anglican and Baptist Churches have different understandings of the Eucharist. The differences centre on what it is believed to happen when the Eucharist is celebrated. The Roman Catholic Church believes in what is known as **transubstantiation**. This view depends upon Aristotelian principles in which the 'accidents' or outward appearance of the bread and wine remain the same while the substance, or actual nature, changes from bread and wine into the body and blood of Jesus. This belief was defined by the Fourth Lateran Council in 1215 and reaffirmed by the Council of Trent in 1551.

The doctrine of transubstantiation was heavily criticised by Protestant Reformers, even though there was no precise eucharistic agreement among them. Luther taught **consubstantiation**: the body and blood are present through the faith of the believer. Zwingli taught that Christ was present not in bodily form, nor in the blood and wine, but among the faithful, in spirit. He argued that it was a mistake to believe that the words of Christ 'This is my body' and 'This is my blood' needed in any sense to be taken literally, pointing out that there were other sayings in the Gospel that cannot be meant literally.

Martin Luther (1483–1546) and Ulrich Zwingli (1483–1531) were two of the most important of the 16th-century Protestant Reformers.

Hinduism

Indus Valley civilisation

The main sources of information about the ancient history of the Indus Valley are the Vedic sacred texts (providing evidence from 1500 BCE onwards, when Vedic tribes entered the area) and archaeology. Excavations beginning in 1920 CE of the cities of Mohenjo-Daro and Harappa revealed the existence of an urban civilisation dating back to c.2500 BCE. Further archaeological work demonstrated that this urban civilisation was extensive and advanced, with a highly organised system of central government.

The Indus Valley is to be found in modern Pakistan; the excavations have been taking place in what is now Sindh and the lower Punjab.

Some evidence of the religious practices of this civilisation has survived:

Religion

- ✦ Statuettes of a female figure suggest the possible worship of a mother-goddess
- ✦ Representations on seals of a male figure with crossed legs that may be a forerunner of the later Hindu god Shiva
- ✦ Veneration of phallic symbols that may relate to later fertility cults in India
- ✦ Veneration of a sacred tree similar to the later worship of the pipal, the Hindu holy tree

Shiva is known as the 'Prince of Yogins', the name of this posture.

Warning. Photocopying any part of this book without permission is illegal.

World faiths **105**

♦ Absence of temples, suggesting that Indus-valley religion was largely domestic, like later Hindu practice.

These similarities suggest continuity, that the roots of Hinduism lie in the Indus Valley civilisation. Indeed Klostermaier claims that some Hindu beliefs and practices may be even more ancient, originating as long ago as 6000 BCE.

See A Survey of Hinduism by K. Klostermaier (University of New York Press 1994).

The Indo-Aryan invasion debate

The dominant theory for many years however maintained that all but the smallest forms of native Indian religion were replaced by new ideas brought in by Aryan invaders from Eurasia. Scholars pursuing this theory pointed to the similarities between Sanskrit and European languages such as Greek and Latin. Some suggested that the Indians of this period were not capable of the religious developments of c.1500 BCE. Those who oppose the invasion theory maintain that there is a lack of concrete evidence for it. This debate has become a highly political one, with some Hindu nationalists seeing the theory as an attempt to minimise the value of native Indian culture and justify more recent invasions.

Modern reform movements

The British were the dominant power in India from the beginning of the 19th century CE. Contact with British government, methods and ideas challenged the Hindu view of life, and resulted in a number of Hindu reform movements.

Brahmo Samaj

Brahmo Samaj (society of the one God) was founded in 1827 by **Ram Mohan Roy** (1772–1833). Influenced by Christian friends – he believed in the virtues of British rule – as well as by the Islamic doctrine of the unity of God, Ram was a staunch opponent of polytheism and the use of idols. His movement was important in campaigning for social reform; it was prominent in advocating the abolition of **suttee** (the process whereby widows would throw themselves on to their husbands' funeral pyre to demonstrate their unfailing fidelity). Brahmo Samaj was never a mass movement, but intellectually it was highly influential. It underwent two revivals in the 19th century: in 1842, when Debendranath Thakur sought to eliminate Christian influences and to give the movement a distinctly Indian basis, and in 1866, when Keshab Chandra Sen attempted to reconcile Indian ideas with Christian theology.

'It [the Brahmo Samaj] was a deeply individualistic protest and signified the rise of individual reason, heart and conscience against what it considered degrading and barbarising customs.' V. P. Varma Modern Indian Political Thought (Lakshmi Narain Agarwal 1964).

Arya Samaj

Arya Samaj (society of the noble) was founded in 1875 in Bombay by **Dayananda Sarasvati** (1824–1883). It hoped to reform Hinduism from within, without resorting to other religions or foreign practices. Dayananda denounced idolatry and advocated a return to the earliest Vedic principles, as well as a cleansing of Christian and Muslim influences from Hinduism. A monotheist, he interpreted the different divine names in the sacred Vedic texts as titles for the one true God. He argued that the study of these texts should be made open to all and not just to the priestly Brahmins. Unlike other reform movements, Arya Samaj made no attempts to convert non-Indians.

Ramakrishna and Vivekananda

Ramakrishna (1836–1886) was a Brahmin devoted to the worship of the mother-goddess Kali, and given to asceticism and meditation. But he was also aware of Christianity and Islam, and held universalist views that all faiths were essentially different routes to the same goal, the worship of the one true God.

Vivekananda (1863–1902) was one of the followers of Ramakrishna. He is best remembered for speaking at the Parliament of Religions (Chicago 1893), where he proclaimed Ramakrishna's universalist doctrine. He established the Ramakrishna Mission in 1897. This is an international teaching body, devoted to charitable work among the sick and the needy. It also promotes a religion of understanding and tolerance.

The militant Hindu **Bal Gangadhar Tilak** (1856–1920) had understood part of the Hindu scripture – the *Bhagavad-Gita* – as emphasising the need for political, and even violent, action in the cause of Hinduism. This had led to violence against non-Hindus. **Mohandas Karamchand Gandhi** (1869–1948), known as Mahatma ('great soul'), returned to India in 1915 after some 20 years abroad as a student, lawyer and newspaper editor. In his time abroad he had felt the influence of Christianity and western political ideas. He interpreted the *Bhagavad-Gita* differently from Tilak and advocated the principle of satyagraha (non-violence).

Gandhi also worked hard on behalf of the untouchables. Indian society has traditionally been divided into four major groups, which are called **varnas**. These are:

- **Brahmins** – priest and scholars
- **Kshatriyas** – soldiers and rulers
- **Vaishyas** – traders and farmers
- **Shudras** – workers, servants and slaves.

Indians who did not belong to one of these varnas were known as the **untouchables**. They were the poorest members of society and their touch was believed to pollute members of other varnas. Gandhi called them **Harijans** (children of God) and sought to raise their standard of living. He led them into temples which they were forbidden to enter and procured for them the right to vote.

Religious concepts

During the Gupta period (320–500 CE) many of the central concepts of Hinduism achieved their classical form. People in south Asia at this point believed in a variety of gods, many of them local or indigenous deities. This diversity does much to explain the particular character of Hindu theology.

Hindus believe in the supreme Brahman, the supreme divinity of the universe. Unlike Jewish, Christian and Muslim concepts of God, Brahman is an impersonal force. It is a 'holy utterance' or 'sacred power' giving life to all human beings and is often described as the underlying fabric of the universe itself.

As Hinduism spread, it tended to gather local deities under this central concept, so that they became universal gods through their identification with the supreme force of Brahman. Each of these gods was regarded as an individual manifestation of Brahman. While at a popular level Hinduism accommodates a wealth of

Gandhi and satyagraha

Further study

Watch *Gandhi* starring Ben Kingsley (Columbia Tri-Star Home Video: DVD (CDR10135), VHS (C9065163)). Compare the treatment of people and ideas with that given in Gandhi's autobiographical *The Story of my Experiments with Truth* (Public Affairs Press 1948).

Proponents of the Aryan Invasion theory see the invasion as the moment when the caste system solidified.

Brahman

When reading this section, keep clear in your mind the differences between Brahma, Brahman, Brahmanism and Brahmins.

Warning. Photocopying any part of this book without permission is illegal.

polytheistic belief, at an intellectual level it offers a form of monotheism.

Om and Trimurti

The symbol *Om* is the most sacred word in Hinduism. It is a nasal sound, made up of the three syllables a, u, m. These are said to represent three things:

See page 105 for more on the Vedic texts.

- The first three Vedas
- The three worlds (earth, atmosphere and heaven)
- Trimurti – the triad of Brahma, Vishnu and Shiva.

Trimurti means 'having three forms'. In the Vedas various gods are grouped together under the title Trimurti.

Trimurti is not worshipped in its own right: it brings together the gods who create, sustain and destroy, and was thought of as a representation of Brahman.

Avatars of Vishnu

A detailed website on the avatars can be found at www.avatara.org.

Vishnu, whose name means 'to spread' or 'to extend', began as a minor Vedic deity. Vishnu is held to have had nine avatars (incarnations or earthly manifestations), with a tenth still to come. The two most important avatars are:

Krishna. Krishna was probably initially a local human hero, whose status took on legendary proportions. Closely connected with herdsmen and known as the protector of cattle, Krishna gradually became a demi-god, and was later regarded as the eighth avatar of Vishnu. In subsequent mythology Krishna is presented as a wonderful child and as a warrior-king. He is the most popular of the Hindu gods and the hero of the *Bhagavad-Gita*.

The Buddha is held to have been the ninth avatar of Vishnu.

Rama. Rama is the seventh avatar of Vishnu. He is the hero of the *Ramayana*, one of the two great epics of Sanskrit literature (the other is the *Mahabharata*). The *Ramayana* tells the story of Rama's struggle to recover his wife Sita after her abduction by Ravana, the ten-headed demon king.

Shiva

Of all the Hindu gods, Shiva is perhaps the most colourful, and is regarded as both the destroyer and the creator in the cyclical Hindu view of reality. This paradox is magnified by the portrayal of Shiva as not only an ascetic but also as a householder and a husband, which is perhaps only comprehensible in the light of the knowledge that meditation can produce a form of sexual energy. Shiva is also known as Nataraja (lord of the dance), and is the father of Ganesh, the elephant-god, and Kartikeya, the war god.

Atman and Brahman

The *Upanishads* teach that each person has a basic divine nature, the atman, or true self, which is itself part of the universal spiritual reality, Brahman. The purpose of life is to reunite the atman with Brahman and so find peace and happiness. The atman will continue to be reincarnated until **Moshka** (happiness/release) is achieved. Meditation and caring actions are the key ways of achieving this.

In a famous passage from the *Chandogya Upanishad*, Svetaketu is instructed by his father to break open a seed and to describe what he sees. On finding nothing, he is told that a great tree will grow from what he cannot yet perceive. Following this parable of the self, the father then instructs the son to dissolve some salt in water, a metaphor for the way in which Brahman permeates the individual and forms an atman within them.

Hindu religious practices

Puja means the worship or reverence that is offered to the gods. In the oldest forms of Hinduism, it denoted animal sacrifice; now it generally means ceremonial worship, such as the recitation of sacred texts and the repetition of the sacred word, Om.

Domestic worship

The home is an important centre for such worship. Every Hindu home has a shrine, which is used to welcome gods as honoured guests. The family offers water for drinking and washing, and food and incense to the god, whose pictures and statues are adorned in garlands and surrounded by flowers. This worship leads to the development of close bonds between a family and their god, although Hindu homes usually have statues of more than one god within them. Local deities are particularly prominent in such domestic worship.

The term 'Ishta-devata' or 'Ishwara' is used to denote a family's god.

Each day presents fresh opportunities for devotion. Every Hindu is invited to begin the day with prayer, calling to mind the day's tasks and asking for the strength to do them properly. In Indian villages, women offer prayers as they go to collect water. On their return, they make small offerings to the roadside shrines which adorn the way. In cities, people make offerings at shrines and temples. Food is often given to **sadhus** (wandering holy men) as part of a long Hindu tradition of supporting them.

Temple worship

The Gupta period witnessed the erection of temples as permanent shrines. The temple connects the mortal world with the realm of the gods and is a god's dwelling-place on earth. Consequently the temple's architecture is sacred. In northern India, temples are often built to resemble mountains, further signifying the connection between the human and divine realms.

Temple rituals are conducted by professional priests. As in the home, the deity is treated as an honoured guest, and is bathed and adorned with flowers. Sometimes images of the gods are carried in procession and offerings are made to them. The most important part of temple ritual is the **arati**, when the priests wave lamps in front of this image and worshippers press their palms together on their foreheads as a sign of devotion. After this puja there is **prasad** (grace), when the offerings that have been made to the deity are distributed among the worshippers. It is especially common for people to worship at the temple when they want to ask a favour of the gods.

There is a variety of holy men in Hinduism:

Holy men

- **Priests** are a professional class concerned with temple worship
- **Sannyasin** is the last of the four **ashramas** (stages) in life, preceded by student, householder and 'forest dweller': this final stage, not attained by every Hindu, involves asceticism, renunciation of family life and severing all ties with one's former existence
- **Rishis** (singers of hymns) are held to have received the sacred Vedic texts from the gods

Warning. Photocopying any part of this book without permission is illegal.

- **Gurus** are spiritual teachers: they have gained enlightenment and are consequently able to help others.

Islam

The development of Islam

Muhammad

Muhammad (570–632 CE) was born in the city of Makkah (Mecca), and suffered early misfortune – his father died before he was born and his mother when he was only six years old. He was brought up by his uncle, Abu Talib.

Muhammad grew up to be a merchant and he was employed at the age of 21 by a wealthy widow, **Khadijah**, whom he later married. The period before Muhammad is often called **jahiliyya** (days of ignorance), for Arabs were mostly polytheists. During his twenties, Muhammad became progressively more dissatisfied with polytheism and began to search for religious truth. In 610 CE he experienced his first revelation, known as the 'Night of Power and Excellence'. The Angel **Jibra'il** (Gabriel) appeared to him and brought him a divine message. The essence of the revelation that Muhammad received was simple. **Allah** was the only God, and life was to be lived in obedience to him. Other revelations followed, and Muhammad was instructed to recite them all. These revelations were later written down to form the **Qur'an**, the holy book of Islam.

Makkah

Muhammad began his public ministry in Makkah in 613 CE. He won some converts to the new religion, but was increasingly seen as a threat to the powerful merchant class of the city. The Muslims (members of the religion of Islam) began to be persecuted. Muhammad continued to have revelations during this period of persecution, one of the most important of which was the 'Night of the Ascent'. In the course of this, Muhammad experienced a spiritual journey from Makkah to Jerusalem, and from there to heaven where he met other prophets. He was also instructed by Allah to increase prayers from three to five times daily.

Hijra

In 622 CE Muhammad led his small group of followers north, away from Makkah, to the city of Madinah (Medina). This journey, the hijra, marks the beginning of the Muslim calendar. Muhammad became political leader of the city, and this led to the formation of a Muslim state based on his teachings.

Madinah

Theocracy: a state ruled by God. Some of Muhammad's rules for the city of Madinah survive in the *Constitution of Madinah* which dates from 640 CE.

Muhammad turned Madinah into a theocracy. Certain rules were laid down: polygamy was encouraged, money lending and alcohol were forbidden. Muhammad was also able to attract many new followers, and he began to act to protect and expand the community. By 628 CE Muhammad was able to march on Makkah at the head of an army. Makkah's leaders initially entered into a treaty with Muhammad, but after they broke this in 630 CE he conquered the city and made it part of the Muslim community. Once established in Makkah, Muhammad continued his military expansion. By the time of his death in 632 CE, Islam was a significant force in Arabia.

Significance of Muhammad

Muhammad's life and teaching became the determining factor for the subsequent development of Islam. Muslims call him 'The Seal of the Prophets'. This means that they believe that Muhammad delivered the final and most complete message of Allah, and that there will be no more prophets after him. Muhammad is also believed to be the ideal human being and is seen as the example that all Muslims should follow: he lived out Islam in the best way possible and was completely submitted to the will of Allah. Muslims do not believe that Muhammad was divine, nor do they see him as the founder of Islam. Islam teaches that Allah founded the religion when he put the first people on earth; Muhammad was a prophet who called for a return to this original religion, the truth of which had been confused and hidden due to human disobedience to Allah.

The old-fashioned term 'Muhammadan' (Muslim) is thus inherently offensive to Muslims.

There are two principal Islamic sects. **Sunna** means custom, and denotes the orthodox practice of Islam. Sunnis recognise the first three **Caliphs** (Abu Bakr, Umar and Uthman) as divinely inspired. Shi'ites reject the authority of these Caliphs and regard Ali, the husband of Muhammad's daughter Fatima, as the first true Caliph. He was hailed as Caliph in 656 CE but assassinated five years later and he is presented in Shi'ite sources as a saint and warrior.

Sunnis and Shi'ites

Caliph was the title borne by the leaders of Islam. There is some talk today of reviving a Caliphate.

Islamic religious concepts

The terms Islam and Muslim come from the Arabic 'aslama', meaning 'submission' and 'peace'. Muslims are people who have submitted themselves to the will of Allah and that submission results in inner peace. Five of the six central beliefs of Islam are found in **sura** 4 of the Qur'an. This states that 'Whoever disbelieves in Allah, His Angels, His Books, His Messengers, and the Last Day has surely gone far astray, far into error'. (A sixth belief in Allah's power to determine what happens to individuals was developed later.)

Beliefs

The Qur'an is divided up into 114 units, which are known as 'suras'. See page 45.

Allah is the creator of the physical universe: several parts of the Qur'an use the Design Argument to emphasise this divine creativity. Islam teaches that God created Adam as a kind of vice-regent, so that human beings are mandated to rule the earth and should keep Allah at the heart of their lives. This should culminate in **taqwa**, the constant awareness of the presence of Allah. **Tawhid** is the Arabic word for the oneness of Allah. Sura 11 of the Qur'an says of Allah that: 'He is God the One and Only, God the Eternal, Absolute. He beggetteth not nor is He begotten; and there is none like unto Him.'

Allah

For the Design Argument, see pages 126–131.

Modern Muslims extend this argument to the sphere of science and argue for a unity in the universe that suggests a common origin. There are some tensions in this belief with the actual teaching of the Qur'an about the creation.

Angels were created by Allah from divine light. They give praise to Allah and, unlike human beings, are incapable of disobeying him. In this respect human beings are seen as superior to angels. Angels can communicate with human beings and act as the guardians of hell. They record what humans do in their lives and there is an Angel of Death who is responsible for ending them.

Angels

The Qur'an is the direct revelation of God and is therefore the nearest thing to God that exists on earth. The tradition that Muhammad was illiterate underlines the revelatory status of the Qur'an: he did not compose it, he was given it. The Qur'an is the basis for the Muslim religion, and has absolute authority among Muslims. It is the most holy thing an individual can possess.

The Qur'an

Since Arabic is the language in which the Qur'an was revealed to Muhammad, it is seen as divine: an English translation is not seen by Muslims as a Qur'an.

World faiths 111

See pages 45–46 for more on the Qur'an.

Muslims keep their copy of the Qur'an on a higher shelf than other books and wrapped up to prevent it getting dirty. Most Muslims read the Qur'an in a **mosque** where special stands are provided so that the Qur'an is kept off the ground when Muslims are sitting on the floor.

Prophets

Prophets are people chosen by Allah to communicate his will to humanity. The Qur'an names the 25 most important prophets but there are many more. The Qur'an teaches that each prophet proclaimed God's word to their generation but that they were ignored, hence the need for further prophets. People like **Ibrahim** (Abraham) and **Musa** (Moses) are recognised as prophets: **Isa** (Jesus) in particular plays an important role in Islamic theology. The Qur'an acknowledges Jesus' miracles, but denies that he died on the cross stating that he was taken up by God to heaven. Muhammad is the greatest prophet, but is depicted as an ordinary man, who did not perform any miracles. His achievement was the delivery of the Qur'an.

Judgement

Judgement takes place on the Last Day, when a trumpet will sound out from heaven, all the dead will rise and Allah will sit in judgement. The good go to Paradise, sinners go to **jenna** (hell). The worst sin for a Muslim is **shirk**, which means to associate a created being with God, the single unique divine being. The Christian belief that Jesus was the son of God counts as shirk. Because of shirk there are no pictures of Muhammad in Islam for fear of a practice of icon-worship developing.

Islamic religious practices

Prayer

There is another form of Islamic prayer, known as 'du'a'. This is more informal than salah and can be offered at any time or place.

There are no fixed hours for prayer in the Qur'an; the prescription is essentially practical and allows for local variation.

The Qur'an advocates the practice of regular daily prayer, known as **salah**. Strict Muslims will say prayers five times a day, for about ten minutes each time. These frequent prayers are a way for Muslims to ensure that their minds are centred on Allah and on the path of Islam. The time of prayer is announced by the **muezzin** (the man who calls the faithful to prayer) from the minaret of the mosque.

Prayer is preceded by careful preparation known as **wudu**, a ritual washing ceremony in which the body is cleansed for the encounter with Allah. Prayers must be said in the correct **qibla** (direction), so Muslims must face Makkah, where the **Ka'ba** (a sacred shrine) is situated. Muslims use a series of ritual movements, such as bowing or kneeling, for each of the five prayer times. While doing these movements they repeat set words from the Qur'an.

Friday is **juma** (day of assembly), a special day of prayer for Muslims. Prayers on this day consists of two prostrations and a sermon, and must be attended by at least 40 male worshippers.

Fasting

Sawm (fasting) is obligatory for Muslims: sura 2 of the Qur'an states that the purpose of fasting is to 'learn self-restraint'. There is a special obligation to fast during **Ramadan**, the ninth month of the Muslim calendar. Adult Muslims who are not sick or pregnant must fast between the hours of dawn and dusk during this period. All Muslims are expected to attend the mosque on the 27th day of Ramadan in memory of the 'Night of Power' when Muhammad received his first revelation from Allah. The end of Ramadan is a day of celebration known as **Eid**.

Sawm is a test of a Muslim's willingness to follow the commands of Allah even when it is not easy to do so, and is seen as an opportunity to deepen faith. During Ramadan Muslims try to be especially devout. Many will offer extra prayers, and some will read through the whole of the Qur'an.

Judaism

Jewish reform movements

The Reform movement in Judaism began after the French Revolution in 1789. Before then Jews had often been denied citizenship in the various countries in which they lived. After the French Revolution it became common for Jews to become integrated in the **gentile** (non-Jewish) communities which surrounded them. This meant that Jews were increasingly influenced by the movement of societies away from religion and towards a view that personal freedom was the basis of a good life.

A major figure in the early Reform movement was **Abraham Geiger** (1810–1874). He organised the first conference of Reform rabbis. Geiger outlined the basic principles of Reform Judaism, which are that every human being has the potential to know and experience God, not just those Jews who follow the traditional interpretations of the **Torah**. It is the spirit of the Torah that matters: God is to be worshipped and we have a moral responsibility to others. The detail of the Torah should be obeyed where it is relevant to modern life and not just because it is part of the Torah.

These principles have led to a number of differences in the lives of Reform Jews. In the home, the **Shabbat** (Sabbath) and festivals (see pages 115–116) are kept in a more informal way and many Reform Jews have abandoned the kosher food regulations (see page 115). In the **synagogue**, men and women sit together, both genders can be **rabbis**, worship uses the native language of the congregation as well as **Hebrew**, and highly repetitive prayers are discouraged.

Those rejecting the Reform movement in Judaism organised themselves as a self-conscious group keeping strictly to the traditional beliefs and practices of Judaism.

Orthodox Jews believe in the ultimate authority of the Torah, an authority which modern ideas of critical scholarship and personal autonomy cannot change. At the heart of the Torah is the revelation of the Law to Moses on Mount Sinai. Interpreting that revelation is the rest of the Scriptures and the oral traditions, codified in the **Mishnah** and interpreted in the **Talmud**, and these too have unchallenged authority for Orthodox Jews.

These beliefs have a great effect on the daily lives of Orthodox Jews. They worship on a daily basis. Women play no part in the worship or the organisation of the local synagogue but sit separately from men in their own gallery. The dietary laws on kosher food are kept strictly. Sabbath observance is exact and the tradi-

You are required to know about the foundations of Judaism, specifically the Abrahamic and Mosaic Covenants: see pages 50–55 for this.

Reform Judaism

The conviction that Jews needed to leave behind a ghetto mentality lay behind modern Jewish reform movements. Moses Mendelssohn (1729–1786) pioneered the marriage of traditional Judaism and modern European culture. He asserted that God's existence and nature could be discerned through the exercise of human reason. His Enlightenment thinking lay behind much of the movement for Jewish reform.

Further study

See *The Blackwell Companion to Judaism* (Blackwell 2000) and *Tradition and Change: A History of Reform Judaism* Anne J. Kershen (Vallentine Mitchell 1995).

Orthodox Judaism

You should also consider the role of Hasidic Judaism. Hasidim today are generally thought to be the staunchest defenders of tradition against secularism: see page 26.

Further study

See *The World of Orthodox Judaism* by Eli W. Schlossberg (Jason Aronson 1996).

Warning. Photocopying any part of this book without permission is illegal.

tional extra day on the major festivals is observed. Most Orthodox Jewish men wear some form of head covering at all times.

Conservative Judaism

Zacharias Frankel (1801–1875) was the founder of Conservative Judaism. Although he was a German it is in the United States of America where Conservative Judaism has had its greatest success, having more affiliated Jews than any other Jewish group.

Conservative Judaism teaches that scholarship can avoid what adherents regard as the extremes of both Orthodox and Reform Judaism. Jewish Law is taken seriously as both a divine revelation and something that human beings have produced.

Conservative Jews use Hebrew in their synagogue services and sabbath observation is strict. Conservative rabbis have a greater degree of freedom than that of an Orthodox rabbi but they must keep to a number of traditional teachings. They are forbidden from accepting male converts to Judaism who have not been circumcised and from accepting anyone as a Jew who does not have a Jewish mother. Women can become rabbis. Conservative Jews observe kosher food laws but make modifications to them if essential.

> **Further study**
>
> See *Conservative Judaism* by Neil Gillman (Behrman House 1996).

Liberal Judaism

Liberal Judaism is a British expression of the Jewish Faith. The movement was founded by **Lily Montagu** (1873–1963) in 1902. She had been a Reform Jew, but was concerned that even the Reform Jews were at risk of holding on to traditions which made Judaism irrelevant to contemporary society.

Liberal Judaism is represented by the Union of Liberal and Progressive Synagogues. The Union teaches that a Jew has almost total autonomy in deciding what aspects of traditional Judaism they will follow. The traditions are respected and being a Jew is seen as being a valuable and worthwhile thing, but there is a great sensitivity to the possibility of religious practice becoming just a matter of habit.

> **Further study**
>
> See *Liberal Judaism: Lily Montagu and the Advancement of Liberal Judaism* by Ellen M. Umansky (Edwin Miller Press 1993).

One difference between Liberal and Reform Judaism in practice is that Liberal Jews will not use traditional prayer objects such as the **tallit** (prayer-shawl, see page 115). Liberal Jews introduced the **Bat-Mitzvah** as the female equivalent of the **Bar-Mitzvah**, the ancient Jewish ceremony in which a Jewish boy becomes a 'Son of the Law'. They also introduced a further service, **Kabbalat Torah** for 16-year-olds as the basis of a more mature acceptance of the faith.

In spite of these differences there is a great similarity between Liberal and Reform Judaism. Together they are known as Progressive Judaism and from time to time there is discussion about the possibility of uniting the two movements. They share a common training college for candidates to the rabbinate, the Leo Baeck College in London.

Central concepts

The nature of God

For Jews God is the creator of the physical universe. In addition he involved himself directly in the history of his chosen people, Israel. Although the most recent scholarship has shown that monotheism was a gradually emergent concept in Israel, and not a matter of absolute observance from the very beginning, monotheism has become the fundamental pinnacle of contemporary Judaism.

God is thoroughly distinguished from the world: he is both omniscient and omnipotent. Yet his engagement with history shows he is not a watchmaker who set the universe going and then retired from the scene. An important Hebrew term is **hashgahah**, which means providence in the sense of God's attentive care. The daily prayer, the **Shema** declares: 'Hear O Israel, the Lord our God, the Lord is One.' This assertion of the divine oneness is also an assertion that God has disclosed himself in historical revelation. Jews believe that the entire Torah was revealed to Moses on Mount

> **Warning.** Photocopying any part of this book without permission is illegal.

Sinai. What human beings need to know about God, God himself has disclosed in the form of a book and the basic structure of Judaism lies in the Torah.

For more on the Torah, see pages 46–48.

This notion of the covenant, with its biblical base and demand for practical expression allied to the doctrine of providence, underpins Jewish life today. This becomes evident as we turn to examine contemporary Jewish religious practices.

For more on the importance of the concept of covenant, see pages 50–55.

Religious practices

The centre of Jewish devotion is the home, and life is determined by domestic rituals and the weekly **Shabbat** (Sabbath) routine.

The word Shabbat means 'to break off' or 'to cease' from ordinary work, because it is a day when Jews must put aside all the ordinary concerns of their working lives. Genesis states that God created the world and its inhabitants in six days and that he rested on the seventh day.

In Jewish households the men go to the synagogue on a Friday evening while the women prepare a special meal at home. This meal begins with the lighting of the Shabbat candles and the blessing of a cup of wine. All forms of work are forbidden on Shabbat, including turning on lights and answering the telephone. This is sometimes thought to be restrictive, but the reverse is equally true. Shabbat gives people a time for:

- Peace
- Rest
- Celebration
- Family life
- Reflection about God
- Study of the Torah.

> 'Remember to keep the Sabbath day holy. You have six days to do all your work. But the seventh day is a sabbath to the Lord your God; that day you shall not do any work.' (Ex 20: 8–11).

Mourning is also forbidden on the Sabbath, which is looked forward to and prepared for like a wedding. These words are chanted in the synagogue at the Friday evening service: 'Come, my friend, to meet the bride; let us welcome the presence of the Sabbath.'

In Orthodox synagogues, services are held three times on Shabbat. Traditionally, women are exempted from attendance because of their domestic duties. The prayers centre round the **Shema** and the **Amidah** (a sequence of blessings). Jews cover their heads when praying in a custom that dates back to the 12th century CE. Another feature of Orthodox activity is the wearing of tallit (fringes) and the practice of wearing **tefillin** (leather boxes which contain parchment scripts of biblical texts). Jewish men wear two tefillin for prayer: one on the left arm and the other on the forehead.

Probably the most distinctive feature of everyday life in a Jewish home is the requirement to keep **kosher** dietary rules. Certain categories of food are completely forbidden to Jews and even permitted categories must be prepared in a particular way. Meat and dairy food may not be eaten together, so that Jewish households have two sets of saucepans and two sinks and fridges.

Deuteronomy prescribes that Jews must celebrate three pilgrim festivals every year: Pesach (Passover), Shavuot (the Feast of Weeks) and Sukkot (the Feast of Booths). These were originally celebrated in the temple; all three festivals have agricultural connections.

High holy days

Pesach celebrates the barley harvest as well as the miraculous deliverance of the Israelites from Egypt. During its seven or eight days Jews eat nothing that is made with leaven or raising agents. The house is thoroughly cleaned, and special crockery and cutlery used. On the first night (and again on the second night, for many Jews) a meal is celebrated in which the story of Moses' liberation from Egypt is narrated (**Seder**). This meal employs culinary reminiscences of the Exodus events, including salt water and radishes, but also eggs and fresh vegetables.

Shavuot celebrates the end of the barley harvest and takes place seven weeks after Pesach. It commemorates the giving of the Torah to Moses on Mount Sinai.

Sukkot takes place in the autumn. It is a harvest festival and also a reminder of the fact that the Israelites spent 40 years in the wilderness after their liberation from Egypt.

In addition **Rosh Hashanah** is the Jewish New Year, which falls in the autumn. It is essentially a call to repentance since it precedes **Yom Kippur** (Day of Atonement) ten days later. The **shofar** (ram's horn) is blown on Rosh Hashanah. Yom Kippur is the most solemn day in the Jewish year. Adults fast from sunset until the end of the following day in what is regarded as atonement for all the sins committed in the previous year.

These festivals provide an annual structure to Jewish life which is reinforced by the weekly routine.

Sikhism

In the 15th century CE northern India was marked by the rise of a number of groups challenging Hinduism and Islam. Sikhism was one such group, and was similar to a number of others particularly in its opposition to ceremonial and ritual practices, especially the use of idols.

> Sikhism rejects all forms of rituals such as fasting, pilgrimages, superstition and idol worship.

Guru Nanak

> The Punjab is the region of northern India between the desert and the Himalayas.

Guru Nanak (1469–1539) was born a Hindu in the village of Talwandi in the Punjab. The information that we have on his life comes from four collections of stories called the *Janam Sakhis*. These were written to demonstrate divine inspiration from the moment of Nanak's birth. They show that Nanak was interested in religion from an early age. As a member of the second highest Hindu caste (the kshatriya), he could study (but not preach from) the Vedas and developed an understanding of Hinduism. Nanak also managed to learn about Islam from the Muslim ruler of his village. Later he apparently spent a great deal of time meditating and asking penetrating questions about the value of Hinduism and Islam of local elders.

> See pages 105 and 107 for more on the Vedas and the Hindu caste system.

> Scholars sometimes present Sikhism as syncretic, drawing on aspects of Hinduism and Islam, with the addition of later independent beliefs and practices, but Sikhs themselves emphasise Sikhism as a direct revelation from God.

When Nanak was 30, he had a vision while bathing. This caused him to leave his family, give away his worldly possessions and become an itinerant preacher, travelling through India, Sri Lanka and Arabia. He conveyed his message in the form of hymns, which he delivered in local dialects so that his listeners could easily understand him. In these hymns he insisted in particular that religion was a matter of the spirit, that it needed neither ritual nor symbol and that salvation comes through religious devotion.

On returning from his travels, Nanak established a settlement called **Kartarpur** (the home of God) where he lived from 1521. Pilgrims came to hear his hymns and preaching. Nanak organised them into a community based on manual work, prayer and hymn singing, which was devoid of any distinctions of caste, birthright or gender.

Nanak was the first of ten Sikh Gurus. Sikhs believe that God is the original guru; the ten Sikh Gurus are earthly representatives and mediating authorities. They also believe that all later Gurus were reincarnations of Guru Nanak and that they all preached the same message. Four important Gurus are:

Guru Arjan Dev (1563–1606) became the fifth Guru in 1581 and occupied the role until his death. He established the **Harmandir** or **Golden Temple** at Amritsar and declared that Sikhs must donate a tenth of their earnings to charity to fund similar building projects. He began the process of organising the first version of the Sikh holy book. He instructed his followers to revere the book as it was divinely inspired.

Guru Har Gobind (1595–1644), the son of Guru Arjan, became the sixth guru on his father's death. He undertook to lead the Sikhs against tyranny and oppression. Sikhs now began to bear arms; Guru Har Gobind encouraged them in physical exercise and weapon handling. He himself displayed considerable physical prowess, leading Sikhs in a number of battles.

Guru Tegh Bahadur (1621–1675) was, from 1664, the ninth Guru. He undertook a number of missionary journeys, preparing wells and communal kitchens for the people. Guru Tegh Bahadur is celebrated for sacrificing himself for the freedom of another religion. He confronted the Muslim Emperor Aurenzeb over the repression of Hindus. He reprimanded the emperor for his deeds and the emperor responded by ordering him to convert to Islam or face death. The Guru refused and the emperor had him publicly beheaded.

Guru Gobind Singh (1666–1708) became Guru after the execution of Guru Tegh. He succeeded in completing the Sikh holy book. He also decided that a degree of reformulation was necessary for the Sikh community and introduced the concept of a higher-level commitment to Sikhism.

In 1699 Guru Gobind Singh founded the Khalsa (the pure), those willing to die for their faith. Those who were willing to do so underwent a form of baptism known as *amrit sanskar*. This led to a distinction between different kinds of Sikhs. Those who accept Amrit are called *amrit dhari*. Other Sikhs are known as *sahaj dhari*; these people do not follow the code of the Khalsa, but follow the traditions of the Gurus, particularly Guru Nanak. Guru Gobind Singh prescribed five symbols for members of the Khalsa, generally called the Five Ks:

- **Kacha:** wearing shorts (as a symbol of self-control)
- **Kara:** wearing a bangle
- **Kirpan:** carrying a sword
- **Kesh:** not cutting one's hair
- **Kangha:** wearing a comb.

The Khalsa remains important today for many Sikhs. The normal

Gurus

A guru is a teacher or holy person. In Sikhism the title is reserved for the ten Gurus and the holy book: see page 118. See also pages 109–110 for gurus in Hinduism.

'For me, there is only one religion – of God – and whosoever belongs to it, be he a Hindu or a Muslim, him I own and he owns me. I neither convert others by force, nor submit to force, to change my faith.' Guru Tegh Bahadur's response to Aurenzeb's demand that he should convert to Islam.

Khalsa

age for admission to the Khalsa is 16 to 18, and the initiation ceremony has to take place in front of five fellow Sikhs. Initiates are instructed that they should never remove any hair from their bodies, that they should not use any intoxicating drug, that they should not eat any meat slaughtered in the Muslim way and that they should not commit adultery. Initiates are also required to wear the symbols of the Khalsa, although nowadays swords and shorts are only requirements on ceremonial occasions.

Note however that for some traditional Sikhs, the symbols of the khalsa are still very much a requirement of daily life.

Sikh religious concepts

Guru Nanak's vision is regarded as the historical origin of what is known as the **Mool Mantra** (the perfect mantra), a short statement of belief with which the Sikh scriptures open.

The Mool Mantra: 'There is but one God whose name is True, the Creator, devoid of fear and enmity, immortal, unborn, self-existent, great and bountiful. The True One was in the beginning, the True One was in the primal age. The True One is, was, O Nanak, and the True One also shall be.'

Sikhs believe that God cannot take on human form and that he must be remembered through daily devotion. The most popular name for addressing God is **Waheguru** (wonderful lord), while God is also frequently called **Sat-Guru** (true guru).

Guru Granth Sahib

Before he died, Guru Gobind Singh is reported to have placed a coconut and five coins on a copy of the Sikh holy book the **Adi Granth** and pronounced that there would be no more human gurus: from then on the Sikh community would have to rely on scripture. Sikhism shifted away from a focus on humans as representatives of the divine towards a book, and the Adi Granth was renamed the Guru Granth Sahib and was treated as the 11th Guru.

Interpretation of the scriptures is done by a **granthi** (expositor or guardian) in the gurdwara (temple). When disputes arise about the interpretation of passages, they are referred to the **Akal Takht** (a religious court) in Amritsar.

Langar and Sangat

Guru Langar (Guru's kitchen) and Guru Sangat (Guru's association, the Sikh assembly or congregation) are important features of Sikh communities. The Langar is a communal kitchen which is organised on a non-hierarchical basis. Only those who eat together in the Langar can become members of the Sangat. The Langar and the Sangat express the idea that all Sikhs are equal members of the community. Equally, the Langar is open to all, Sikhs and non-Sikhs.

This was a tradition established by Guru Nanak at his settlement in Kartarpur.

Sewa

A fundamental Sikh principle is that of sewa (service to the community). This is not just designed to help members of the Sikh community, but is a service offered to everyone, including non-Sikhs. It can involve giving time or money, or some form of community service, such as helping to prepare meals in the communal Langar. In some cases, sewa involves talking to other people about religious matters.

Sikh religious practices

Sikh worship is known as **diva** and is centred on the Guru Granth Sahib. As the Guru Granth Sahib must be treated with respect, a household needs a separate room in which to keep it, so many Sikh families do not have a copy.

Gurdwara

The literal meaning of gurdwara is the guru's door and usually refers to the Sikh temple, although in fact any place where the Guru Granth Sahib is kept can be called a gurdwara.

Every gurdwara flies the Sikh flag with its **khanda** (two-edge sword) which demonstrates that Sikhs are expected to struggle against spiritual and temporal forces. Many worshippers touch the flagpole as a sign of respect before entering the gurdwara. Some Sikhs also touch the steps of the gurdwara and then their foreheads, while everyone is required to remove their shoes and cover their heads. Sikhs must bath before attending the gurdwara. In the Punjab, there are generally washing facilities outside, although this is not necessarily the case with gurdwaras in Britain. Pride of place in the gurdwara is given to the Guru Granth Sahib. Men and women sit on the floor of the gurdwara, with their feet facing away from the Guru Granth Sahib. The Sikh principle of equality dictates that there are no special places.

Services

Sikhs do not have a special holy day, but meet together whenever proves convenient. In Britain, this is usually on a Sunday. The service in the gurdwara lasts several hours, and people can come and go while it is going on. There is no formal order of service; instead the Guru Granth Sahib is opened at random and a text is taken from it. This text is chanted, and the congregation are led by ragis (musicians).

There is a set order for the close of service. The congregation joins in two poems:

✦ The **anand sahib** (hymn of joy), which declares that sorrow has vanished

✦ The conclusion of the **japji** (the passage at the beginning of the Guru Granth Sahib which contains the essence of the teachings of Guru Nanak), which states that humans are composed of earth, water and air, and which warns that humans will one day be judged by God.

All then stand for **ardas** (prayers) which fall into three parts. The first recalls the gurus and the five original members of the Khalsa, and concludes with the hope that worshippers be freed from attachment to this world and its vices. Secondly, special prayers are said for those in need. Finally, there is a random reading from the Guru Granth Sahib which is believed to be especially significant.

The Langar

When entering the gurdwara each person makes an offering of food or money, with the food generally being used in the Langar. While the service takes place, some members of the congregation prepare the Langar. Although it is not held after every service, it is always prepared on Sundays and festivals. A special kind of food called **karah parshad** is placed next to the Guru Granth Sahib and blessed at the end of the service. This food is a sweet confection composed of sugar, water, butter and semolina. Its sweetness is held to express God's kindness, and that everyone shares in it demonstrates the Sikh principle of equality.

Test yourself

Buddhism

1. Outline what is meant by 'taking refuge' in the Buddha, the Dhamma and the Sangha, and explain why it is important for Buddhists to do this.
2. 'Mahayana Buddhism is so different from Theravada Buddhism that it is hardly the same religion.' To what extent do you agree with this statement?

Christianity

1. (a) Outline the key differences in interpretation which have led to divisions within the Christian Church.
   (b) Do you think that these differences are important to 21st-century Christians?
2. (a) Describe the main differences in belief about EITHER the Eucharist OR Baptism between TWO Churches.
   (b) Assess whether of these differences are best understood today as matters of tradition and practice rather than theology and faith.

Hinduism

1. 'It is in domestic worship not temple worship that the heart of Hinduism is to be found.' Explain and assess this observation.
2. 'The Indo-Aryan invasion debate ignores the complexity of Indian culture, and is nothing more than a justification of invasion, past or future.' To what extent do you agree with this assertion?

Islam

1. Why is the Qur'an so important to Muslims, and what does its nature reveal about Muhammad's status in Islam?
2. 'For Muslims, fasting is more important than prayer.' Assess this claim.

Judaism

1. 'A Liberal Jew is no Jew at all.' Assess this Orthodox view.
2. Examine the argument that, for Jews, the home is infinitely more important than the synagogue.

Sikhism

1. Explain how Sikhs express their membership of the Khalsa and assess the importance of Khalsa membership for Sikhs today.
2. 'Today, the true meaning of the Langar has been forgotten.' Explain what the Langar means to Sikhs today and assess how far this statement is accurate.

Warning. Photocopying any part of this book without permission is illegal.

Religion and science

The origins of the universe

Religious concepts of creation

Not everyone is agreed that the universe has an origin in the sense of a beginning in time. Stephen Hawking for one has suggested that the universe had no clear beginning and therefore has no need of a creator. But whether it did or not, it can be argued that the universe still requires an **ontological** grounding to sustain it in existence. The theology of creation could describe equally well a universe that was infinitely old. **St Thomas Aquinas** (see page 126) suggested in the 13th century that the real issue is not whether there was a temporal beginning but that the universe exists as an expression of the primordial love that Christians call God.

> Ontology is the branch of metaphysics that deals with the nature of being. An ontological argument is one which argues that the existence of the concept of God entails the existence of God.

In this section, we will be looking at the accounts of the creation of the universe in the Jewish and Christian traditions. There are several conflicting opinions about how to understand the accounts of creation given in the key scriptural texts Genesis 1 and 2. These chapters can be understood as a straightforward scientific record about the chronology and mechanism by which the early universe appeared. They can also be read as stressing the universe's ontological dependence on God: the point of the Genesis 'beginning' narratives is to answer the question of why there is something rather than nothing and to say that the very existence of the universe is a gift from God, held in being by God's sustaining power.

Religious fundamentalists, biblical literalists and creationists take the view that Genesis 1 and 2 are literal history and scientifically true. These groups see no need or scope for interpreting the documents symbolically or mythologically. In these chapters, as in the rest of the Bible, God speaks to humans, and because the Bible contains the words of God, it must (by definition) be true and cannot be tampered with or changed.

Literal truth

According to this literalist view, the universe is much younger than modern (secular) science suggests. The 17th-century CE Irish Archbishop Ussher calculated, by looking at the genealogies in the Bible, that the universe was created by God in 4004 BCE.

Some scholars understand the creation accounts to be symbolic. It is possible to see a direct and specific correlation between the biblical accounts and a scientific understanding of the Big Bang (see pages 123–125). The physicist and theologian **Gerald Schroeder** says that they are 'identical realities... described in vastly different terms'. For example he argues that the wind or breath of God moving over the waters is symbolically equivalent to the inflationary mechanism by which the universe expanded. He reads God's command 'Let there be light' as equivalent to the separation of photons in the early moments of the universe.

Symbolic truth

See Gerald Schroeder *Genesis and the Big Bang* (Bantam 1992).

Many scholars now think that there are two separate mythological stories in Genesis. In the first, God creates everything in six days. Human beings (both man and woman) are the last thing to be created and are seen as the pinnacle of creation (Gen 1). In the second story, God creates a garden (Eden) into which he places all the animals and plants, then man (Adam) and finally woman (Eve). Adam and Eve are given responsibility for the maintenance of the garden and 'dominion' over the animals (Gen 2).

Mythological/theological truth

See pages 65–67 for an outline of the approaches adopted by different schools of biblical scholarship.

Until the 18th century CE, it was believed that Genesis 1 and 2 were scientific, historical accounts of the divine origin of the universe. Bibical scholars now attempt to reach a fuller understanding of these passages by taking into account such issues as the nature of the literature, the date at which it was written, the intellectual environment of the writers and the purpose for which they were writing. It is now argued that these are theological documents, written at a particular time and place for particular groups of religious people. Bearing all this in mind, it is possible to analyse the theological ideas in these creation accounts.

It is very important to remember that, if the biblical accounts are not to be taken historically, the ideas they put forward must have to do with the question: 'Why is there anything at all?', not with the question: 'How did the world and everything else come about?'. That is, they deal with the question of *ontological* existence, not of *temporal* existence. What they can tell us about is something of the nature of God, the creator of the universe, and the reason why he created it. The following four points are central to the accounts:

God is the sole creator. Genesis says that God is the only creator of the universe. There is no other being which makes the universe. Genesis 1 stresses the power of God in creating the *entire* universe, not just part of it. He is thus not a local deity nor one with a special responsibility for one element of the universe alone. This God is the foundation of everything that goes on within the universe and his creative activity is seen in every part of the universe.

This is a different view from most of the other civilisations at the time these accounts were written, when polytheism was the norm.

The universe depends on God The universe in Genesis is ontologically dependent on God for its continued existence as well as for the first moment of creation. The Christian view is that God not only created the universe ex nihilo (from nothing), but also is continuously creating it at every moment. If God were to stop this creative activity, the universe would cease to exist. The idea that God created the universe ex nihilo does not appear in Genesis, but developed during the early Christian period. A group accused of heresy by the Catholic Church, called the Gnostics (who believed that they had received special, secret knowledge), claimed that the present material world was evil and only the world of the spirit was good. Thus the god who created the world was inferior to the god who redeemed it. It was in the attempt to clarify Christian belief that the early Christian scholars developed the idea that God directly created everything that exists ex nihilo. This removed entirely the Gnostic idea of demiurges (intermediate divinities) and meant that the creator and the redeemer were the same.

'It is irrelevant to a doctrine of creation 'ex nihilo' whether the universe began or not: that the universe began was usually accepted because of a particular reading of Genesis 1. The doctrine of creation 'ex nihilo' simply maintains that there is nothing other than God from which the universe is made, and that the universe is not God and wholly dependent on God for its existence.' Keith Ward, quoted in *Science and Religion: From Conflict to Conversation* by J. F. Haught (Paulist Press 1996).

The universe is ordered by God. According to Genesis, the universe is not chaotic but ordered. God is the source of order in the universe. He is the source and guarantor of the laws that govern this order. To say that the world is created is to say that it is ordered. In Genesis 1, the creation is divided into several sectors, and each of these has a number of appropriate life forms within it:

Further study

Gnosticism takes its name from the Greek word 'gnosis' or 'knowledge'. Some scholars have seen Gnosticism as a heresy within Christianity, some as a separate religion that predated Christianity. There are countless books on this subject. You could try *The Gnostic Gospels* by Elaine Pagels (Penguin 1990) and *The Medieval Manichee* by Stephen Runciman (Cambridge University Press 1982).

Sector	Life forms
Heavens	Sun and moon; birds
Earth	Humans, animals, plants, trees
Waters	Fish, sea creatures

In the light of other ancient views of the world, this emphasis on the order of the creation is very striking. God orders time as well as the life forms. By arranging time into seven blocks (days), God asserts his sovereignty over the created world.

A personal God. Both creation stories in Genesis signal that God is a personal God. He is described anthropomorphically as walking in the garden and speaking to Adam (Gen 2). He is also a God of relationships: he created human beings to be in relationship with himself and created woman to be in relationship with Adam. The statement that humans are made in the image and likeness of God (Gen 1: 26–27) suggests that the relationship between humans and God is one of dignity, responsibility and intimacy. Furthermore, God's command to 'subdue the earth' (Gen 1: 28) implies that humans are God's representatives – they have the power and responsibility to maintain and control God's created order.

> 'Anthropomorphically' means that something is being understood in human terms or described as possessing human qualities.

Scientific theories of the origin of the universe

The Big Bang theory suggests that the universe came about as the result of something like an initial large explosion. An explosion as we understand it is where some physical material is blasted into the surrounding space. However the Big Bang was an explosion that actually created space and time itself. This theory also claims that the entire universe began to condense out of this original explosion between 10 and 20 billion years ago, and (this is an important point) that it is still expanding.

> **Big Bang theory**

Among the strands of evidence which are presented in favour of the Big Bang theory is the fact that the universe appears to be expanding at a rapid rate as if in the aftermath of a large explosion. Very distant galaxies seem to be moving apart from each other. The galaxies furthest away are moving faster than those nearest to us. From this evidence we can infer that at one time all the galaxies were closer together and that they are now moving further and further apart. It is possible to calculate how far away a galaxy is by measuring how fast it is moving. The frequency (colour) of the light we see coming towards us from a star varies according to whether that star is approaching or receding. It varies further according to how fast the star is travelling. Because we can measure how far away stars are, how fast they are travelling and how old they are, we can also calculate the age of the universe.

The Big Bang theory states that the conditions at the beginning of time must have been very hot indeed. The Big Bang was in effect a huge fireball. Scientists believe that they have detected the remnants of this fireball in the background microwave radiation in the universe. This was discovered accidentally by **Andrew McKellar** in 1941 and then observed again by **Arno Penzias** and **Robert Wilson** in the 1960s and confirmed in the early 1990s by satellite observations. This radiation seems to be coming equally from all points in space at the same time. This observation is consistent with the Big Bang theory, because all parts of the universe were equally created by the same initial explosion.

It takes time for the light from distant galaxies to reach earth. This means that observing objects through a telescope is like looking back in time. We can see directly the way the universe looked long ago. Observations show that it looked different from how it does now. This is exactly what one would expect from the Big Bang.

Cosmologists are relatively clear about what happened just after the Big Bang, with the rapid expansion of the universe. However the actual moment of the Big Bang is unknowable. This is because, at the first moment, the universe was an infinitely dense, dimensionless point. This is called a **singularity**. Certain physical attributes (notably density) take infinite values at a gravitational singularity. The laws of physics (in their present, imperfect form), which depend on the values of these attributes, tell us nothing about what happens under these conditions.

> The academic physicist Paul Davies has said: 'A singularity is the nearest thing that science has found to a supernatural agent.' *God and the New Physics* (Pelican 1984).

Steady State theory

This theory of the origin of the universe is associated with the physicists **Hermann Bondi**, **Thomas Gold** and **Fred Hoyle** (1915–2001). Its central idea is that, instead of the single large initial explosion of the Big Bang theory, there was a series of small 'bangs'. There was no beginning and will be no end to the universe. New matter is created from nothing. As the universe expands, new particles of matter are spontaneously and continuously created. This means that the density of the matter in the universe remains constant. When a star burns out, it is replaced by newly-created matter. The rate of expansion remains unchanged and the rate at which matter appears is just enough to maintain a constant density. A helpful example for understanding this theory is of a river that looks the same on the surface, even though the water is constantly flowing through it. The moving river is clearly not static, but it is in 'steady state'.

> Steady State theory has been undermined by the evidence and is currently a minority view in scientific circles. Radio telescopes have shown that the universe has not always looked the same and the cosmic background radiation is not consistent with the Steady State theory.

Steady State theory is even less like the biblical story of Creation than Big Bang (which at least was a story with a beginning): it removes any need for an 'explanation' of the universe. If there was no beginning of the universe, then there was no creation and therefore no creator. A universe in which matter is continuously being generated is effectively in perpetual motion and has no need for an interventionist God to keep it going. In Big Bang, something happened; in Steady State, the universe 'just is' and thus requires no explanation of its existence. Nevertheless some theologians have welcomed this theory as it replaces an image of a God who lights the blue touchpaper and stands back with one of a God that is constantly pouring his divine creative energy into the universe.

Oscillating Universe and continuous creation

The physicist **John Wheeler** and others have suggested that the universe is part of a cycle of cosmic oscillations. According to this view (a modified version of the Big Bang theory), the universe begins with a Big Bang, expands at a diminishing rate as gravity overcomes the energy of the explosion and then starts to contract again. The contraction mirrors the expansion so that the contraction gets faster and faster. Eventually the universe disappears in a 'Big Crunch' – a Big Bang in reverse. A new expanding universe emerges from this and so the cycle continues for ever. If the physical conditions of each successive cycle vary randomly, then a combination with the conditions necessary for intelligent life will eventually come up by chance. This theory assumes that the

> The Oscillating Universe theory is now disputed by many scientists, who argue that there is not enough matter in the universe to cause the oscillating effect. They believe that the universe will continue to expand forever.

> Warning. Photocopying any part of this book without permission is illegal.

universe has neither a beginning nor an end; for some, this means that there is no place for a creator.

Christian responses to scientific theories

Depending upon their theological viewpoint, Christians give different responses to the Big Bang and other theories of the origin of the universe. For Christian fundamentalists, who uphold the literal truth of Genesis, the logic of the Big Bang is flawed. They point to the paradox of nothing exploding into everything. **Creation Science** is an attempt to construct a rival version of science, dedicated to showing how the Bible is literally and wholly true.

Some Christians understand the Bible to be symbolically true. They believe that the insights of science can enhance their view of creation and teach humans about God. In 1951 Pope Pius XII accepted the scientific findings of the Big Bang theory as providing solid support for the Christian doctrine of creation. Other theologians point to the following similarities:

- The universe is not infinitely old – it had a beginning. Like Genesis 1 the theory explains that the universe came into existence abruptly out of nothingness. **Robert Jastrow** argues that scientific and theological accounts are complementary. Both can be true even though they may appear superficially different. They represent different approaches to describing aspects of the same reality

- If the universe came into existence from nothing, this raises the question of what caused the Big Bang. Cosmologists answer this by saying that space and time arose out of the singularity, and that the question does not make sense because causes can only be understood *within* space and time

- The singularity represents the point at which physics must stop. It is impossible to go beyond this. Physicists acknowledge that there is something real beyond the singularity, but it is inaccessible to science. For some theologians, this scientifically inaccessible point is where God is (but see *right*).

Other Christians believe that there is no clash between science and religion about the origin of the universe. They argue that there is simply no relationship at all between the two disciplines. They believe that theology and cosmology are talking about two completely different sets of truth, and that apparent similarities between Genesis and the Big Bang are irrelevant.

According to this approach science is not in the business of dealing with the ultimate questions of life. It attempts to answer the 'how?' questions, not the 'why?' questions. Big Bang cosmology does not explain anything about what the concept of creation actually means in its religious depth. Conversely, the narratives in Genesis have nothing to do with cosmology and have no value for explaining the scientific origin of the universe.

This group of Christians therefore sees the theology of creation as having nothing to do with the question, 'How did the universe begin?', but rather with viewing God as the sustainer,

Fundamentalism

Creationism is a minority position both in the scientific and the Christian communities. For a selection of links to websites and essays which argue for and against the fundamentalist view, see www.atheism.about.com and look for the section entitled Evolution vs. Creationism.

Symbolic reading

God and the Astronomers by Robert Jastrow (W. W. Norton 2000).

The language used in descriptions of the Big Bang may find symbolic echoes in Genesis 1. See page 12⁀.

Is this just another example of a phenomenon known as the 'god of the gaps'? This term was coined by C. A. Coulson in his *Science and Christian Belief* (Oxford University Press 1955), and is used to describe attempts to seek out gaps in scientific knowledge and point to them as indicating the limits of human knowledge, thus proving the existence of God.

No clash, no connection

purpose-giver and spiritual dimension of the universe. It is this view of God that gives meaning to the physical processes of the universe.

Arguments for the existence of God

The Design Argument

Many different design arguments for the existence of God have been put forward by philosophers and theologians. In this chapter, we shall be looking particularly at those of Aquinas, Paley and Swinburne. They are examples of natural theologians: they look at the natural world for evidence concerning the existence and nature of God. Proponents of the Design Argument find apparent evidence of order and purpose in the world, and conclude that this evidence points to the existence of an ordering and purposeful God. These arguments do not appeal to any kind of revelation from God, for example the Bible.

> The Design Argument is closely related to the Teleological Argument, from the Greek word *telos*, meaning 'end' or 'purpose'. The name makes clear that this is an argument that is pursued backwards to the beginning (a creator God) from the end (a created world). Design arguments tend to emphasise the analogy between the world and a mechanism, while teleological arguments tend to point in a more general way to the order and complexity in the world as evidence for the existence of God.

Aquinas

St Thomas Aquinas (c.1225–1274) was the greatest of the Medieval scholastic theologians. His many writings influenced Christian theology for several centuries and his system of philosophy came to be known as Thomism. The Roman Catholic Church regards him as one of its greatest theologians. He was made a saint in 1323.

Medieval theologians and philosophers were influenced by the ancient Greek philosophers: Aquinas actually refers more often in his writings to **Aristotle** (384–322 BCE) than to the Bible. Aquinas became very influenced by Aristotle's works and adapted his ideas for the Church's use. On the other hand Aquinas rejected Plato, who had influenced earlier Christian thinkers like St Anselm (1033–1109). Anselm had formulated an ontological argument for the existence of God, based on reason alone. Aquinas rejected this because his philosophy was rooted in the world of evidence and not solely on reason.

As was typical for the Middle Ages, Aquinas was both a philosopher and a Christian theologian. He believed that philosophy would confirm Christian teaching. Along with others at the time, he taught that reason was subordinate to religious faith and that philosophy was subordinate to theology. Aquinas believed that his system was like a two-storey house: his use of Aristotelian philosophy was the foundations and the ground floor, while Christian theology perfected the house by adding the upper floor and the roof.

> These are Latin terms. *A posteriori* proofs are those which argue backwards; *a priori* ones are based on reason alone and argue forwards from first principles. A further Latin term Aquinas used was 'demonstratio', meaning a strong and conclusive proof.

For Aquinas, the existence of God was not self-evident. After all no human being could see, hear or touch God. However Aquinas did believe that the natural world provided a lot of evidence for God's existence. He set out **Five Ways** of proving God's existence from this evidence. These proofs were concerned with the things people observed and experienced every day. They are *a posteriori* proofs, rather than *a priori* ones. It is in the fifth of the Five Ways that Aquinas puts forward his version of the Teleological Argument. He says that the natural world seems to exhibit purposeful order and infers from this that there must be an intelligent designer. Things do not simply exist and behave randomly, but instead act for some specific end (*telos*). He does not give any examples, but he meant things like the earth moving round the sun and plants growing in the proper conditions. Animals appear to be self-regulating mechanisms designed to maintain themselves and to reproduce. The individual parts of an animal seem to be designed to contribute to the overall end of the animal – the heart pumps blood round the body, the stomach digests food and provides energy, and so on.

Aquinas mentions two things present in nature which, taken together, imply design. The first is order ('things act always, or nearly always, in the same way'). The second is that the order in nature seems to be beneficial. He thinks that the regular, orderly processes in nature which bring about a beneficial result are evidence that there is an intelligent design in the world. Beneficial order cannot occur by chance. This intelligent designer is what everyone understands by God. Aquinas argues thus: that there is order implies design, and that there is design implies a designer, God.

In the 18th and 19th centuries, the most popular way of arguing for God's existence was to use an analogy between the production of things in nature and the production of things by humans. If one could demonstrate a resemblance, then one could, by using the principle that similar effects imply similar causes, argue that the causes of those effects resembled each other. So if one could show some kind of similarity between a man-made object and the natural world, then since we know that the former is the product of planning, design and purpose, we could infer that the same is true of the latter.

Probably the most famous version of the Teleological Argument was put forward by the English theologian William Paley (1743–1805), in a book called *Natural Theology*, published in 1802. Paley argued that if one came across a stone while walking and was asked how it came to be there, it would be tempting to assume that it had lain there for ever, and thus think nothing more of it. If one came across a watch, however, the intricacies of its design and composition would immediately indicate the existence of a watchmaker.

For Paley, the conclusion from this analogy is obvious: if we must argue from the watch to a watchmaker, we must argue also from the world to a worldmaker. The watch and the world have two things in common – **order** and **purpose**. Because of the complexity of the order and the purposeful arrangement of the parts, we are obliged to think of an intelligent designer. The only difference is in scale. The known designer (the watchmaker) and the postulated designer (God) are therefore similar *in kind,* but dissimilar *in degree.* Most of the remainder of Paley's book is devoted to piling up examples of design in the natural world.

It is important to note four points about this argument:

✦ It treats the world and its parts as mechanisms, comparable to the ones we ourselves produce

✦ It is concerned with order (the accurate adjustment of parts to one another) as well as with purpose (the adaptation of means to ends) in natural mechanisms

> 'The fifth way is taken from the governance of the world. We see that things which lack knowledge, such as natural bodies, act for an end, and this is evident from their acting always, or nearly always, in the same way, so as to obtain the best result. Hence it is plain that they achieve their end, not fortuitously, but designedly. Now whatever lacks knowledge cannot move towards an end, unless it be directed by some being endowed with knowledge and intelligence; as the arrow is directed by the archer. Therefore some intelligent being exists by whom all natural things are directed to their end; and this being we call God.' From Aquinas' *Summa Theologica*.

Paley

- It uses the principle of 'similar effects, similar causes'. This forms the backbone of the argument

- It is concerned with proportion: although the makers of artificial and natural mechanisms are similarly intelligent, there is a huge difference between them. This corresponds to the huge difference between their products. This is essentially a matter of scale: the unknown designer must be like the known human designer, only much more so, since the work of the former so completely dwarfs the work of the latter which it otherwise closely resembles.

Swinburne

Richard Swinburne also sees miracles as constituting evidence for the probable existence of God as part of his broader argument. See page 23.

Richard Swinburne has attempted to provide a stronger version of the Design Argument. He discards the 18th-century starting points of the argument as unsatisfactory and instead suggests two possible lines of argument. The first is from spatial order and the second is from temporal order.

His suggestion about **spatial order** (Swinburne calls this 'regularities of co-presence') concerns the existence of things with complex structures. So, when Paley and others argued from the huge complexity of animal and plant life to the existence of a designer, they were arguing for 'spatial order'. However Swinburne recognises that this kind of argument is bound to fail as a result of Darwinian evolutionary theory. The theory of Natural Selection provides a viable alternative explanation for the complexity to be found in the universe.

The British naturalist Charles Darwin (1809–1882) put forward his theory of Natural Selection in his famous *Origin of the Species by Means of Natural Selection* (1859). See page 130.

Instead, Swinburne's arguments concern the **temporal order** in the universe, that is the sheer fact that there are laws of nature throughout the universe (Swinburne calls these 'regularities of succession'). These laws of nature are more fundamental than spatial order laws. The universe could very easily have been chaotic, but it is not. It is the orderliness of the universe that Swinburne finds a very remarkable fact – the universe conforms to very simple scientific laws that, in the case of our own world, provide the conditions for life. Without these laws, there could be no life at all. The existence of orderliness and uniform laws of nature throughout the universe suggests that it is more probable than not that the universe was designed. Hence it is more probable than not that God (the designer) exists.

> **Further study**
>
> Find out more about Richard Swinburne's views by reading his *Is there a God?* (Oxford University Press 1996).

Swinburne explains why the temporal order in the universe should point to God. He says first that the simplicity of a hypothesis makes its probability greater, and second that theism, which is an extremely simple hypothesis, is therefore more probable than any other explanation. God is a very simple hypothesis because his characteristics are of the most simple, basic or fundamental kind: omnipotence, omniscience, omnipresence, benevolence and freedom. These fundamental characteristics increase the probability of its being true because it is much more simple than any alternative explanation. Even if we say that the probability of God creating the universe is not very high, the fact that we have a universe at all still makes it more likely that its designer was God than not.

Swinburne's argument therefore invokes Occam's Razor, a principle attributed to William of Occam (c.1285–c.1349). This principle rules that we should avoid assuming the existence of more things or events than is necessary to explain something. The simplest hypothesis may not actually be the correct explanation, but it is better to start with that and only move beyond it when absolutely necessary.

Criticisms of design arguments

The various versions of the Design Argument have created a great deal of discussion and debate through several centuries, and lots of criticisms have been made of them. The classic opponent of the argument is the Scottish philosopher **David Hume** (1711–1776). Hume's book, *Dialogues Concerning Natural Religion*, was published some 23 years before Paley's famous statement of the argument, though Paley does not mention Hume. He wrote in the form of a dialogue, using three characters (Cleanthes, Demea and Philo) to portray different positions. Hume used Philo to voice his own highly critical views of the Design Argument. His criticisms may be summed up as follows:

> These names are borrowed from the history of Greek philosophy, as is the method of pursuing a philosophical argument through a dialogue, which was Plato's method of presentation.

- The Design Argument asserts too much. If there is design in the universe, then it ought to be explained. But to do so by appealing to some design-producing entity, and to equate this entity with the God of classical theism, goes far beyond the evidence available

- When we make inferences from a specific thing to a general principle, we do so on the basis of experience. In terms of Paley's analogy, it is experience that has taught us that watchmakers design watches. If we are in doubt, we can go and observe them being made. However we have no experience – and could have no experience – of a universe being made. There is no way of checking that our world and the order in it were made by a creator or worldmaker

- If we argue that the order apparent in the universe is the result of a divine mind, then this mind must itself be complex and we can legitimately ask what or who created this complex mind. In other words, why should we stop at God when asking for explanations?

- The Design Argument leads to a form of anthropomorphism. If the strong point of the argument lies in the analogy between the world and a mechanism, consistency would lead us to assume that the worldmaker resembles a human designer in some ways. Does God then have a body or gender? Is he, like humans, limited? Is God mortal? If we deny that there is a close resemblance between the worldmaker and a human designer, then the whole strength of the analogy on which the argument is based is undermined

- Why should there only be *one* worldmaker? There is no logical reason in the Design Argument why many gods should not have been involved. Perhaps different gods took responsibility for different aspects of the universe. Further, when a human being makes something, he can leave it or put it to one side. Perhaps God has done the same, or perhaps a trainee god, who was practising his worldmaking skills, made the universe

- Hume also suggests that we cannot tell whether God is perfect from looking at the world. Some aspects of the world, like earthquakes, war, disease and torture do not suggest an omnipotent, benevolent God. Hume claimed that a better hypothesis was that of a God who had no moral character.

Hume is not the only person to criticise the Design Argument. The neo-Darwinist biologist **Richard Dawkins**, in *The Blind Watch-*

> **Further study**
>
> Like Moses Mendelssohn (see page 113) and Jeremy Bentham (see page 80–81), Hume (see also page 132) is an Enlightenment philosopher. Find out more about the Enlightenment. You might find the following books helpful:
>
> *The Enlightenment* by Norman Hampson (Penguin Books 1990).
>
> *The Enlightenment (Studies in European History)* by Roy Porter (Palgrave 2001).

> Warning. Photocopying any part of this book without permission is illegal.

Dawkins' most famous book is *The Selfish Gene* which caused a considerable stir when published in 1976, and which has been a scientific bestseller. On the first page he declares that 'all attempts to understand humanity before 1859 are useless' – that being the date of Darwin's publication of the *Origin of Species*, the first proper expression of an evolutionary biology.

maker (1986), deals with the apparent design in the world. He claims that the Design Argument is completely mistaken.

Dawkins agrees with Paley about the staggering complexity of the world and that it needs to be explained. But for Dawkins, **Natural Selection** satisfactorily explains why species appear to be designed for a particular environment. Natural Selection is not an intelligent designer, but it does select in the sense that natural forces tend to lead to the extinction of certain species in the face of intense competition with other species, all fighting for existence in the same environment. Evolution is a race where only the winner is seen and they look as though they had been designed for the race.

For Dawkins, the appearance of design is an illusion. There is no God masterminding the process, only 'the blind, unconscious, automatic process which Darwin discovered'. God, then, is superfluous and redundant. According to Dawkins, the Design Argument should therefore be regarded as an inferior explanation to that of Natural Selection because Natural Selection is self-explanatory and self-contained.

Responses to the criticisms

Most philosophers and theologians accept that some of Hume's criticisms are valid, in particular those concerning the analogy-based argument. Furthermore most thinkers have accepted the theory of evolution, in one form or another and, as we have seen, scholars like Dawkins believe that this renders the Design Argument useless. However other scholars think that evolution does not eliminate God. This is because they argue that evolution may be understood as the means by which God achieves his purpose.

Scientific observations and the success of the theory of evolution have led to the development of a new version of the Design Argument based on the Anthropic Principle.

The **Weak Anthropic Principle** is a philosophical rule that states that the very fact that we are here observing means that what we observe is limited by the conditions necessary for our presence as observers. The principle is a response to the accusation that the amazing fact of our being here is the result of a series of staggering coincidences. The **Strong Anthropic Principle** asserts that the existence of intelligent life forms was inevitable and that life will necessarily spread to take control of not only our but all (and all possible) universes.

> **Further study**
>
> The arguments can be found in *The Anthropic Cosmological Principle* by John D. Barrow and Frank J. Tipler (Oxford University Press 1996): a challenging read.

This last claim has led to authors referring to a Final Anthropic Principle.

The Strong Anthropic Principle thus argues that the universe is evidently constructed specifically for the development of intelligent life. Physicists agree that if there had been very small changes in the amounts of the elements that make up the universe (eg hydrogen, carbon) the universe could not have supported any form of life. Similarly, if the force of gravity had been very slightly different from what it is, the universe would have been sterile and lifeless. As **John Polkinghorne**, a nuclear physicist who became a priest, puts it:

> A universe capable of evolving carbon-based life is a very particular universe indeed, "finely tuned" in the character of its basic physical processes, one might say. (*Science and Theology: an Introduction* by John Polkinghorne, SPCK 1998).

This 'fine tuning' is also seen in the biological processes of the universe. For example the mechanisms that keep the earth's oxygen content, its temperature and the salinity of the seas within tolerable limits are delicately balanced and suggest a very careful construction of the universe. Polkinghorne summarises the scientific consensus as follows:

> For the development of fruitful complexity one needs: the right laws (neither so rigid that nothing really new can happen nor so floppy that only chaos can ensue – quantum mechanics seems ideal from this point of view); the right kind of constituents (a universe consisting just of electrons and photons would not have a rich enough potential for varied structure); the right force strengths (e.g. nuclear forces able to generate the elements inside stars); and the right circumstances (eg a big enough universe). The Anthropic Principle is widely accepted in this scientific sense. (*Science and Theology: an Introduction* SPCK 1998).

Polkinghorne has put forward a version of the Anthropic Principle which he calls the **Moderate Anthropic Principle**. He claims that a universe that has produced life is a 'fact of interest calling for an explanation' precisely because of the huge number and complexity of conditions necessary for the emergence of intelligent life. He believes that chance factors are too unlikely as an explanation for the existence of the universe and of intelligent human life within it. Instead, he offers an explicitly theistic explanation:

> I believe... anthropic considerations are... part of a cumulative case for theism... I believe that in the delicate fine tuning of physical law, which has made the evolution of conscious beings possible, we receive a valuable, if indirect, hint from science that there is a divine meaning and purpose behind cosmic theory. (*Beyond Science* Cambridge University Press 1996).

It is clear why many theologians should be interested in the Anthropic Principle: it suggests design rather than random chance.

The French priest and scientist, **Pierre Teilhard de Chardin** (1881–1955) attempted to see the theory of evolution in a Christian theological framework. For him, evolution was a process willed by God and possessing its own inbuilt dynamic (in a way, he anticipated the Anthropic Principle). The evolutionary process led in a trajectory from inanimate matter to human life, the high point of which was the person of Jesus Christ.

The philosopher and theologian **F. R. Tennant** (1866–1957), in his book *Philosophical Theology* (1928), developed the Anthropic Principle by arguing that evolution is part of a cumulative design argument. Tennant takes Darwin's evolutionary theory into account in his revised and extended Design Argument and concludes that Natural Selection is entirely in accordance with the divine purpose. Evolution is thus the work of God. He observes that the world is intelligible to the human mind, and says that this may be evidence that something akin to the human mind planned the world. He sees the inorganic chemistry of the earth as a theatre prepared for the emergence of life. So for Tennant evolution appears to be a process designed to push creatures to greater heights of complexity. It is a loaded dice designed specifically in favour of human life.

Further study

Go to www.polkinghorne.org, where you will find extracts from Polkinghorne's work. Having read some of these, evaluate the strengths and weaknesses of his position.

Teilhard de Chardin's works were suppressed by the Roman Catholic Church during his lifetime and were published posthumously. The best known of these are *The Phenomenon of Man* (1959) and *The Divine Milieu* (1960).

Miracles

Concept of miracles

See also pages 74–76.

'Miracle' comes from the Latin word for 'wonder'. A miracle is an event which fills people with a sense of surprise and amazement. Miracles are generally classified as being one of two types.

Miracles which break the laws of nature

Sometimes people claim to have been present at an event which should not have happened according to the laws of science as we presently understand them. The story of Jesus walking on the water is an example of this sort of miracle and in today's world there are frequent claims of people being healed of a range of illnesses because someone prays for them. If miracles like these can happen then it would suggest that there is a God responsible for them.

Miracles which change lives

R. F. Holland suggests that an event does not have to break a law of nature to be classified as a miracle. He defines a miracle as an extraordinary coincidence that does not involve any contradiction of laws of nature. He cites the following example:

> Imagine that a child is playing in his toy car, then that it gets stuck on a railway level crossing. The mother sees the child and also sees an express train hurtling along the track. Suddenly, the train's emergency brakes are applied and it comes to a halt only a metre from the child. The mother says a prayer of thanks to God for this miracle. However, later investigation reveals that the driver fainted. This faint was explicable on medical grounds, without appealing to divine intervention. In spite of this, however, the mother continues to believe that God acted to stop the train so that her child would be saved. ('The Miraculous' *American Philosophical Quarterly* 1965).

If someone was healed of a painful disease, and it was believed to be the work of a loving God, then it may be considered miraculous. The important criterion here would be the significance of demonstrating God's nature to humans.

No law of nature has been broken. What makes it a miracle is the mother's sense of divine purpose and religious significance. The events that occur are consistent with natural processes but their timing is extraordinary and may properly be called miraculous. Holland calls this the 'contingency concept' of the miraculous – there is no expected or necessary link between the events, but this linking happens contingently and is labelled miraculous. But where a theist sees a miracle, an atheist sees a coincidence or lucky chance.

A different way of understanding miracles is explained by **Donald MacKay** (1922–1987). The Bible teaches that God is the creator of the universe, and also its sustainer. Without the continuous creative activity of God, the world and everything in it would cease to exist. This goes against the idea that there was only one moment of creation and leads to a more dynamic view of God's creation. MacKay uses the model of an artist to explain this idea:

> Imagine an artist able to bring his world into being, not by laying down paint on canvas, but by producing an extremely rapid succession of sparks of light on the screen of a television tube. The world he invents is now not static but dynamic, able to change and evolve at his will. Both its form and its law of change (if any) depend on the way in which he orders the sparks of light in space and time. The scene is steady and unchanging just for as long as he wills it so; but if he were to cease his activity, his invented world would not become chaotic; it would simply cease to be. (*The Clockwork Image* IVP 1997).

When this view is related to miracles, we can see that, because God is constantly active in creation, miracles are not interventions by God in the world. Instead they are instances of where God is not acting in his normal, sustaining way, but is acting in a different way from usual. According to this view, miracles can be described as unusual events, not supernatural ones.

Hume

David Hume is usually cited as a trenchant critic of belief in miracles. Strictly speaking, rather than saying that miracles cannot happen at all, he argued that belief in these miracles should not be used as a basis for religious faith. Here are some of his objections:

- Miracles are extremely unlikely events. The world seems to work in a regular way (night always follows day, ill people do not abruptly get better) and the vast majority of people never claim to witness anything like a miracle. Hume thought that miracles were so unlikely that it is always more likely that the people who claim to have seen the miracle are mistaken than that the miracle actually happened

- Many people desperately want miracles to be true and thus believe in miracles even when proper evidence for them does not exist

- They have not taken place in conditions where they can be carefully checked and observed. Hume talks of the 'ignorant and barbarous nations' where miracles are supposed to occur; now we might say that miracles do not happen in places where they can be scientifically checked

- They are used to support contradictory claims. Christians believe in the miracle of the resurrection of Jesus while Muslims believe in the miracle of the Qur'an being dictated to Muhammad. If one of these two claims is true then the other must be false. If Jesus was resurrected then what the Qur'an says about him cannot be true, as the Qur'an denies his crucifixion. If the Qur'an is true then Jesus could not have been resurrected. Each claim cancels out the other.

Criticisms of Hume on miracles

Hume was correct in that people do demand more evidence to back up claims to have witnessed an extraordinary event than for an ordinary one. According to Hume, there could *never* be sufficiently strong evidence to establish the existence of something that is contrary to the laws of nature. But is Hume right?

For example if someone said, 'I saw an angel on my way to school' you would be justified in requiring a greater number of witnesses and a greater checking of their truthfulness than if someone else said, 'I saw a milkman on my way to school'.

- Laws of nature are concerned with repeatable events. To use Hume's example, it is a law of nature that 'lead cannot, of itself, remain suspended in the air' because we have repeatedly observed that lead falls to the ground. Laws only apply to such events because of the way in which laws are established. By contrast, a miracle is a *unique* event and therefore cannot be judged as if it were a candidate for a new natural law. We cannot make judgements about the probability of a unique event, ie God breaking into the laws of nature

In 1969 the American astronaut Neil Armstrong became the first man to walk on the moon.

◆ Hume's argument could be used to discount events that very obviously have occurred. In Hume's day, the uniform experience was such that no one had ever walked on the moon. Within Hume's system, we would be right to reject predictions about Neil Armstrong, but we know that those predictions would have been justified. Universal observation of a particular phenomenon does not, therefore, necessitate that the unusual will not happen

◆ Are miracles highly improbable? Hume might say that they are rare and unusual, but any event may be so and is still to be expected in certain circumstances. It is rare for a person to reach the summit of Mount Everest, but under certain conditions (following years of training and then a long climb) it is to be expected. Miracles are highly unusual, but are they not to be expected once in a while given the existence of a God who wishes to help his creation? Moreover Hume does not even consider the extent to which belief (theism or atheism) affects one's assessment of the probability of a miracle occurring

◆ Hume takes belief in miracles to be an expression of a rival description of how the world works. Obviously we could never establish as a new law of nature that dead men in certain circumstances come back to life. However a miracle is a case of God breaking into the natural order and doing something different, so that the question of the probability of the event occurring naturally is, in this sense, irrelevant

◆ Hume is assuming that all religious claims to miracles should be given equal weighting. But what if the evidence for one religion's claims to the miraculous were actually much stronger than another religion's? Is there more historical evidence for the miracles of, say, Jesus than for those surrounding the Buddha? If we could establish a comparison like this then Hume's criticism collapses. Secondly, what if we leave aside the sectarian claims and decide that God does different miracles in different religions so that humans in all cultures will turn to God in some way? Again, Hume's criticism would cease to function.

In defence of miracles

Many religious people would cite miracles as evidence for the existence of God. God intervenes in the normal course of events to remind people that he exists and has authority over creation. **Richard L. Purtill** uses the following illustration: 'If I claim to have authority in a certain organisation, strong evidence of my authority would be an ability to suspend the rules or make exceptions to usual procedures.' Similarly, Purtill argues, God shows his existence and authority through performing miracles.

See Richard L. Purtill *Thinking about Religion* (Prentice Hall 1978).

See *God, Chance and Necessity* by Keith Ward (Oneworld 1996). See also *The Existence of God* by Richard Swinburne (Oxford University Press 1979) for another view of miracles.

Keith Ward argues that if the world is as Christianity says it is, then there are good reasons to believe that miracles that appear to break the laws of nature will happen. Christianity says that the world was made by a God who has complete power over it. God also cares for the world and is free to change what happens in the world when it is the right thing to do. So when we hear or read about stories of miracles which help people in their lives then it is reasonable to conclude that at least some of these stories are true.

Religious people often go on to use miracles as evidence for the existence of a particular God as defined by a particular religion. This is a definite progression in the argument, extending it beyond the establishment of the existence of some force beyond the natural universe. Purtill makes this progression when he states that in the resurrection 'Christ's words were backed up or authenticated by God'. Thus a miracle is seen as part of the Christian God's revelation to humanity. Some people believe that the purpose of miracles is to show the power of God. Examples from the Bible, like the crossing of the Red Sea or Jesus calming the storm, could be cited here.

> **Further study**
>
> See the discussion on miracles in *Reason and Religious Belief* by Peterson, Hasker, Reichenbach and Basinger (Oxford University Press 1998).

However **Peter Vardy** succinctly points to a problem with this approach:

> A God who intervenes at Lourdes to cure an old man of cancer but does not act to save starving millions in Ethiopia; who helps an individual believer by giving him/her guidance about a new house/ job, but does not prevent the mass murder of the Jews at Auschwitz – such a God needs, at the least, to face some hard moral questioning.

See *The Puzzle of Evil* by Peter Vardy (Fount 1992). David Jenkins, a former Bishop of Durham, upset some people when he argued this point but in stronger language. He wrote that a God who would perform the Gospel miracles but allow, for example, the Holocaust to take place 'must be the very devil'. *God, Miracle and the Church of England* (SCM 1987).

In the end, the view we take of miracles will depend on the view we take of God (including whether or not such a being exists).

Test yourself

1. (a) Outline the reasons why science and religion are often assumed to be opposed to one another on the subject of creation.

    (b) Explain and assess the claim that this conflict between religious and scientific views of creation is unnecessary.

2. (a) 'It is commonly held that a miracle is an intervention by God to make something happen which would never have happened had nature been left to itself. A miracle is therefore a violation of natural law. When a violation is reported, it is always more reasonable to believe that the witnesses were lying or mistaken than to believe that the event really happened.' Explain what is meant by 'a violation of a natural law'.

    (b) 'If we accept that violations of natural law do happen, then the conclusion follows that God causes them.' Assess this view.

3. (a) Outline and explain the Design Argument for the existence of God presented by Aquinas and Paley.

    (b) 'The Design Argument has been seriously weakened by science.' Explain and assess this view.